Transcending Time

Kālacakra with consort Viśvamātā.
Photo by Peter Nebel.

Transcending Time

The Kālacakra Six-Session Guru Yoga

Gen Lamrimpa
(Ven. Lobsang Jampal Tenzin)

Translated by
B. Alan Wallace

Edited by
Pauly B. Fitze

Foreword by
His Holiness the Dalai Lama

Wisdom Publications • Boston

Wisdom Publications
199 Elm Street
Somerville MA 02144 USA

Library of Congress Cataloging-in-Publication Data
Gen Lamrimpa, 1934–
Transcending time : the Kālacakra six-session guru yoga / Gen Lamrimpa ; foreword by His Holiness the Dalai Lama ; translated by B. Alan Wallace ; edited by Pauly B. Fitze.
p. cm.
Includes bibliographical references and index.
ISBN 0-86171-152-1 (pbk. : alk. paper)
1. Kālacakra (Tantric rite) 2. Yoga (Tantric Buddhism)
I. Wallace, B. Alan.
BQ7699.K34G46 1999
294.3'4436—dc21 99-19501

ISBN 0-86171-152-1

04 03 02 01 00
6 5 4 3 2

Cover image: Vajradhara, 17th century, from the collection of Shelley and Donald Rubin. Photo courtesy of Moke Mokotoff.

Designed by: Jennie Malcolm

Wisdom Publications' books are printed on acid-free paper and meet the guidelines for the permanence and durability of the Committee on Production Guidelines for Book Longevity of the Council on Library Resources.

Printed in the United States of America

Contents

Foreword ix
Editor's Acknowledgments xi
Preface xiii
Introduction 1
Homage 9

Part 1 Preparing for Practice
1 Reflections on the Path 13
2 Receiving Tantric Teachings 20
3 Overview of the Kālacakra Tantra 25

Part 2 The Kālacakra Six-Session Guru Yoga
4 Beginning the Practice 37
5 Guru Yoga 54
6 Recollections and Practices 75
7 Receiving Initiation 88
8 The Seven Self-Entries of a Child 104
9 The Higher and Greatly Higher Initiations 127
10 The Purification of Death 141
11 Generating Oneself as Kālacakra 155
12 Deepening Your Understanding 168
13 Hooking the Hearts of All Kālacakras 178
14 Bindu Yoga and Subtle Yoga 184
15 Mantra Recitation 188
16 Offerings 194
17 Praise and Dedication 198

To be read only by those who have received the Kālacakra initiation.

May this be an expression of gratitude
And reverence and love for the Revealer,
And the spiritual mentors, for preserving this
Precious body of wisdom, and may the
Blessings received be passed on to all who
Read this, and thereby to all beings.

Publisher's Acknowledgment

The publisher gratefully acknowledges the contribution of the students of Gen Lamrimpa (Venerable Lobsang Jampal Tenzin), who, through the Dharma Friendship Foundation Education Fund, helped make production of this book possible.

Foreword

THE DALAI LAMA

The Kālacakra Tantra is a Buddhist practice belonging to the class of highest yoga tantras, which are among the most profound teachings of the Bodhisattva Vehicle. According to tradition, Buddha Śākyamuni appeared in the south of India as Kālacakra and set forth this tantra at the request of King Sucandra of Śambhala.

King Sucandra then propagated the teachings of Kālacakra widely among the citizens of Śambhala. The tradition is said not to have reappeared in India until shortly before it was brought to Tibet in the eleventh century. Thereafter, until the upheavals of the present century, it thrived not only among Tibetans, but also among their neighbors in the Mongolian regions to the north, as well as in Sikkim, Bhutan, and Nepal and the Himalayan regions to the south and west.

For those who attend the initiation and wish to cultivate a daily practice of meditation based upon it, it is common to begin by performing a method of six-session guru yoga. This typically presents a concise review of the important points of the generation stage yogas of the Kālacakra path, within the context of a prayer to the spiritual master and meditation. Practices of this nature are called "six-session yogas" because they are meant to be recited and contemplated three times during the day and three times at night.

However, we should not limit our practice to this minimal level of endeavor. The six-session yoga provides the basis for our daily meditation in which we should try constantly to expand our familiarity with the practice of Kālacakra.

An increasing number of individuals who do not have access to the original Tibetan commentaries are taking interest in this practice. Therefore, it is indeed timely that a book has been prepared containing an explanation of the practice of the *Kālacakra Six-Session Guru Yoga*, based on his own experience, by Gen Lamrimpa Jampal Tenzin. I offer my prayers that it will enable readers to deepen their understanding and appreciation of this sublime teaching of the Buddha.

Tenzin Gyatso, the Fourteenth Dalai Lama

Editor's Acknowledgments

It is with a sense of continuing gratitude that we think of His Holiness the Fourteenth Dalai Lama. With sympathy and understanding for our needs he granted the request made by B. Alan Wallace and the Dharma Friendship Foundation and encouraged Venerable Lobsang Jampal Tenzin, Gen Lamrimpa, to travel to Seattle to lead a one-year *śamatha* retreat in 1988. Gen Lamrimpa's two-year stay (1987–1989) was a rich experience for those fortunate ones able to participate. Besides the śamatha teachings and retreat—which is the subject of another book entitled *Calming the Mind*, edited by Hart Sprager—we received teachings on many quintessential subjects, including the *Kālacakra Six-Session Guru Yoga*, the subject of this book. With great skill, patience, and generosity he imparted his treasure of knowledge and insight. It brought about not only a tremendous enrichment in our lives, but also gave us much food for reflection and meditation in the future.

We were also most fortunate to have the excellent translation skills of B. Alan Wallace. His vast background in the Dharma and excellent knowledge of Tibetan and English made the teachings a truly profound experience.

To reflect Gen Lamrimpa's penetrating erudition as well as profound realizations, we attempted to preserve the traditional Tibetan format of teachings he used. There was some minor shifting of introductions to individual classes to fit into the major chapters.

Tibetan words used in the text are spelled to reflect the pronunciation, and the transliteration in parenthesis is in accordance with the Wylie system. Sanskrit words are spelled according to the standard transliteration system.

I would like to express my gratitude to the many individuals who have made contributions to this project.

First I would like to thank Venerable Lobsang Jampal Tenzin, Gen Lamrimpa, for the many hours he gave during his second stay in Seattle in 1993 to go over the text and to clarify aspects that were unclear to me. The kindness and assistance of Tenzin Tsultrim at that time is also gratefully remembered.

My gratitude also goes to T. G. Dhongthog Rinpoche for checking the entire document and making suggestions for improvements.

Thubten Jampa has earned my undying gratitude for his continuing willingness to help over the many years. Special mention should be made of Ivanka Jakic for her untiring efforts on behalf of the Kālacakra and to thank her for requesting the teachings.

It gives me great pleasure to acknowledge my indebtedness and gratitude to my two co-editors. Brenda Loew studied the entire manuscript and contributed suggestions for presentation and clarity. Jean Paone also scrutinized the entire manuscript and made many valuable changes. She had an uncanny knack to pinpoint weak areas and improve them.

During the times when I needed specialized expertise in computer technology it was my dear friends Elizabeth Heath and Thomas V. Ashbrook IV who came to my aid. A big thank you to both of them.

I cannot overestimate my debt of gratitude to my husband, Werner Fitze. Without his continuous and untiring encouragement and generous support of many kinds, this work would not have been accomplished.

Great care has been taken to report the teachings accurately as given. Any errors that may have crept in are mine alone and are infinitely regretted. May I be permitted to repeat the sentiments voiced by Gen Lamrimpa: "I hope this teaching will be of benefit to all and serve as a seed and as a basis to analyze."

Preface

This preface focuses on the activities of the Dharma Friendship Foundation, a nonsectarian group whose members appreciate all traditions. It is located in Seattle, in the northwestern part of the United States, a world power in these modern times.

Its spiritual director, American scholar Alan Wallace (Jhampa Kelsang), requested permission from His Holiness the Dalai Lama to invite me to Seattle. With incomparable kindness he granted permission. Even though I am impoverished in good qualities from former lives and from learning in this life, I was regarded as valuable as gold. For one year beginning in March 1987 I taught Dharma there to the best of my ability. The following year I taught meditative quiescence and guided fifteen practitioners in a year-long retreat. Between meditative quiescence (Skt. *śamatha*) and insight (Skt. *vipaśyanā*), it is in the practice of meditative quiescence that the mind is truly stabilized internally.

Then the Dharma Friendship Foundation and its altruistic program director Ivanka Jakic (Jampa Lhamo) from Yugoslavia fervently requested that I teach the *Kālacakra Six-Session Guru Yoga* for the purpose of practice and meditation. This was given for the daily practice of His Holiness the Fourteenth Dalai Lama by his senior tutor Ling Rinpoche, who was the Ninety-seventh Holder of the Ganden Throne in the Gelug order. His Holiness the Dalai Lama kindly gave the permission. As holy scholars and adepts are very rare in that area, I was conceited enough to feel like a fine-looking man among dwarfs and I gave these teachings for fifteen days to fifteen people, some of whom participated in the year-long retreat. During the preliminary teachings, I tried to emphasize the common path practices, such as the spirit of awakening, the spirit of emergence, the correct view, and so forth. To the best of my ability I explained the specific points of Kālacakra, including the initiation that brings maturation, the stages of generation and completion that bring liberation, the basis to be purified, the practices that purify, and the results of purification. However:

Having dipped the *kuśa* grass tip of my childish intelligence
Into the deep and limitless ocean of treatises,
I worship the merciful and compassionate beings
And confess my errors in the nature of nonobjectivity.

Having entered the midst of the great ocean,
Even though I cannot fathom its depths or breadth,
Is it the custom of articulate and educated people
Not even to speak of the ocean?

Though a great bird's wings have no power
To reach the far side of the sky,
What intelligent person would say
It should not fly in the sky?

From beginningless time until now,
My body, speech, and mind have been messengers of *saṃsāra*.
Now, by chance, I have striven for the sake of beings throughout space.
Why isn't this a good thing?

When I was teaching at that time, I was ignorant of the English language, so Alan Wallace, who is fluent in both English and spoken Tibetan as well as Dharma terminology, translated well everything I taught, occasionally helped by the Tibetan Thubten Jampa. Those teachings were recorded on tape by Pauly and Werner Fitze, who were born in Switzerland but presently live on Vashon Island near Seattle. With great altruism, diligence, and rugged endurance, they accepted the responsibility of transcribing the teachings from the tapes, then edited them again and again, many times over.

There are not many such writings about Kālacakra in English. His Holiness the Dalai Lama's initiation brings great blessings, and a number

Place
Stamp
Here

Wisdom Publications

199 Elm Street • Somerville MA 02144 USA

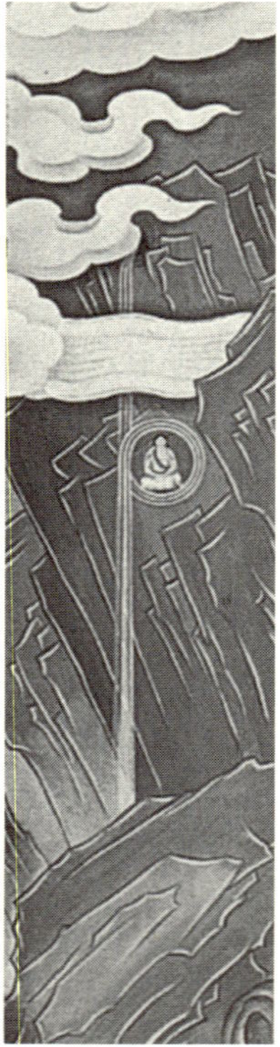

Please return this card if you would like to be kept informed about our current and future publications.

Name ______________________

Street ______________________ New Address? ❒

City ______________________

State/Prov. ____________ Zip ____________

Country ______________________

Email ______________________

In which book did you find this card? ______________________

How did you learn of this book? ______________________

If you bought this book in a bookstore, which one? ______________________

of Westerners are very interested in learning more about Kālacakra. So I hope this teaching will be of benefit as a basis, or seed, for study.

The Point of the Practice

Even if one does not have very much time for meditation, any practice of Kālacakra brings a blessing. In particular, practicing the *Kālacakra Six-Session Guru Yoga* brings tremendous blessings. Moreover, the six-session guru yoga synthesizes all the essential points of practice of both the sūtras and the tantras.

Once you have received the Kālacakra initiation, it would be very helpful for you to gather together for a couple of days at a time to engage in this practice and discuss the teachings. By doing so, you will acquire experience in the six-session guru yoga practice as well as gain some familiarity with the stages of generation and completion. It would be much to your advantage. Many of you are especially attracted to Kālacakra. If you express this faith in the practice, this will place very powerful propensities upon your mindstreams. On the other hand, if you practice with little faith, few benefits arise.

The point of the practice is chiefly to counter the mental afflictions, which should be the ongoing emphasis of your practice. In short, what we need to do is to try to diminish the force of the mental afflictions and cultivate wholesome qualities.

Although the chief task is transforming the mind in order to totally eradicate the mental afflictions, we should also give very strong emphasis to diminishing unwholesome tendencies of speech and physical actions. The reason for this is that even though the mind is the source of all three, if one does not attenuate verbal and physical actions such as harsh or abusive speech and other nonvirtues, these will enflame the mental afflictions. It is very hard to counter the mental afflictions without restraining the unwholesome actions of body and speech. Moreover, the body and speech are easier to subdue. So start there as a basis, and with that, counter the mental afflictions.

Now, in terms of a really practical procedure along the path, it is very good to develop the spirit of awakening, the altruistic wish to be of benefit to others. As the basis, if one can emphasize being honest, this is extremely important. Without countering the mental afflictions to some extent, it is impossible to be honest. If one really becomes accustomed to being honest to oneself and to others, it is much easier for authentic loving kindness and compassion to arise.

These things are to be practiced.

General Remarks about Tantric Teachings

Although I have given the teachings on Kālacakra, I feel, in fact, that I cannot teach this material very well. Nevertheless, these teachings were requested by Ivanka Jakic and the Dharma Friendship Foundation. Moreover, there are very few people who teach the Kālacakra practice. Before offering these teachings, I made a lot of effort to study and prepare the material. As I put together the things that I have studied and heard, I tried to teach in accord with what is written in the authoritative scriptures on Kālacakra. According to my ability, I have done as well as I can. In comparison to the instructions of a great sage, these would not be considered good teachings.

In the explanations I have taught explicitly about transforming sensual experiences into the path. The reason for being so very explicit and unambiguous is because nowadays there are a lot of people who say they are practicing tantra, transforming sensual experience and pleasure into the path. When people have no clear idea what such transformation entails, all they are doing is confusing themselves and others. If one does indeed have the proper, extensive preparation that I have discussed at length, and one transforms sensual pleasure into the path, this is very good.

I have spoken very clearly about these points in order to protect people from following a deviant path. As I was giving these teachings, I was not presenting something that I dreamed up. My comments were based upon authoritative scriptures that have been practiced for over a thousand years. Also, throughout the whole history of such practice, there have been generations of *siddhas* who have gained authentic experience by such means.

If people unfamiliar with Buddhist teachings should take a paragraph here or there out of context and just focus on that, this could be dangerous. Therefore, care should be taken that these teachings do not get into the wrong hands.

When appropriate, if one can clarify these issues to other people, this would be a service to humanity, for this is a very precious body of knowledge. It seems that in the West, already a lot of books on tantra have been written and translated. Some of these may state that in the tantric context one should not abandon mental afflictions. It would be good to clarify these issues. If there is an opportunity to go into deeper explanations, then the people you speak with should have received initiation and have strong, irreversible faith.

The Lineage Background

Concerning the lineage from which I have received these teachings, I received the Kālacakra empowerment itself from His Holiness the Dalai Lama. I also received brief instructions from His Holiness on the generation and completion stages of the Kālacakra Tantra. These teachings were given to only a few people, by invitation only.

Three people were invited as representatives of large regions of Tibet. One was Kirti Tsenshab Rinpoche, an older monk who was invited to represent Amdo. A second was Chamdo Geshe, a representative of Kham. I was the third, and I was invited as a representative of southern and central Tibet. We represented all of Tibet. Then there were the abbot and three other monks from Namgyal Monastery, His Holiness' personal monastery. Seven people in all received the oral transmission of the teachings, the explanation, and private instructions by His Holiness. Thereafter, His Holiness encouraged those seven to engage in a propitiatory retreat, which we did. That is one lineage I have received.

Following that, I received another lineage of the oral transmission of the *Kālacakra Root Tantra*, the *Vimalaprabhā*, and the voluminous annotations and subcommentaries of Butön. That was a vast undertaking. At that time there was just one person, as far as we know, at least outside of Tibet, who had received this complete oral transmission, and this was Kirti Tsenshab Rinpoche, who had been invited to the previous teaching. His Holiness then instructed Kirti Tsenshab Rinpoche to pass on the oral transmission to three people. Those three again represented all of Tibet. One was Kirti Rinpoche, a younger monk, representing Amdo. Then there was Banglang Rinpoche, representing Kham, and I was again invited to represent central and southern Tibet.

I really do not know why these individuals were chosen to represent those regions of Tibet. There are many lamas and geshes superior to me from central and southern Tibet. I have no special ability, and His Holiness knows that, but perhaps I was chosen due to some karmic connection from my previous lives.

Every year since then at least some of the monks of Namgyal Monastery engage in the self-initiation rite of Kālacakra, and each time I have been instructed to come and take the self-initiation with them. And that I have done.

I encourage you to dedicate the merit of your reading and engaging in this practice to the best of your ability. Because this particular tantric practice is intimately related to Śambhala, it is very beneficial to dedicate some of the merit to your being reborn in Śambhala.

Since His Holiness the Dalai Lama has given permission to publish this teaching, Pauly and Werner Fitze asked me to write an introduction. In accordance with the common tradition, I have written a homage and preface at the beginning and a prayer of dedication at the end.

I, who am known as Lobsang Jampal Tenzin, am a monk from the Chusang Hermitage (Tib. *chu bzang sgrub sde*), located in the Latö Shelkar (Tib. *la stod shel dkar*) district in the western region of the snowy land of Tibet, which is a realm subdued by Ārya Avalokiteśvara. Even though I am single-pointedly devoted to the sublime Dharma, my Dharma behavior is artificial and ordinary. With the thought to benefit all, I have written this in the *ārya* land Sikkim, the secret land of Ācārya Padmasambhava, at Dechen Ling on the fifteenth day (commemorating the Buddha's teaching of the *Kālacakra Paramādhibuddha* at Dhānyakaṭaka in India) of the third Tibetan month of the Tibetan royal year of 2120.

Lobsang Jampal Tenzin
May 6, 1993
May joy and goodness prevail

Introduction

B. Alan Wallace

The practice of Kālacakra belongs to the general category of Buddhist practice known as *Vajrayāna*, or Buddhist tantra, which originated in India and further developed over the past twelve hundred years in Tibet. According to the *Sampuṭa Tantra*, there are four classes of Buddhist tantra: action (Skt. *kriyā*), performance (Skt. *caryā*), yoga, and highest yoga (Skt. *anuttarayoga*). In the first three classes of tantras, one generates a coarse consciousness combining skillful means and wisdom, and then meditates on emptiness. Only in the highest yoga tantras are methods taught to bring forth subtle levels of consciousness arising from the union of skillful means and wisdom. To utilize such subtle consciousness, one must first subdue coarse levels of conceptualization, which may be done either by directing the vital energies within the body into the central channel, or by engaging in totally nonconceptual meditation, as is done in the practice of Dzogchen. Highest yoga tantras are further subdivided into the two categories of father and mother tantras. The former emphasize the generation of an illusory body that is transmuted into a form body (Skt. *rūpakāya*) of a buddha when one achieves spiritual awakening. The latter are principally concerned with bringing forth the subtle consciousness of clear light (Skt. *prabhāsvara*) with which one realizes emptiness, and this subtle mind is ultimately transformed into the mind of a buddha (Skt. *dharmakāya*).

The Kālacakra Tantra belongs to the class of highest yoga mother tantras and, like other tantras of this class, it includes two stages of practice: the stage of generation and the stage of completion. This particular system of theory and practice includes three Kālacakras: the outer Kālacakra, the inner Kālacakra, and the other Kālacakra. The outer Kālacakra constitutes the elements of the external environment in which we live; the inner

Kālacakra constitutes the psychophysical aggregates that make up an individual; and the other Kālacakra consists of the stages of generation and of completion, which purify the first two Kālacakras.

According to Buddhist tradition, the *Kālacakra Mūlatantra*, or *Root Tantra* (also known as the *Paramādibuddha*), was taught by the Buddha Śākyamuni in his mystical manifestation as the deity Kālacakra to King Sucandra of Śambhala, who had traveled to India to request these teachings from him. From Sucandra, this lineage was passed down through a line of seven Great Kings and twenty-one Kalkī Kings of Śambhala, beginning with Yaśas Mañjuśrī, who composed the *Kālacakra Laghutantra*, or *Condensed Tantra*. His son Puṇḍarīka composed a great commentary to this father's work, entitled the *Vimalaprabhā*, or *Stainless Light*, which remains the primary commentary on Kālacakra to this day.

According to the legend of Śambhala, based on the *Kālacakra Tantra*,[1] when Yaśas Mañjuśrī reincarnates as the twenty-fifth Kalkī King, Śambhala and our world will unite and a time of great material and spiritual bounty will begin. In order that as many people as possible might receive karmic imprints related to this momentous event, the Kālacakra initiation was openly given in Tibet, and His Holiness the Fourteenth Dalai Lama has, in this same tradition, granted this initiation openly on many occasions throughout the world. Whether Śambhala is located on our planet but can be experienced only by those whose minds and karmic propensities are pure, or whether it exists elsewhere is a question still debated by devout Tibetan Buddhists. But it is certainly true that for almost a millennium Tibetan Buddhists have been praying to be reborn in Śambhala or in our world when the twenty-fifth Kalkī King appears and the golden era of Śambhala begins.

According to Tibetan tradition, the Indian Buddhist yogin Cilupa, who lived probably in the eleventh century, learned of the existence of Śambhala and the Kālacakra Tantra and went in search of this fabled land and the teachings of Kālacakra. On his way there, he encountered a manifestation of Mañjuśrī, who granted him the initiation, tantra commentaries, and oral transmissions of Kālacakra. As far as we know, the *Kālacakra Mūlatantra* was never brought from Śambhala to India, but the *Kālacakra Laghutantra* and the *Vimalaprabhā* were, and they were later included in the Tibetan

Buddhist canon. An Indian lineage of this tradition thus arose and was passed down from one Indian guru to another, eventually being transmitted to the Nepali *paṇḍit* Samanta Śrībhadra. In the twelfth century, the Tibetan yogin Ra Chörab traveled to Nepal to study Kālacakra with Samanta Śrībhadra, who later accompanied him back to Tibet, where they translated the main Kālacakra treatises into Tibetan. This lineage was passed on down to the great fourteenth-century Tibetan Buddhist scholar Butön (Tib. *bu ston rin chen grub*), who wrote extensive commentaries and annotations to the *Kālacakra Laghutantra* and the *Vimalaprabhā.* This lineage has been preserved to the present, and the Fourteenth Dalai Lama received the initiations and oral transmissions of the stages of generation and completion from his senior tutor, Vajrācārya Kyabje Ling Rinpoche.

With the Chinese Communist invasion of Tibet and its genocidal assault on Tibetan Buddhism, the study of Kālacakra in Tibet has declined during the latter half of the twentieth century, though there are a few monasteries in eastern Tibet (in the present-day Chinese provinces of Qinghai and Sichuan) where it is actively studied and practiced to this day. The lineage of the complete oral transmission of the *Kālacakra Laghutantra*, the *Vimalaprabhā*, and the Tibetan scholar Butön's sub-commentaries and annotations to these treatises were taken from Tibet to India by Kirti Tsenshab Rinpoche, who, at the request of His Holiness the Dalai Lama, passed it on to Gen Lamrimpa and a few other Tibetan monks in Dharamsala.

Over the past few decades, the Kālacakra Tantra has drawn increasing interest from scholars and practicing Buddhists throughout the world, largely as a result of the Dalai Lama granting this initiation many times in Asia, Europe, and North America. This has led to the publication of a number of popular and scholarly works in Western languages on the theory and practice of Kālacakra. Among the first of these is Geshe Ngawang Dhargyey's *Kālacakra Tantra*, consisting of his oral teachings on Kālacakra theory and practice, which I translated. This work is especially valuable for its detailed discussion of the vows and pledges pertaining to this practice. *The Wheel of Time: The Kalachakra in Context* by Geshe Lhundub Sopa, et. al., provides an excellent introduction to the history, the process of initiation, and the general practice of Kālacakra. The *Kalachakra Tantra: Rite of Initiation* by Tenzin Gyatso, the Fourteenth Dalai Lama, and Jeffrey

Hopkins presents the context for the practice of Kālacakra and gives a very detailed account of all the stages of the initiation, as well as the first English translation of the *Kālacakra Six-Session Guru Yoga*, which was formulated by the Fourteenth Dalai Lama and versified by Kyabje Ling Rinpoche. In his book *The Practice of Kalachakra*, Glenn Mullin offers an overview of Kālacakra within Tibetan Buddhism as a whole and presents translations of various short Tibetan treatises covering different aspects of this tradition. Barry Bryant offers an engaging account of the Kālacakra tradition in his visually stunning book *The Wheel of Time Sand Mandala: Visual Scripture of Tibetan Buddhism.* Most recently, Alexander Berzin has published two very helpful works entitled *Taking the Kalachakra Initiation* and *Kalachakra and Other Six-Session Yoga Texts*, which well complement the earlier literature in these fields. Recent works of a more scholarly nature include Günter Grönbold's *The Yoga of Six Limbs: An Introduction to the History of Ṣaḍaṅgayoga*, translated from the German by Robert L. Hütwohl; John R. Newman's unpublished dissertation entitled *The Outer Wheel of Time: Vajrayāna Cosmology in the Kālacakra Tantra*; and Vesna A. Wallace's unpublished dissertation entitled *The Inner Kālacakratantra: A Buddhist Tantric View of the Individual.*

This present work by the Tibetan monk and contemplative Gen Lamrimpa (Lobsang Jampal Tenzin) provides an unprecedentedly detailed explanation of the *Kālacakra Six-Session Guru Yoga.* The motivation for presenting this material is to make the practice of Kālacakra accessible to sincere practitioners who have received the Kālacakra initiation but who do not have the time or ability to practice the elaborate Kālacakra *sādhana*, or means of actualization of the body, speech, and mind of Kālacakra, which may take many hours each day to complete. This six-session guru yoga, first translated into English by Jeffrey Hopkins and newly translated here, is based on a shorter and more generic six-session guru yoga composed by the First Panchen Lama (Tib. *blo bzang chos kyi rgyal mtshan*, 1567?–1662). The purpose of this type of yoga is to provide a concise matrix of highest yoga tantra practices that include the stages of generation and completion as well as all the specific tantric pledges (Skt. *samaya*) associated with the five families of buddhas, namely, Vairocana, Ratnasambhava, Amitābha, Amoghasiddhi, and Akṣobhya. By properly practicing this yoga each day, all those pledges are fulfilled. Thus, although the various kinds of six-session yogas are nowadays affiliated especially closely with the Gelug order, they are equally pertinent to all those who have taken highest yoga (or, in the Nyingma order, *mahāyoga* and *anuyoga*) tantric initiations and their accompanying pledges.

In this eminently practical explanation of Kālacakra practice, inspired by years of scholarly training and decades of solitary contemplative retreat in Vajrayāna practice, Gen Lamrimpa begins by emphasizing the importance of a compassionate motivation for spiritual practice. In Mahāyāna practice in general and Vajrayāna practice in particular, compassion must be more than a mere appendage to one's spiritual practice to balance one's cultivation of contemplative insight. Rather, compassion is the very motivating force behind one's spiritual practice as a whole. By carefully examining the range of suffering to which all sentient beings are vulnerable, one becomes moved by a powerful urge to protect everyone from fear and suffering. With one's present, limited abilities, how can one do anything more than temporarily relieve the pains and sorrows of others, never truly protecting them from the underlying causes of misery? With faith in the power of the spiritual awakening of a buddha and in one's own buddha nature, which enables one to realize that state of enlightenment, in which one's deepest capacity for wisdom, love, and power is fully manifested, one brings forth the motivation of a bodhisattva: to achieve perfect spiritual awakening for the benefit of all beings. This is the spirit of awakening that lies at the core of the entire Mahāyāna tradition, including Vajrayāna.

In order to fully ground this spirit of awakening in a deep understanding of the nature of sentient existence, Gen Lamrimpa delves into the nature of the cycle of existence in which all sentient beings are trapped. While one may uncritically believe that all one's difficulties will naturally vanish at death, generations of Buddhist contemplatives attest to the truth of a continuity of individual consciousness that precedes this present life and carries on after death. Thus, this present human life is but one in an unimaginably long sequence of lives reaching into the unknown past and potentially extending indefinitely into the future. But this present life, he explains, is one of immeasurable value, for by applying one's human intelligence to effective spiritual practice, one may become forever healed from all mental afflictions, such as craving, hostility, and delusion, and their resultant miseries. By engaging in Mahāyāna practice, one may set out on the bodhisattva path of the six perfections, or the Pāramitāyāna, which takes countless eons of dedicated practice before perfect awakening is achieved. However, by practicing the swift path of the Vajrayāna, such as the Kālacakra Tantra, one may achieve the enlightenment of a buddha in one short human life span. One's incentive for practicing Kālacakra should not be merely impatience at the thought of having to practice for eons, but rather an urgent sense of compassion, the wish to effectively serve the needs of sentient beings as soon as possible. No motivation other than a spirit of awakening is suitable for Vajrayāna practice as a whole.

Gen Lamrimpa then proceeds to discuss the role of "pure vision" and "divine pride" in Kālacakra practice. According to Vajrayāna Buddhism, the world does not inherently exist in the ways we perceive it and think of it; nor does our sense of our own identities and that of other beings reflect anyone's intrinsic existence. Rather, our experience of ourselves, others, and the world around us is a creation of our own conceptual frameworks and languages. We are literally "making up" ourselves and our environment based upon experiences that are themselves products of our own previous habitual propensities. This is not to say that no one else exists and there is no universe apart from our conceptual constructs, but that all that we experience and imagine is structured by our concepts: neither we nor our environment inherently exist apart from conceptual designation.

The habitual propensities that structure our ordinary sense of personal identity and our environment can, however, be overcome through the ingenious practice of pure vision, by which—inspired by our own faith in or intuition of the all-pervasive buddha nature—we imagine all appearances to be expressions of the Buddha's body, all sounds to be the Buddha's speech, and all mental events to be the mind of the Buddha. This practice is coupled with the cultivation of divine pride, in which we identify our Vajrayāna guru, ourselves, our spiritual friends, and all other beings as emanations of the Buddha, in this case, Kālacakra. By so purifying our vision and identification of ourselves and others, the world increasingly arises to our experience as a pure manifestation of enlightened awareness, and our progress to spiritual awakening is enormously expedited.

In order to engage in such profound Vajrayāna practice, in which the motivation of a spirit of awakening is thoroughly integrated with one's understanding of the lack of inherent existence of all phenomena, one must rely upon a qualified spiritual mentor and receive tantric initiation. Gen Lamrimpa therefore gives a detailed explanation of all the stages of the Kālacakra initiation, each of them designed to purify obscurations of one's body, speech, or mind and establish within one the potencies for actualizing the body, speech, and mind of Kālacakra. This explanation, which is closely based on the ancient commentary the *Stainless Light*, can be enormously helpful to those who receive this initiation from the Dalai Lama or any other qualified lama. For without such understanding, the complexities of this rite may simply leave one bewildered.

In his discussion of the stage of generation, Gen Lamrimpa explains how this phase of practice is related to the processes of taking birth, living, and dying, and how it transmutes each of these phases into spiritual awakening. This entails a presentation of the vital energies, channels, and drops (Skt. *bindu*, Tib. *thig le*) that constitute the subtle body according to the Kālacakra system. Although none of these may have any direct correlation to human anatomy and physiology according to modern medicine, this does not necessarily mean that either system invalidates the other. Medical science is based on the objective observation of the human body, using a wide range of technological instruments that detect only those phenomena known to the physical sciences. No "vital energy" *(vis vita* or *élan vital)* has been, or perhaps can be, detected by such physical instruments. One can therefore conclude that if anything like the vital energies attested to in Tibetan Buddhism exist, they do not exist in the same manner as cells, electric currents, or electromagnetic fields. However, there are many known phenomena that also cannot be detected by the instruments of technology, the principle one, perhaps, being consciousness itself. Just as consciousness is known through first-hand experience, so do generations of Vajrayāna yogis claim that the vital energies, channels, and drops described in this system can be experienced directly through such practice. Thus, this view of the subtle body may be regarded as complementary to, and not necessarily in conflict with, medical science's view of the human body.

Gen Lamrimpa concludes his explanation of this practice with a remarkable account of the six-phase yoga, including retraction, meditative stabilization, *prāṇayāma*, retention, recollection, and *samādhi.* To the best of my knowledge no such detailed account of these secret practices has previously appeared in English, and it was only with the permission of His Holiness the Dalai Lama that we ventured to present them here. These are the unique practices of the Kālacakra stage of completion, and by bringing these practices to culmination, all the material components of one's body are said to be exhausted, and one achieves the empty form body, which is the primordial wisdom body of Kālacakra. In this process, all karmic energies are extinguished, all cognitive obscurations are abandoned, and with the realization of the empty form of Kālacakra with consort, one attains the immutable bliss of a buddha. From that point on, Gen Lamrimpa states, there is no moment in which one, as the Buddha Kālacakra, is not dedicated to the welfare of sentient beings, and one's enlightened body, speech, and mind pervade space.

With the motivation that all beings may achieve this state of spiritual awakening, these teachings are offered to all those who have received the Kālacakra initiation and wish to follow this profound path.

Homage

Lobsang Jampal Tenzin

Namo Guru Munīndra Vajradhara

In the nature of the broad pathway of the divine, free of conceptual elaboration,
All phenomena are displayed with the brush of conceptualization.
I reverently worship those beings of incomparable kindness
Who withdraw them back into the nature of the pathway of the divine.

My spiritual friends, more than twenty—including three who are foremost—
Embodiments of the primordial wisdom and enlightened activities of all the merciful *jinas,*
Have variously manifested in accordance with the dispositions, capacities, and inclinations of sentient beings.
Look after me until the end of sentient existence.

Siddhārtha, who dispels the darkness of beings of the final five hundred years,
Please dispel the darkness of the beings of the land of Tibet, without closing your eyes.
You, who have been praised for your courage by all the *jinaputras,*
Look after me until the end of sentient existence.

To emptiness free of taint, in union with the immutable enlightened mind free of stains,
To Kālacakra and your consort in primordial union,

And to the lineage of Kulika Dharma kings I pray:
Look after me until the end of sentient existence.

I reverently worship those *āryas* who have devoted themselves to the beings in Tibet—
The abbot, the teacher, and Dharma king; Atiśa, Ngog, and Drom;
Marpa, Mila and Dakpo; the three Sakya patriarchs;
And the father and spiritual sons of the Ganden order.

From beginningless time until the end of the world,
May such destructive foes as self-grasping and self-centeredness
Be vanquished, and may we be blessed by a myriad of enlightened activities
Of those who heed the vajra command.

Part 1

Preparing for Practice

The Kālacakra maṇḍala
Photo by Peter Nebel

1

Reflections on the Path

Motivation

In Mahāyāna practice as a whole, motivation is of paramount importance. In the highest yoga tantra in particular, aspiring for one's own spiritual development is inappropriate. Rather, one should sincerely seek to eliminate the unbearable pain and suffering experienced by all sentient beings. One must develop the courage and compassion to dwell in a hell realm for many, many eons without being depressed by that prospect in order to bring even one sentient being to the state of enlightenment. In addition, when one considers that the general Mahāyāna practice will require three countless eons on the path to enlightenment, one thinks: "I cannot bear the suffering of beings during all this time without being able to help them and serve them effectively. Therefore, I must attain full awakening as quickly as possible."

Simply wishing to attain individual full awakening, however, is insufficient for Mahāyāna practice in general and for the practice of highest yoga tantra as well. With the motivation to attain full awakening as quickly as possible in order to dispel the suffering of others, think, "Therefore I shall engage in this practice of Kālacakra; therefore I am attending this retreat; therefore I am sitting in this session; and therefore I am practicing this hour." This motivation needs to be cultivated and maintained in each individual practice session.

Bodhisattvas of sharp faculties are on the ordinary Mahāyāna path. Great merit is required to approximate their compassion (Skt. *karuṇa*, Tib. *snying rje*), wisdom (Skt. *prajñā*, Tib. *shes rab*), and superior resolve (Tib. *lhag bsam*). To be a fully appropriate practitioner for the highest yoga tantra, however, one's compassion, wisdom, and superior resolve should be one hundred thousand times greater than that of a bodhisattva of sharp faculties.

The Unsatisfactory Nature of the Cycle of Existence

The *Kālacakra Root Tantra* (Skt. *Mūlatantra*, Tib. *rtsa rgyud*) states that each of us abides in the beginningless cycle of existence. The text also explains the difficulty of obtaining a human rebirth and, within the human realm, the rarity of possessing a Dharma motivation. Even among people who feel an aspiration toward Dharma, it is unbelievably exceptional to be drawn toward the Vajrayāna. The text implies that among those who are drawn to the Vajrayāna, it is again rare to have a connection with the highest yoga tantra. The point is that it is extremely wonderful and amazing to have the opportunity to aspire to full awakening, to have the means to pursue that goal, and to have available the path for attaining the state of immutable bliss, the mind of a buddha.

The rarity and difficulty of obtaining this human life of leisure and endowment may be understood in terms of its nature, numbers, and causes. First of all, consider the difficulty of obtaining a fully endowed human rebirth in terms of its nature. We can look at the world population of roughly five billion people, and compare that figure with the number of those who have obtained a human life of leisure and endowment and are drawn to the Dharma. We can see that the latter group is quite small. We can continue by comparing a person with a human life of leisure and endowment not only with other human beings, but with all sentient beings. Consider insects, which seem to be everywhere. Indeed, forgetting size for a moment, if the five billion human beings on this planet were tossed into the insect population, the humans would simply vanish. Moreover, according to modern science there are microorganisms living in the soil as well as in the air and in water. The comparison of the human population with the numbers of all sentient beings enables us to understand the difficulty of obtaining a human life of leisure and endowment in terms of its nature.

In terms of numbers, it is said that most sentient beings exist in the hell realm, followed by fewer in the *preta* realm, fewer still in the animal realm; the fewest can be found in the human realm. So human existence is extremely uncommon.

The causes for rebirth in the miserable realms are unwholesome activities. If we look into our minds, we find mental afflictions replete with the causes for unwholesome activities. During the course of the day, it is most unusual to experience the arising of a wholesome state of mind. From the time we get up in the morning to the time we go to bed at night, the day is filled with unwholesome mental states. Thus, the causes for this human rebirth are difficult to acquire.

Even for human beings, the occurrence of a truly spiritual state of mind is extremely unusual. Out of the five billion people in the world, just a few have the appropriate attitude required for spiritual practice. And among those who do experience the mind of Dharma, if the ability to discriminate between proper Dharma and improper Dharma is absent, the presence of a spiritual attitude does not make much difference.

It is said that among those who do experience a Dharma mind, the ones who are drawn to the Mahāyāna are a strikingly small minority. And among those, the ones who are drawn to tantra are an even smaller minority. In this context, whether one experiences a mind of Dharma and is drawn to this form of Dharma depends on whether a fully awakened being has appeared in the world. But the appearance of a buddha in the world is very rare. Out of 16,300 great eons, a buddha appears only four times in four eons, or sixteen times. Most of these eons are said to be eons of darkness.

In one great eon there are eighty intermediate eons. These eighty fall into four types: twenty are empty eons; twenty are eons of creation, when things are in the process of becoming; twenty are eons of existence; and twenty are eons of destruction. A buddha can appear only during the twenty eons of existence. In each eon of existence, half the time the human life span is increasing, and during the other half the human life span is decreasing. A buddha manifests only when the human life span is decreasing. Thus there are only ten intermediate eons in which a buddha could appear.

One intermediate eon encompasses the following: When the human life span is on the increase, every one hundred years, the optimum life span increases by one year, ranging between ten years and eighty thousand years. Then it decreases in like fashion.

In this present eon, we are now in the phase when the human life span is decreasing. It has come from eighty thousand down to its present level and during this whole phase only four buddhas have appeared. One manifested when the human life span was forty thousand years, the second when the life span was thirty thousand, the third when the life span was tweny thousand, and the fourth, our historical Buddha, came when the optimal life span was one hundred years.

If you can take birth on one of those brief occasions when a buddha has taken birth, you have something precious. Of course, we have missed that opportunity.

Our Rare Opportunity

In terms of a human existence, it is quite remarkable to have the chance to practice Dharma. Many human beings do not even accept Dharma at all. Among those who do, many develop misconceptions. In addition, there are those whose senses are not complete. There are many factors that decrease our opportunity to practice Dharma. We now have an almost unimaginably rare opportunity: to have a human rebirth, to be drawn to Dharma, and to have a mind drawn to Vajrayāna. It is imperative to make this event meaningful.

Human beings have profound intelligence, and we should use this intelligence to enable us to avoid the causes for having to wander about in miserable states of existence. Assuming that one is an appropriate vessel, or trainee, for the practice of tantra, and one fully receives initiation, then it is said that even if one does not apply oneself to the practice but simply keeps the vows and tantric pledges purely, one can attain full enlightenment within seventeen lifetimes. And it is said that if one does apply oneself very assiduously to the practice, then it is possible to attain full enlightenment in one or two lifetimes. Even if one encounters difficulty in attaining full enlightenment in one lifetime, there are great hopes of attaining it in two.

If we can train ourselves well in the common path, properly receive initiation, and apply ourselves to the best of our abilities to the stages of generation and completion, potent imprints will be left on the mind. Even if we do not fully awaken in this life, we will be able to take rebirth in the next lifetime as a human being with real capacity to practice tantra and to attain full enlightenment at that time.

We have the ability to serve not only our own needs but also the needs of others. We have a very profound mental capacity in this lifetime, and if we do not make use of it, this is a great loss. The essential point is that it is very important to take advantage of our opportunities for practicing

Dharma. We are extremely fortunate to have the chance to engage in the practice of highest yoga tantra.

REFUGE

The actual *sādhana* of the six-session guru yoga begins with taking refuge, which is said to be the criterion that determines whether one is a Buddhist. Understanding one's state of suffering and experiencing the fear of being unable to free oneself from suffering causes one to look elsewhere for protection and refuge. It is important to reflect upon the nature of the three causes of the fear that impels us to take refuge, namely: (1) the suffering nature of the three miserable states of existence; (2) the unsatisfactory nature of the entire cycle of existence; and (3) the disadvantages of having cognitive obscurations when trying to serve the needs of other sentient beings. In the context of Kālacakra, the chief fault to consider is the unsatisfactory nature of cognitive obscurations.

What is it that brings about this unsatisfactory cycle of existence? A mistaken state of mind. In order to fulfill our desires and to avoid what we do not desire, we engage in actions of the body and mind. In this process imprints are placed upon the mind, and these habitual propensities become the causes of our body, environment, and experiences of pleasure and pain in future lifetimes. As these habitual propensities in the mind ripen in future lives, we again use the body and the mind to engage in actions, which again store habitual propensities. In this way the cycle is perpetuated. Whether people are in high or low positions, or have great or little power—indeed, no matter what the circumstances—we are all in the same situation. If one reflects upon the twelve links of dependent origination, the nature of the cycle becomes very clear.

Reflecting upon this, we should meditate until we come to the conclusion that there is no end to this compulsive cycle. It self-perpetuates until a wish arises to bring it to an end. If we think in this way, it becomes clearer and clearer why the cycle of existence is called an ocean of suffering from which there is no escape without Dharma. There are no mundane activities that lead to the cessation of this self-perpetuating cycle. If you want to make an effective nuclear bomb, make one that would cut that cycle. That would be a true bomb. This is exactly what Buddhist practice is all about—"bomb making." The realization of emptiness is the bomb that destroys the cycle of existence.

To cut this continuum of the cycle of existence, there are Hīnayāna methods that have their own strengths. However, the methods of the Pāramitāyāna are more effective, and the most effective methods are found in the Vajrayāna.

If we look for the ultimate source of the suffering, we find that it stems from ignorance. It is very difficult to recognize one's own ignorance and delusion. Why? Because the actual nature of that ignorance is a veil of obscurations. For everyday activities we can have a plan, but rarely do the results of our actions come out exactly according to plan. For that to happen, we would have to have a perfectly clear vision of the reality that is involved, but we do not. Nor do we have a perfectly clear vision of what needs to be done to accomplish our goals. Therefore, reality usually does not conform closely to our plans. Because we cannot see what is coming in the future, we do not see our whole situation very clearly on our own. That really is the essential reason for relying on someone else, and for taking refuge. There are two causes of Mahāyāna refuge, namely, the inability to bear one's own suffering and the compassion by which one is not able to bear the suffering of others. We must rely upon a teacher who is very familiar with the path.

The teacher we rely on should be one who is fully endowed with the ability to protect us from suffering. This person is called an object of refuge. One's objects of refuge should be the Three Jewels—the Buddha, the Dharma, and the Saṅgha. We can have utter trust and confidence that the Three Jewels know the actual nature of reality.

In terms of taking refuge, it is necessary to have a teacher who shows the way. In this context, of course, the teacher is the Buddha. Even if one has a teacher, however, if one does not put into practice what is taught, the teacher cannot be effective. That which is taught, the actual Dharma that one puts into practice, is the refuge of Dharma. It is very difficult to progress if one does not have some examples to look to, people who are farther along on the path. Those to whom one looks as role models are called the Saṅgha.

The chief of these objects of refuge is the Buddha. There are four criteria demonstrating that the Buddha is a true, authentic object of refuge. The first attribute is that he is free from fear. One who is not free from fear of danger is not able to protect others from fear. The chief cause of external danger is actually the elements of one's own mind, namely, one's own delusion, desire, and anger. When one has freed the mind of these distortions, then one is freed from external dangers. It should be clear that great desire makes one quite vulnerable. For example, the body, which is grasped by the mind and to which one is attached, is vulnerable to all kinds of suffering. If one has no more desire for the body than one has for a stone, one is free from physical suffering. When someone steps on a stone or grinds it into little pieces of sand, we do not get concerned. In the same way, things that happen to your body would not cause you to suffer if you were not attached to it. The Buddha is totally free of such mental afflictions as desire, anger, and ignorance, along with the habitual propensities for them.

The second attribute of the Buddha is skill in leading others out of suffering. One who does not employ skillful means in leading others cannot provide protection to them. It is important that the teacher's methods accord with reality. A mother who is very compassionate but does not know how to take care of her child may give her infant any kind of available food, in which case the child might die. A skillful mother, knowing that the child's digestive powers are weak, would give easily digested food that would gradually increase the strength and digestive powers of the child.

The third quality is that the object of refuge, the Buddha, must be endowed with compassion.

Fourthly, the object of refuge must not discriminate between those who are close and those who are far. The Buddha serves the needs of all sentient beings without regard for whether an individual has been of service to him.

The accounts of the Buddha's life establish that the Buddha was endowed with all of these qualities. Moreover, the Buddha and all the objects of refuge are without fraudulence. Because the teacher himself is without fraudulence, deceit, or deception, the teaching and its true followers will also be without deception.

In this practice, then, first of all visualize the objects of refuge. Bring to mind the causes for taking refuge and the excellent qualities of the objects of refuge. Then, while reflecting upon your own suffering and the suffering of others, beseech the objects of refuge for protection.

2

Receiving Tantric Teachings

We now begin the concise teachings on the *Kālacakra Six-Session Guru Yoga*, specifically in relation to the stages of generation and completion. Generally speaking, while listening to teachings of tantra, one should cast aside ordinary appearances. For example, do not think that you are sitting in an ordinary house, but imagine this dwelling to be the palace of Kālacakra. Moreover, do not look at the teacher as an ordinary person, but as an emanation of Kālacakra. This is true also for the students who are listening to the teachings. We should generate ourselves in the nature of Kālacakra.

Vajrasattva Purification

Tradition holds that teachings on the stages of generation and completion are preceded by the practice of the one-hundred-syllable Vajrasattva *mantra*, and also the offering of the *torma* (Tib. *gtor ma*). Therefore, after cultivating the highest Mahāyāna motivation, we follow tradition and proceed to the one-hundred-syllable Vajrasattva mantra practice. Do this as completely as you can by engaging in the Vajrasattva meditation, including the mantra and the visualization.[2] If you know the one-hundred-syllable mantra, recite that:

> *Oṃ vajrasattva samayam anupālaya vajrasattva tvenopatiṣṭha dṛḍho me bhava sutoṣyo me bhava supoṣyo me bhava anurakto me bhava sarva siddhiṃ me prayaccha sarva karmeṣu ca me cittaṃ śrīyaṃ kuru hūṃ ha ha ha ha hoḥ bhagavan sarvatathāgata vajra mā me muñca vajri bhava mahāsamaya sattva āḥ hūṃ phaṭ*

Otherwise, you can recite the abbreviated Vajrasattva name mantra:

> *Oṃ vajrasattva āḥ*

Please cultivate the all-encompassing motivation to attain the highest possible spiritual awakening for the benefit of all beings throughout space, and with that motivation listen to the teachings. After cultivating the motivation, please engage in the Vajrasattva practice.

The Teachings in Context

Traditionally, the teachings are given sequentially. A presentation of the teachings of the path in general is followed by explanations of the distinctions between the Mahāyāna and the Hīnayāna, between the Sūtrayāna and the Vajrayāna, and among the four different classes of tantras. If you fail to cover all the topics, you may miss the particular profundity of the path of tantra, which could lead to misconceptions.

Mahāyāna and Hīnayāna

It is said that the teachings of the Buddha, including the 84,000 aspects of the teachings as antidotes for the habitual propensities of desire, aversion, and ignorance, all flow into the ocean of reality. Just as there may be many streams from diverse directions traveling to the ocean, similarly the vast number of teachings given by the Buddha culminate in the reality that is the attainment of the *tathāgatas.*

Our experience of suffering occurs because of the confusion of the mind; mental delusions create our suffering. Insofar as we dispel the delusions of the mind, we emerge from the suffering and attain liberation.

The attainment of liberation is approached in different ways. For example, in the Hīnayāna, desire for sensual objects is identified as the chief cause of deception, and the antidote is the elimination of desire for objects such as food, and the cultivation of contentment and satisfaction by simply accepting alms to eat. The cultivation of contentment for one's clothing or one's abode is extremely important. Internally, the Hīnayāna practitioner focuses on the practice of the three high trainings—ethical discipline, concentration, and wisdom—and especially on the abandonment of mental afflictions (Skt. *kleśa*, Tib. *nyon mongs*), which are regarded as adversaries. The goal of the practice is simply liberation for oneself.

Within the Mahāyāna, there is the Pāramitāyāna, or the vehicle of the perfections, and the Vajrayāna. The Pāramitāyāna, which is based on the

Mahāyāna sūtra teachings, places an even finer emphasis on the rejection of desire for sensual objects. One is encouraged not to have the slightest desire for such things as food, clothing, and lodging for one's own sake. The bodhisattva abandons all concern for self and focuses entirely on others. The chief objects to be abandoned are not mental afflictions but cognitive obscurations (Skt. *jñeyāvaraṇa,* Tib. *shes sgrib*), which obscure the omniscient potential of awareness. In order to eliminate the cognitive obscurations, it is necessary to eliminate afflictive obscurations (Skt. *kleśāvaraṇa,* Tib. *nyon sgrib*), which are hindrances to liberation. On this path, one engages in the practice of the six perfections, and these practices in turn are qualified by special methods and wisdom.

It is said that one engages in the six perfections for the sake of one's own ripening, and one engages in the four means of assembly for the sake of others. All the other practices of a bodhisattva can be included in the perfection of ethical discipline. For the bodhisattva, there are three types of ethical discipline: keeping one's precepts, serving sentient beings, and applying oneself to wholesome behavior.

A person following the path of the Hīnayāna is never permitted to engage in any of the ten nonvirtues. In contrast, a bodhisattva on the Mahāyāna path is occasionally permitted to have desire for sensual objects for the sake of sentient beings. That is, one does not need to abstain from sensual objects if one is acting for the sake of others. Similarly, there are occasions when a bodhisattva is permitted to engage in unwholesome actions of body and speech for the benefit of sentient beings.

You may ask if the distinction between Hīnayāna and Mahāyāna is one of view or behavior. The distinction is one of behavior. How so? In the Mahāyāna, the basis of the motivation is the spirit of awakening (Skt. *bodhicitta,* Tib. *byang chub kyi sems*), and it follows that the bodhisattva has the intent to act for the sake of sentient beings. The Hīnayāna practitioner does not have the basis of the spirit of awakening. Rather, such a person's motivation is based in the trainings of the spiritual path to attain individual liberation.

Sūtrayāna and Vajrayāna

Within the Mahāyāna, the distinction between the Pāramitāyāna and the

Vajrayāna lies, once again, in one's behavior. Whether or not one has entered the Mahāyāna path is determined by one's development of the spirit of awakening. There is, however, a strong distinction in terms of the nature of the spirit of awakening involved. In tantra, there is an explicit usage of sensual objects and sensual events along one's spiritual path. In the Pāramitāyāna, the sūtra path, one does not explicitly transform sensuality into the path.

An additional distinction is that in the Vajrayāna, one must fully and authentically receive initiation. Furthermore, the Vajrayāna has the distinction of the four complete purities (Tib. *yongs dag bzhi*): (1) Seeing one's abode as the abode of a buddha (to accomplish this, one imagines one's abode as the palace of the deity); (2) seeing one's body as the body of the deity; (3) seeing one's actions as emanations of light that serve the needs of sentient beings; and (4) seeing one's enjoyments as being in the nature of ambrosia. At the time of fruition, this is the reality: that is, one's abode, body, actions, and enjoyments are of that pure nature. While one is still practicing on the path of tantra, one imagines these purities as they will be present in the state of fruition.

The Four Classes of Tantra

With regard to the time of fruition, there are no distinctions among the four classes of tantra. There are distinctions, however, in terms of how sensual objects are used explicitly on the path. For example, the four ways of using sensual attraction toward the meditation goddess are through gazing, smiling, holding hands, and sexual union. These four aspects correspond to the four tantric classes, from action tantra up to highest yoga tantra.

The first class of tantra, namely action tantras, places a strong emphasis on outer action, such as keeping pure hygiene and external rituals. The class of performance tantras places a somewhat greater emphasis on inner yoga. For the third class, yoga tantras, there is a definitely stronger emphasis upon inner yoga. The highest yoga tantras overwhelmingly emphasize the inner yoga over the outer actions such as ritual purification.

In highest yoga tantra, there are two branches known as the father and the mother tantras. That branch explicitly concerned with cultivating the body of a buddha is called the father tantras. The mother tantras are chiefly concerned with attaining the mind of a buddha. The two are equally advantageous in terms of attaining both the body and mind of a buddha, and they are equal in the sense that they are both equally founded in the Vajrayāna. The distinction is simply the degree of emphasis in this regard. Generally speaking, the Kālacakra Tantra is chiefly concerned with the attainment of the buddha body because it places a special, unique emphasis on what is called the pure body of *empty form* (Tib. *dag pa'i stong gzugs kyi sku*). Nevertheless, the Kālacakra Tantra is included in the class of mother tantras. The reason is that the attainment of empty form is used as a means for attaining *immutable bliss* (Tib. *mi 'gyur ba'i bde ba*), which refers to the mind of a buddha.

In other highest yoga tantras, the goal is to transform the extremely subtle primordial energy into the illusory body and by this means attain the body of a buddha. In the Kālacakra system, however, there is not such an explicit transformation of the extremely subtle primordial energy. Rather, the Kālacakra Tantra provides another means to attain the body of a buddha, through the empty form body.[3]

3

Overview of the Kālacakra Tantra

Kālacakra's Extraordinary Qualities

It is said that Kālacakra is exceptionally profound. One of the exceptional qualities of the Kālacakra is that from the time that the Buddha taught the Kālacakra up to the present, the lineage of teaching and practice has been maintained by *āryabodhisattvas*. The lineage has not degenerated, so the continuum of the blessing has not deteriorated.

Other profound qualities will become apparent in the future. There are said to be four sequential historical eras: the era of fulfillment (Tib. *rdzogs ldan*), the era of threefold endowment (Tib. *gsum ldan*), the era having two qualities (Tib. *gnyis ldan*), and finally the era of conflict (Tib. *rtsod ldan*). At the end of the era of conflict, the age of Śambhala, which is an age of fulfillment, will begin. At that time, Rudra Chakrī, the King of Śambhala, will bestow initiation. Receiving initiation from him will enable easy entry into the practice of Kālacakra, leading to the swift attainment of full enlightenment without great effort. Those who can take advantage of this opportunity will have a very good chance of attaining enlightenment within three hundred years.

Another extraordinary quality of the Kālacakra is its unique means for ripening disciples. For instance, at the time of receiving the initiation, disciples generate the five elements (Tib. *khams lnga*) of their bodies as deities. Specifically, the five elements are generated as the five consorts. Then all the initiating deities of the *maṇḍala* (Tib. *dkyil 'khor*) are invited to confer initiation. Meanwhile, the initiating guru generates the waters of the vases used in the initiation as the form of the five consorts. The five consorts then dissolve into the nature of the water and the five vases, and the initiation is bestowed by the initiating deities of the maṇḍala. Then the five consorts dissolve into the five elements of the disciple's body, and the elements in turn transform into the nature of the five consorts.

Later on, as one is practicing the stage of generation, one visualizes those five consorts in a similar fashion. The five elements, the twelve sense bases (Tib. *skye mched bcu gnyis*)—the six sense faculties, or subjective sense bases (Tib. *nang gi skye mched drug*), and the six sense objects, or objective sense bases (Tib. *phyi'i skye mched drug*)—and all other aspects of the discipline are dissolved into emptiness. They then appear from emptiness and are transformed into deities. The actual deities are drawn into these imagined beings, which thereby become the actual deities. The deities are present in the visualized maṇḍala.

In other tantras, the five psychophysical aggregates are transformed, but not by the process used in the *Kālacakra Tantra,* which is by generating one's sense bases into the nature of the deities, transforming the nature of the initiating substances into deities, and then taking the substances as deities, and so forth. These very profound aspects of the ripening process are not present in other tantras.

Kālacakra practice carries great blessings because one generates the many parts of one's being into deities. The five buddhas purify the five aggregates (Tib. *phung po lnga*); the five consorts purify the five elements; the ten *śaktīs* (Tib. *nus ma bcu*)—female embodiments of power—purify the ten channels; the six male bodhisattvas and the six female bodhisattvas purify the twelve sense bases. The twelve male and female wrathful deities (Skt. *krodha,* Tib. *khro bo, khro mo*) transform the different faculties of action and activities. On the other hand, a maṇḍala with only five deities directly purifies only the five aggregates. Although the other constituents of one's being are included in the aggregates, such a simple practice is not a direct purifier of the other constituents. Thus, the more detail there is in the visualization, the greater the blessing there is in the generation stage. The more clearly and precisely one visualizes a maṇḍala with all the deities present, the more profound one's practice.

When one generates the deities for each of the faculties (eyes, ears, and so forth) and brings them to mind during the visualization, the energies that are associated with the different faculties are made fit for action. Then in the completion stage it is much easier to bring these energies into the central channel.

In the practice of Kālacakra, many, many deities can be visualized, even at very subtle constituents of the body such as joints and so forth. All this visualization enhances the process of bringing the energies into the central channel. These intricate visualizations in the generation stage act as a favorable circumstance for the swift ripening that can occur in the completion stage. By contrast, generating a single deity without consort, be it male or female, is insufficient as a ripener for the completion stage.

Swift realizations arise as a result of training well in the common path, authentically receiving initiation, and engaging extensively in the stage of generation. Without such a blessing of the various energies, it is difficult for the ripening process to occur. Generally, tantric practice must be preceded by guru yoga practice, which is the vital essence of the path. In the *Kālacakra Six-Session Guru Yoga* one finds the essential elements of the generation stage.

Kālacakra, the Cycle of Time

In the Sanskrit term *Kālacakra* (Tib. *dus kyi 'khor lo*), *kāla* means time and *cakra* means wheel or cycle. Therefore, the word translates into English as *cycle of time.*

Kālacakra has three aspects: the outer, inner, and other Kālacakra. In the outer Kālacakra, *kāla* refers to a year, or the 360 days of the calendar year.[4] This annual cycle is symbolized by the wheel. The outer Kālacakra is that which is external to what is directly grasped by the minds of sentient beings, namely, everything in the environment apart from our bodies and minds.

The inner Kālacakra is that which is grasped by consciousness. In this context, kāla refers to the twelve subsidiary channels at the navel cakra—six of them on the right and six on the left—and to the vital energies, or breaths, that flow through them. Six inhalations and exhalations alternately flow on the right and left sides.

There are twelve shifts of vital energy each day. For every shift of energy there are 1,800 breaths, and within a twenty-four-hour period there are 21,600 breaths. During each of the twelve shifts, 56.25 breaths go into the central channel, totaling 675 breaths in each twenty-four-hour period. The term *cycle* in the inner Kālacakra refers to the twelve shifts of energy and the 21,600 breaths per day.

In the other Kālacakra, the etymology is understood in terms of the generation stage, the completion stage, and the fruition, or full enlightenment. In the fruition, Kālacakra refers to immutable bliss; *cycle* refers to the pure body of empty form, which is of the same nature as immutable bliss. In terms of the union of the body and mind, the fruitional state of enlightenment entails the union of immutable bliss, or mind, and empty form. In the completion stage, immutable bliss refers to the path rather than the fruition. That experience of immutable bliss on the path is called *time,* and empty form is given the name *cycle.* In the generation stage, imaginary great bliss is called *time,* and the imagined empty form is called *cycle.*

That is the etymology of Kālacakra.

Tantra, the Continuum

One of the various meanings of the term *tantra* is continuum, namely, the continuum of the reality and the continuum of the words that express reality. The continuum of the words expressing reality refers to the *Root Tantra,* which has 12,000 verses. The synthesis of the *Root Tantra* is called the *Condensed Tantra.*

Among the various tantras, the *Kālacakra Tantra* is regarded as being especially clear. Many other tantras, such as Cakrasaṃvara and Guhyasamāja, are called *hidden tantras* because their actual meaning is not explicitly revealed but is more veiled. For example, other tantras refer to the fourth initiation as being similar to the third initiation, but the point is not elucidated. The *Kālacakra Tantra* on the other hand, is lucid in this respect because it very clearly states that the fourth initiation is the integration of immutable mind and empty form. Because the Kālacakra is so clear and explicit, it is more accessible, especially for beginning practitioners.

The tantra that is the continuum of reality can be understood as the reality of the ground, the path, and the fruition. The tantra of the ground refers above all to the innate mind (Tib. *gnyug ma'i sems*). It is called a continuum because this innate mind is present as the ground throughout the path and at the fruition. At the time of fruition, this innate mind is called primordial wisdom (Skt. *jñāna,* Tib. *ye shes*). It appears as both inanimate and animate phenomena, that is, as the divine palace as well as the deities who abide in it. The term *tantra* can be applied in a similar way to the stages of the path: it refers to empty form, to the innate mind, and to the inanimate environment created by that mind in the stage of completion. This is also true for the generation stage, when all this is merely imagined.

Structure of the Kālacakra Tantra

Within the five chapters of the *Kālacakra Tantra*, this threefold classification of outer, inner, and other has two approaches: one in terms of teachings and the other in terms of reality. Make sure that the distinction between the teachings and reality is clear. The teachings consist of words, while reality consists of the referents of those words. The inner, outer, and other Kālacakras are to be understood in both these contexts.

Let us first examine the outer and the inner. The outer reality is the outer universe. The inner reality is one's own being, composed of the five aggregates and so forth. In terms of the teachings, the first of the five chapters of the *Kālacakra Tantra*, the chapter on the universe, is the outer Kālacakra. The second chapter, known as the inner chapter, is the teaching of the inner Kālacakra.

The reality with regard to the third classification of other Kālacakra includes the initiation, stage of generation, and stage of completion. In the other Kālacakra, the teachings refer to the remaining three chapters of the *Kālacakra Tantra*, namely, the third chapter, which is the chapter of initiation, the fourth chapter on the practice, and the fifth chapter on primordial wisdom.

There are three types of initiations. First there is the causal initiation, which ripens. The ripening elements are the path and the fruition of the path. The causal initiation is called ripening because if the student has received the initiation, it is appropriate for the student to engage in this practice. If the initiation has not been received, it is wrong for the student to enter into the practice. Second, there is the path initiation, which empowers one to become freed from the two obscurations. Third is the resultant initiation of liberation. It is not the process that liberates as in the previous ones, but rather it is the fruit of the process.

Related to the resultant initiation of liberation is the fourth initiation, which entails the body of unification of immutable bliss and empty form. That body is free of obscurations, as stated in the fifth chapter of the *Kālacakra Tantra*, the primordial wisdom chapter.

Since it is not possible to obtain the resultant initiation of liberation without having already received the path initiation that liberates, it is indispensable to engage in the practices of the stage of generation and of completion. These are taught in the practice chapter, which is the fourth chapter of the text. To practice the stage of generation, it is indispensable to have previously received the initiation. Consequently, preceding the chapter on practice is the third chapter on initiation.

As stated in the second chapter, the inner chapter, in order to receive initiation, one has to be a practitioner who has the basis to be purified, that is, the five aggregates and so forth.

The practitioner has to have a place to live and practice, and that place is known as the universe. Therefore, the first chapter is on the nature of the universe.

This explains the five chapters of the *Kālacakra Tantra*.

The Kālacakra System

The *Kālacakra Tantra* emphasizes the attainment of a buddha body by means of the empty form body, which is used to attain immutable bliss, the mind of a buddha. This differs from other highest yoga tantras, in which the buddha body is attained by transforming the extremely subtle primordial energy into the illusory body.

Tantric systems use different terms, such as the *union of body and mind*, the *union of the two truths*, and the *union of method and wisdom*. There are many distinctions regarding these between Kālacakra and other systems, as shown in chart 1.

Empty Form and Immutable Bliss

In the Kālacakra system, immutable bliss acts as the instrument for the utter annihilation of the material realm. Every day 21,600 types of energy course through the body. Each breath corresponds to one type of energy, and during one day there are 21,600 breaths. As one stops one of these 21,600 vital energies, one brings to cessation one of the 21,600 material constituents of the body. Each of these cessations corresponds to one great bliss. The process culminates with the stopping of the so-called karmic energies (Tib. *las rlung*). When one brings to a cessation all the karmic energies, one brings to an end all the 21,600 material constituents and actualizes the 21,600 great blisses. This is the culmination of the path of Kālacakra. At this stage there is a union of the body, which becomes empty form, and the mind, which becomes immutable bliss. This union is eternally indivisible. In order to attain this fruitional union of body and mind, it is necessary to practice the union of body and mind on the path.

There are three types of *mudrās,*[5] or consorts: action (Skt. *karma,* Tib. *las*); primordial wisdom, or visualized mudrā (Sk. *jñānamudrā,* Tib. *ye shes kyi phyag rgya*); and the great mudrā, or empty form *mahāmudrā* (Tib. *stong gzugs kyi phyag rgya chen po*), arising from the power of meditation. To engage in the direct practice for immutable bliss, the only mudrā that is appropriate is the empty form mahāmudrā because it is the only one that is effective for bringing about immutable bliss. This is the significance of representing the deities in union with the consorts in highest yoga tantras. The use of such pleasure in tantra in general is for the development of immutable bliss. The action mudrā and the primordial wisdom mudrā lead only to mutable bliss.

In the practice, while in union with the empty form mahāmudrā, the white *bodhicitta*[6] comes down from the crown of the head to the tip of the jewel, the sexual organ. Simultaneously, one brings the red bodhicitta up to the crown of the head. The body is filled from the top to the bottom. The bindus are exercised in this way, and with each of the 21,600 bindus one experiences the immutable bliss and primordial wisdom.

The Attainment of Immutable Bliss

It is necessary to overcome all types of obscurations, and to do so, one must attain immutable bliss. To do that, one must practice with the empty form mahāmudrā. In order to do that, it is necessary first of all to engage in the practice of recollection (Skt. *anusmṛti*), the fifth phase of the six-phase yoga of the completion stage. How is this practiced? At the recollection phase of the completion stage of Kālacakra, one visualizes Kālacakra with consort in the center of the navel cakra so vividly that they are lifelike.

Immutable bliss first arises from the visualization of Kālacakra in union with the consort at the navel cakra. At that phase of the practice of recollection, although one has attained the empty form, the connection between the body of the yogi and the empty form has not been cut. Sometimes, when you are actually practicing it, it seems that you are in empty form, but later it becomes apparent that the connection between the empty form and ordinary body is still present. Eventually, with the culmination of the path, the relationship between the two is severed.

The stage of recollection is reached after attaining a very firm hold of the energies at the navel cakra through the practices of *prāṇayāma* and retention (Skt. *dhāraṇā*), the third and fourth phases of the six-phase yoga. In order to retain a firm hold on the energies, it is necessary first of all to purify the central channel through the first two phases of the six-phase yoga, namely, the practices of retraction (Skt. *pratyāhāra*) and meditative stabilization (Skt. *dhyāna*). The purification of the central channel is done by focusing on the middle of the forehead until signs arise. As the energies converge, different signs arise, and one experiences different types of empty forms, and gradually one experiences the body of empty form.

Prior to these practices, however, one engages in the practice of the generation stage. If one fails to bless the various energies in the body through the practice of the generation stage, it is not possible for the energies to converge in the manner described. In order to engage in the practice of the generation stage, it is necessary first of all to receive full initiation. To do that, one needs to practice on the common path, and to do that, one must listen to the teachings of the common path, reflect upon them, and put them into practice.

The Place of Practice

The practice of Kālacakra guru yoga may take place in many possible environments. For engaging in actions of power, a forest is an appropriate place. For engaging in the practices that lead to the eight great *siddhis,* it is important to dwell in an abode that has been blessed by a buddha. Other possible locations would be temples or shrines, cemeteries, areas near lakes, or simply very pleasant surroundings. Beginning practitioners should practice in a pleasant environment, while the other places are appropriate for more advanced yogis.

There is a lot of discussion in the *Kālacakra Tantra* about other types of favorable external conditions. In one's dwelling it is important to have an altar, upon which is placed a representation of the body of the Buddha, a vajra and bell symbolizing the mind of the Buddha, and something symbolizing the speech of the Buddha, such as scriptures. It is also good to set out offerings.

The yogi's seat should be comfortable and soft. While actually practicing, sit in the posture of Vairocana with the seven essential points, the chief of which is having the body erect. An erect and straight body allows the channels to be straight and the vital energies to flow freely. This facilitates greater clarity of the mind and is very helpful for making one's channels and energies fit for use.

After sitting on your cushion, cultivate a proper motivation. You can begin the practice by focusing upon the breath, which will subdue the mind if it is in an unwholesome state. On the basis of that, cultivate a virtuous state of mind. From there we enter into the actual practice, the practice of the Buddha Kālacakra.

Part 2

The Kālacakra Six-Session Guru Yoga

4

Beginning the Practice

Please cultivate the motivation to aspire to the highest possible spiritual awakening for the benefit of all sentient beings, and then do the Vajrasattva practice.

Homage

Namo Guru Śrī Kālacakrāya

Having bowed to the original Buddha, the union of the vajra of great bliss with the aspectless mahāmudrā, I will elaborate herein the mode of practicing the very profound guru yoga in connection with the six sessions.

The guru yoga begins with a homage that points to the Sanskrit origin of this practice, the homage to the guru Śrī Kālacakra. The "vajra of great bliss" refers to the definitive meaning of Kālacakra, which is the immutable bliss. There is a mahāmudrā with aspect and a mahāmudrā without aspect. The mahāmudrā without aspect refers to emptiness. First set your motivation, then recite this verse slowly. Do not rush through it.

Refuge

With great adoration I take refuge in the Buddha,
The master from whom the supreme empowerment is received,
The Dharma of indivisible method and wisdom which he reveals,
And in the two types of Saṅgha who abide therein.

Visualize in the space in front of you your own root guru, of the same nature as the original Buddha, the glorious Kālacakra, who synthesizes all of the buddhas of the ten directions and the three times. They are all embodied in this one being, Kālacakra, inseparable from your own guru. In a more elaborate visualization, you may imagine the whole space in front of you to be filled with all the buddhas. Then imagine all around you, to your sides, behind you, and so forth, all the sentient beings, for whom you serve as a representative. You can take refuge while reciting the verse, and imagine doing this on behalf of all the sentient beings.

"The master" refers to your own spiritual mentor, or guru. Imagine your own guru being of the same nature as the Buddha.

Secondly, take refuge in the Dharma. Method and wisdom, which are without distinction, are unified. It is said that only in tantra does one find the indivisible method and wisdom used as a means for attaining the indivisible body and mind of the buddha at the time of fruition. It is a unique quality of tantra. When taking refuge in the Dharma in this practice, you take refuge in the wisdom of the *āryas,* whereas the more symbolic refuge of Dharma refers to the teachings of the Buddha and related treatises and commentaries.

In the teachings of the four noble truths, the Buddha taught, "Know the truth of suffering and abandon the truth of the source of suffering." Two different minds are doing this. Likewise he says, "Actualize the truth of cessation, and cultivate the truth of the path." In the context of the four noble truths, each of these is a separate event. In tantra, immutable bliss recognizes suffering, abandons the source of suffering, actualizes the cessation of suffering, and practices the path to the cessation of suffering all at once. Therefore it is said to be a Dharma of inseparable method and wisdom.

Finally, take refuge in the Saṅgha. The Saṅgha includes the trainees and non-trainees, those who are still on the path and those who have reached the culmination of the path. Other twofold distinctions can be made, including buddhahood attained by means of the sūtras or tantras; Dharma divided into the sūtras and tantras; and Saṅgha classified in terms of those who are practicing the sūtras or tantras. Another set of twofold classifications can be made in terms of the chief object of refuge and the ordinary object of refuge. The actual Buddha is the chief object of refuge; the ordinary object is a representation of the Buddha, such as a statue. For the Dharma, the realization of an ārya is the actual Dharma refuge, and the teachings and the scriptures are the ordinary refuge. The principal Saṅgha refuge is the āryas, whereas the ordinary Saṅgha refuge is practitioners who have entered the path but are still ordinary beings, not yet having become āryas.

An awareness of the excellent qualities of the objects in which one has faith is called admiring faith. It can also be understood as a great clarity of faith without obscurations. There are three types of faith: admiring faith, aspiring faith, and the faith of belief. There are three qualities that may darken the mind of faith, namely, lack of admiration, lack of aspiration, and lack of belief. Any of those three qualities obscure the mind, causing it to become like a pool of water with algae that makes the water unclear. Great clarity refers to faith free from all three.

The first line in the refuge verse, "With great adoration I take refuge," implies that one must follow the practices concerned with refuge. These include the nineteen pledges associated with the five classes of buddhas.[7] The pledge of taking refuge, associated with Vairocana, requires one to take refuge six times a day. Reciting this verse fulfills this pledge.

After reciting the refuge verse slowly, pause to reflect on its meaning.

The Basis for Refuge

The great Indian sage Dignāga said that since there is no doubt that there is no end to this ocean of *saṃsāra,* why do you think that you have not sunk into this ocean? What is meant by the term *ocean of saṃsāra*? It is a condition of existence in which one is dominated by mental afflictions and the actions they cause. As a result, one is caught up in the cycle of birth, aging, sickness, and death. The metaphor Dignāga uses for saṃsāra is an ocean, the depth and breadth of which is virtually impossible to measure. Similarly, as long as one is still under the domination of mental afflictions and their ensuing actions, the breadth and depth of suffering to which one is still subject is inestimable. Dignāga then chides himself, asking, "When you yourself have sunk into the depth of this ocean, why is it that you do not experience fear?" He compares himself to a child who is unable to imagine vast undertakings because he is unable to grasp the magnitude of his situation.

In relation to the whole of saṃsāra, the suffering that one experiences in one lifetime with a maximum span of about one hundred years is relatively insignificant. What one can experience in that time is trifling. In fact, right now we are in the midst of a sequence of former and later rebirths, but because the body acts as a basis for awareness and the body is again and again discarded, we are not able to recollect previous lifetimes. Nevertheless, they have occurred. As stated in the sūtras, if we were to pile up the skeletons of all the bodies we had in the past, it would reach high into the sky. It is also said that if it were possible to put into one vessel the milk we have drunk from our mothers' breasts in previous lives, the four oceans of the world would not be sufficient to hold it. Likewise, if we were to collect all the tears we shed in previous lives, again the four oceans would not be big enough to contain them. We cannot see or experience the degree of suffering that we experienced in previous lives, but if we were able to see it, we would be stunned by its extent.

So, as long as we continue to have mental afflictions, there will be no end to this repeated cycle of existence. Even in this lifetime, we tend to forget much of our experience. If we kept in mind all the suffering, discomfort, and misery we experienced just in this lifetime, we would be overwhelmed. Even in the course of one day, a subtle sense of dissatisfaction is pervasive. In the morning we are not satisfied with staying in bed, we need to rise; but we can't just stand up the whole time, so we have to sit down. And after a while we have to stand up again. We have to be in motion, we have to stop, and then we have to be in motion again. None of these actions is satisfactory. We are simply moving from one state of dissatisfaction to another. If one really were to investigate the nature of ordinary life, one would find it is overall simply a hassle. It goes from one state of discontentment to another. If we could hire someone to experience these discomforts, we would have to give them a lot of money, and it would be difficult for that person to keep everything in order.

In response to the claim that ordinary life is pleasurable, the great Indian sage Nāgārjuna comments that if there is a little bit of pleasure in scratching a rash, would it not be better not to have the rash in the first place? Even though there is some satisfaction in scratching a rash, the rash itself is unsatisfying.

As long as we are still under the domination of desires, it is inevitable that we experience dissatisfaction. The main cause for the cycle of existence is *karma*, or action. Karma comes to fruition and results in repeated rebirths due to craving and grasping.

We must reflect on this again and again to realize that we indeed are subject to this condition. Otherwise, it is difficult to experience deep compassion for others. Though we can certainly feel compassion or sympathy at times, this tends to be a state of mind mixed with mental afflictions, sometimes with the eight mundane concerns and so forth. Reflecting on this state of dissatisfaction also brings about an authentic taking of refuge. And the realization that Dharma is the only remedy for our situation results in an authentic refuge in the Dharma as well. Similarly, meditating in this way gives rise to very profound compassion, and since the very root of the spirit of awakening is compassion, this has very good results. If one fails to reflect on one's own suffering situation, although one can practice and do reasonably well, the practice has no essence.

The Spirit of Emergence

As Śāntideva says, the root of all virtuous action is aspiration, or yearning. How does this arise? From the belief that suffering is the result of unwholesome action and that wholesome action is the cause of happiness and well-being. Śāntideva says also that yearning depends upon one's continual reflection upon the nature of the full fruition of action, in other words, the nature of karma.

The point is that it is important to cultivate a spirit of emergence. This is the aspiration to liberation. Unable to bear the miserable nature of the cycle of existence, one aspires to a liberation that brings an end to that suffering. It is very important to reflect upon this.

Meditating on the nature of suffering brings great benefit. For example, reflecting upon one's own suffering tends to subdue any sense of pride. It also easily gives rise to compassion for others. Recognizing the source of suffering gives rise to an aspiration to free oneself by avoiding unwholesome action, and it gives rise to the yearning to engage in wholesome action.

The Buddha, after attaining full awakening and beginning to teach Dharma, did not say, "Life is great." Rather, he said that life is of the nature of suffering. He followed this by saying that the suffering we experience does not arise simply by accident but comes from an identifiable source, that the cessation of suffering is known as liberation (Skt. *mokṣa*, Tib. *thar pa*), and that the means for accomplishing this is known as the truth of the path. The truth of the path requires a recognition of the nature of reality and of the fact that ignorance is incompatible with that nature. The way in which ignorance grasps reality is incompatible with reality itself.

As long as we are still under the domination of mental afflictions, there are very few occasions when the buddhas and bodhisattvas can look upon us with real pleasure. In a family, when the children are very well behaved, the parents are very pleased with them. The buddhas and bodhisattvas look upon us with compassion, but without much rejoicing or pleasure. Because the buddhas and bodhisattvas have our well-being as their sole concern, they direct all their activities toward this end. So our taking refuge is, no doubt, a source of pleasure or satisfaction for them.

When taking refuge, imagine limitless quantities of light coming from the objects of refuge, entering your body and purifying all types of impurities, obscurations, and unwholesome habitual propensities.

The Spirit of Awakening

From this time until enlightenment
I shall develop the spirit of awakening
And the pure resolve,
And I shall cease grasping onto I and mine.

Recite this verse three times, and then again pause to reflect. This is the verse for the cultivation of the spirit of awakening. According to the pledges of the five classes of buddhas, one must cultivate the spirit of awakening three times during the day and three times at night. To recite the verse more fully, imagine yourself repeating it after the objects of refuge visualized before you, which is how it is done in the actual ritual for taking the precepts of the spirit of aspiring to awakening. If you are doing it in accordance with this ritual, imagine taking the commitment to follow these precepts.

The Two Aspirations

It is said that the prerequisites for the spirit of awakening are causal and resultant aspirations. Causal aspiration is the basis for serving the needs of sentient beings; resultant aspiration is the resolve to attain full awakening. Focusing upon the well-being of others causes the aspiration to achieve perfect awakening.

One looks first to sentient beings with the aspiration to relieve them from suffering and to bring them to a state of well-being. This is the causal aspiration, from which arises the wish to attain full awakening. The wish, "Might I attain perfect awakening," is the aspiration to enlightenment (Skt. *bodhi,* Tib. *byang chub*). However, we must understand that the actual spirit of awakening is difficult to ascertain. What is the measure of an authentic spirit of awakening? In an authentic spirit of awakening, the aspiration to attain enlightenment for the sake of all sentient beings arises spontaneously and without effort. This occurs, however, only after sustained practice.

The aspiration to release sentient beings from suffering and bring them to a state of well-being is known as the superior resolve. Having developed this resolve, you must recognize that, at present, you are incapable of carrying out that task. Then, recognizing this, you aspire to full awakening. If you do not have that superior resolve, the actual spirit of awakening will not arise.

A person with this superior resolve takes responsibility for relieving suffering and bringing about happiness. The superior resolve must be preceded by the yearning for sentient beings to be free from suffering and to experience happiness. In other words, it must be preceded by loving kindness and compassion. If one does not already have the wish that sentient beings be happy and free from suffering, then the wish to accomplish this will not arise. Moreover, the thought "Might sentient beings meet with happiness and be free from suffering" would not arise had one not already reflected upon the manner in which beings are bereft of happiness and satisfaction. Therefore, loving kindness, compassion, and the superior resolve are the means for bringing about the well-being of others.

Also, it is said that if you have not reflected upon the manner in which you yourself are devoid of genuine happiness, subject to the cycle of rebirth, and under the domination of mental afflictions, then this reflection on others will not be very effective.

When you feel affection for someone, that person appears lovable. If sentient beings do not appear lovable, the thought of wishing for their well-being and freedom from suffering will not arise. We can see this in the case of animals. Father and mother animals have a fondness for their own young, see their offspring as being lovable, and take care of them. When it comes to other animal offspring, however, this loving aspect is missing, especially among carnivores, who only have the thought of killing and eating others.

Because the most lovable of persons and our greatest friend is our own mother, it is appropriate to think of sentient beings as being our mothers. Before meditating on all sentient beings as our mothers, it is important to cultivate a sense of even-mindedness to bring an end to the distinction between friend and foe.

If you follow the practice of developing a sense of equality between yourself and others and then exchanging yourself for others, then you come to view others as being lovable by recalling that other sentient beings wish to be happy and free from suffering, just as you do.

If you do not engage in these meditations, an authentic spirit of awakening will not arise. The meditations can be done in either forward or reverse order. In forward order, you first cultivate a sense of even-mindedness regarding all sentient beings, then meditate on sentient beings as being your mother, and proceed to the actual spirit of awakening. To consider this in reverse order, finally there is the aspiration for perfect awakening; for that to arise, there must be the superior resolve; for the superior resolve to arise, loving kindness and compassion must be cultivated; that requires seeing other sentient beings as lovable; and for that to arise, even-mindedness must be present. This meditation can be effective in either order.

A spirit of emergence, or renunciation, is cultivated by reflecting upon the unsatisfactory nature of the cycle of existence and by developing the aspiration to be free from it. The above verse also introduces the element of time by emphasizing the intent to cultivate a spirit of awakening until one reaches enlightenment.

The Two Accumulations

In the context of the Kālacakra guru yoga, it is said that in addition to reflecting on the spirit of awakening, one should reflect upon what are called the three roots. The term root implies a beginning. The root of the two accumulations—of merit and knowledge—is ethical discipline. The root of ethical discipline is the spirit of awakening. Ethical discipline refers to the ethical discipline of the bodhisattvas, so it is perfectly correct to say that this stems from the spirit of awakening.

The root of the accumulation of merit is superior resolve. If one's actions are not motivated by compassion, they do not lead to an accumulation of merit that is a cause of perfect awakening. Similarly, if one's pursuit of knowledge is not motivated by compassion, it does not lead to buddhahood.

Superior resolve, once again, is the aspiration to take upon oneself the responsibility to bring others to a state of eternal well-being and to relieve their suffering forever. This intent gives rise to compassion and to altruistic actions such as the practice of generosity, ethical discipline, patience, and so forth. In this sense, it is said that superior resolve is the root of the collection of merit. The root of the accumulation of knowledge is the realization of emptiness.

The last line of the verse for cultivating the spirit of awakening, "I will cease grasping onto *I* and *mine*," suggests that in order to abandon the concepts of *I* and *mine* as existing intrinsically, one meditates upon the absence of intrinsic existence, or emptiness. It appears from this verse that both the relative spirit of awakening and the ultimate spirit of awakening are cultivated by means of this meditation.

During the process of the initiation, the ultimate spirit of awakening is symbolized by a five-pointed vajra at one's heart. The relative spirit of awakening is symbolized by a moon, also at the heart. The vajra rests on the moon. These are blessed during the process of initiation by the guru, who says, "Never be separated from these." This verse in the guru yoga refers to the tantric pledge never to be separated from the relative and ultimate spirit of awakening.

When reciting, "I will cease grasping onto *I* and *mine*," reflect upon the lack of inherent existence of all phenomena. The emphasis on abandoning the concept of an inherently existent *I* and *mine* points out a crucial facet of the practice. One may grasp onto the true existence of a pen, for example. Although this grasping onto true existence is a mental affliction, it does not seem to give us much harm or much benefit. Grasping onto the true existence of *I* or *mine*, however, has a very powerful impact on our lives. It produces many other mental afflictions, unwholesome behavior, and further consequences. Therefore, there is special emphasis on meditating on the lack of inherent existence of these.

Having recited the verse, again pause to reflect on the meaning.

The Four Immeasurables

I will cultivate loving kindness wishing that sentient beings be endowed with happiness,
Compassion wishing that they be free of suffering,
Delight in their dwelling forever in joy,
And the equanimity of impartiality.

Recite this three times, and then pause to reflect.

This verse refers to the cultivation of the four immeasurables. The first line refers to loving kindness, the second to compassion, the third to empathetic joy, and the fourth to equanimity, or even-mindedness.

In terms of the actual stages of practice, even-mindedness should be cultivated first. Great even-mindedness is cultivated by reflecting upon the lack of inherent existence of friend and foe. The main point of the practice of cultivating great even-mindedness is to counter the attachment toward people we call friends, and to counter the aversion to those we call enemies. The reason for leveling these imbalanced views is to recognize that friends may not remain friends, and that enemies may turn into friends. To counter attachment to some and aversion to others, it is also appropriate to reflect upon the fact that these beings are not intrinsically our friends or foes.

Following the cultivation of even-mindedness, one cultivates the wish that sentient beings who are bereft of happiness may experience happiness and well-being. Then let the yearning that sentient beings be free from suffering arise. Finally, for those sentient beings who have found well-being, yearn that they may continue to experience joy.

Among the pledges associated with Ratnasambhava are the four types of generosity. Reciting and reflecting on this verse fulfills the generosity of giving love. It is said that cultivating even-mindedness fulfills the pledge of giving fearlessness. How so? By cultivating even-mindedness, one overcomes attachment and aversion toward others and thereby offers them fearlessness.

The Spirit of Aspiring to Awakening

In order to liberate all sentient beings from the dangers of mundane existence and peace,
From now until buddhahood is achieved

I will maintain the attitude of wishing to achieve perfect enlightenment
And not forsake it even at the cost of my life.

Recite this slowly three times.

This verse refers to cultivating the spirit of aspiring to awakening. To recite it according to the actual ritual of taking the precepts for the spirit of aspiring to awakening, imagine reciting it after the Buddha in front of you, and imagine accepting the commitment to follow these precepts.

What is the difference between the spirit of aspiring to awakening by itself and the commitment of the spirit of aspiring to awakening? What is the difference between the spirit of aspiring to awakening and the aspiring mind together with the commitment? This can be understood from the verse.

Whether by means of the six causes and one result or of exchanging self for others, one arrives at the aspiration to attain full enlightenment for the benefit of all creatures. This is the spirit of aspiring to awakening. Before actually taking the bodhisattva precepts, one might have the thought, "Might I attain full enlightenment for the benefit of all creatures." This aspiration without any other characteristics is called the spirit of aspiring to awakening.

Assuming that one has not yet taken the actual bodhisattva precepts of the spirit of venturing toward awakening, one may resolve, "I commit myself to not relinquishing this motivation until I attain full awakening." Reciting this verse is similar to engaging in the ritual for taking the precepts of the spirit of awakening. The spirit of aspiring to awakening does not require any ritual. One simply engages in the meditation leading to the aspiration for full awakening for the benefit of all beings. When it arises, it arises. There is no special recitation.

Commitments of the Spirit of Aspiring to Awakening

Taking the precepts of the spirit of aspiring to awakening entails certain commitments, which include abandoning the four nonvirtuous actions, devoting oneself to the four virtuous actions, and not abandoning sentient beings, among others. In this case, first of all, one has the aspiration to full awakening for the benefit of all creatures. Then, one further resolves not to relinquish that state of mind until full awakening has been attained. These precepts, however, are not the actual precepts of the spirit of venturing toward awakening, that is, the bodhisattva precepts. The basis for attaining full enlightenment is the spirit of aspiring to awakening together with the actual bodhisattva precepts. Cultivating the spirit of aspiring to awakening is followed by taking the bodhisattva precepts.

There are six practices pertaining to keeping the commitments of the spirit of aspiring to awakening: (1) reflecting upon the benefits of the spirit of awakening in order to increase it; (2) cultivating the spirit of awakening three times during the day and three times at night; (3) applying oneself to the two accumulations of merit and knowledge; (4) not abandoning any sentient being; (5) avoiding the four nonvirtuous actions that cause the spirit of awakening to degenerate; and (6) applying oneself to the four virtuous actions that bring about the increase of the spirit of awakening in future lifetimes.

The first of the four nonvirtuous actions[8] is to deceive or mislead such holy beings as one's own spiritual mentor, people of exalted nature, people of spiritual realization, and so forth. The antidote for that is the first of the four virtuous actions, namely, to refrain from lying or deception. Because it is not so easy to tell who does and who does not have spiritual realization, it is better to be on the safe side and avoid deception altogether.

Speaking abusively out of anger or hostility toward Mahāyāna practitioners is the second of the four nonvirtuous actions. The antidote for that is the second of the four virtuous actions, namely, to look upon all sentient beings as buddhas. Again, because we really do not know exactly where people are in terms of their practice, it is best to look upon all sentient beings as if they were buddhas. We do not know who is a bodhisattva. Looking upon all beings as if they are buddhas will subdue harsh and abusive speech.

The third of the four nonvirtuous actions is to discourage others from engaging in virtuous actions or to cause them to regret previous virtuous acts. For example, if someone told you that he had been reading the Mahāyāna sūtras, you might scold him for reading when he could have been meditating. If the person took this seriously, he would regret reading the scriptures, and you would be committing one of these four nonvirtuous actions. There are many such occasions when one might discourage another person from practice. To counter that, it is important to encourage people in whatever practice they are able to do, recognizing that people are practicing in accordance with their ability. Be very careful not to discourage them or to lead them to regret the practice they have done. The related virtuous action is to encourage people in the study and practice of Mahāyāna. When the time is appropriate, this is a very skillful thing to do.

There are many people who are drawn exclusively to the Hīnayāna and believe there is no other Buddhism apart from that. To tell people who steadfastly hold this view that they should actually practice Mahāyāna would be fruitless and inappropriate. If you do encourage people in the practice of Mahāyāna, make sure that the occasion is right.

To a certain extent, there are grounds for people drawing the conclusion that only the Hīnayāna teachings are the Buddha's teachings. While the Buddha was living, he did not publicly give many teachings on the bodhisattva path. Most of the Buddha's teachings concerned the *śrāvaka* path. Due to the different way the Buddha taught Mahāyāna, it is easy to draw the conclusion that the Buddha's teachings are only those leading to individual *nirvāṇa.* In fact, there were bodhisattvas to whom the Buddha was giving other types of teachings. People who hold exclusively to the Hīnayāna path are not aware of other facets of the teachings as in, for example, the *Heart Sūtra,* which contains a lengthy dialogue between Śāriputra and Avalokiteśvara regarding the nature of ultimate truth.

The fourth nonvirtuous action is acting deceitfully or hypocritically, and not out of superior resolve. This entails trying to give the impression that one does not have the faults one actually possesses, and trying to give the impression that one has excellent qualities one actually lacks. For example, if someone extravagantly praises a bodhisattva, and the bodhisattva, out of attachment to praise and honor, acknowledges it, this is a form of hypocrisy. Another person may constantly fidget during meditation and have no realization at all, but out of embarrassment, he may claim he was moving about due to a headache. That, too, is hypocrisy.

The antidote is to be straightforward, motivated by the superior resolve. This straightforward quality, involving both self-honesty and honesty toward others, is very important. It has great significance from the outset, because if one practices upon that basis and then begins cultivating the superior resolve, the practice will be sound. If one's practice is not straightforward from the beginning, but is combined with self-deceit as well as dishonesty toward others, then as one is cultivating compassion, superior resolve, and so forth, one's practice is bound to go awry because it gets mixed up with the eight mundane concerns.

Cultivating this straightforward, honest approach alone would tend to counter the four nonvirtuous actions. The first one would already be eliminated because you would not deceive realized beings. For the second one, if you, motivated by hostility, had the urge to speak abusively, your self-honesty would cause you to recognize this as being afflicted and you would avoid such speech. Thus, being straightforward acts as a restraining factor.

Similarly, the third nonvirtuous action would be less likely to occur because if one witnesses another person engaging in virtuous actions, the honest response is more than likely to be one of taking satisfaction and rejoicing. Likewise, being straightforward and honest will preclude the pretense and hypocrisy involved in the fourth type of nonvirtuous actions. We must judge whether we can practice this for ourselves. It is a very profound point.

The virtuous action of looking upon all sentient beings as if they were buddhas requires skill because it is not an attitude to be practiced at all times, on all occasions. Doing so would block your compassion, since you do not have compassion for a buddha. One needs to be very skillful to see when the time is right to generate that thought and when it is the time to retract it. When one has the impulse to speak abusively about someone, that is the time to look upon that person as if he or she were a buddha.

Counting the avoidance of the four nonvirtuous actions as one practice and the devotion to the four virtuous actions as another one, these, in addition to the preceding four, make a total of six practices for keeping the commitments of the spirit of aspiring to awakening.

The Spirit of Venturing toward Awakening

The distinction between the spirit of aspiring to awakening and the spirit of venturing toward awakening can be made in terms of whether one has received the bodhisattva precepts. From the moment that one takes the bodhisattva precepts and keeps them, one has cultivated the spirit of venturing toward awakening. Prior to that point, the spirit of awakening is called the spirit of aspiring to awakening.

There are different ways to understand the distinction between the two types of spirit of awakening. The distinction made here is based on the teachings of Śāntideva, which in turn are based on the sūtras. There are also corroborating sources in the tantras and in the great commentaries, such as the great commentary to the *Kālacakra Tantra*.

According to Śāntideva in his work *A Guide to the Bodhisattva Way of Life*, the two are like the attitudes of intending to go and actually going. In both cases the intention to go is present, but only in the latter case is the intention coupled with the process of going. Similarly, the spirit of aspiring to awakening is the intention to attain enlightenment for the benefit of all creatures. When this intention motivates one to actually engage in the practice, the result is the spirit of venturing toward awakening.

If one receives the commitments associated with either spirit of awakening from another person, that person must also have the commitments. In other words, the person from whom you receive precepts must have the precepts as well. If, however, one has the wish to take the bodhisattva precepts but cannot find a person who has them and thus can give them, one may take them from the Buddha or a representation of the Buddha. Moreover, if one actually has the spirit of awakening, one can directly take the bodhisattva precepts, and they will be generated in one's being.

What is involved in taking the bodhisattva precepts? Aspiring to full awakening for the benefit of all creatures and, with that aspiration, committing oneself to following all the practices adopted by bodhisattvas. The spirit of aspiring to awakening alone has no commitment. It is simply the aspiration to attain enlightenment for the benefit of all creatures.

The Bodhisattva Precepts

Gurus, jinas, and jinaputras,
Please attend to me.
Just as the sugatas of the past
Have developed the spirit of awakening
And dwelt by stages in the trainings of bodhisattvas,
I, too, will develop the spirit of awakening for the sake of sentient beings

And will gradually engage
In the trainings of the bodhisattvas.

By reciting this verse, one takes the bodhisattva precepts of the spirit of venturing toward awakening, taking upon oneself the commitment to avoid the eighteen root downfalls of a bodhisattva and the forty-six faults. To do this in accordance with the actual ritual, recite the verse three times and imagine repeating it after the Buddha in front of you. In this way you affirm the intention to keep not only the bodhisattva precepts, but also the tantric precepts, including those that are given in *Kālacakra Tantra.* It would be good to accustom yourself to reaffirming the commitment to keep the precepts of Mahāyāna, Vajrayāna, and Kālacakra.

Following the threefold recitation, again pause and reflect. As you become more acquainted with this it will become more natural, and when you take the initiation, you can take it in stride.

Two of the eighteen downfalls—abandoning the spirit of awakening and holding on to false views—are also transgressions of the bodhisattva precepts. By incurring either of these two, one abandons the spirit of aspiring to awakening. For the other sixteen, a downfall has occurred but one does not lose the precepts altogether, and one does not abandon the spirit of aspiring to awakening. Recall that aspiration itself is the spirit of aspiring to awakening, whereas the precepts are of the spirit of venturing toward awakening. By abandoning any sentient being, however, one abandons both the spirit of aspiring to awakening and the bodhisattva precepts.

Upon the conclusion of the third recitation, imagine having received the bodhisattva precepts. If you think, "Now I take them," and if you do so with at least a facsimile of the actual spirit of awakening, then this is very good. It is very potent.

Review the eighteen and forty-six bodhisattva precepts to see if you can keep them before taking the precepts of the spirit of venturing toward awakening. If it seems feasible, then it is good to go ahead and take them. If, however, you feel the precepts are overwhelming, intimidating, or not feasible, then it is better to wait and simply continue in the practice of the spirit of aspiring for awakening.

It is the tradition to explain the bodhisattva precepts to trainees before they take them, so we can become familiar with them and judge for ourselves whether we are able to keep them. The process is very open. But the precepts for individual liberation and the tantric precepts and pledges are not taught to trainees beforehand. You learn about them after you have received them.

While taking the bodhisattva precepts, consider by way of example the bodhisattvas of the three times, those who have cultivated the spirit of awakening, engaged in the bodhisattva precepts, and attained the path. One states, "Just as they practiced, so shall I practice and follow this path to full awakening."

Now my life is fruitful.
Human existence is well achieved.
Today I have been born in the family of the buddhas
And I have become a child of the buddhas.

In this verse we rejoice in virtue. It is also a reflection upon the benefits of the spirit of awakening. Recite this three times and pause to reflect.

Now, whatever happens,
I will embark on deeds that accord with this family,
And I will not contaminate
This flawless, noble lineage.

This verse pertains to the cultivation of conscientiousness. Recite this verse also three times and pause to reflect.

Dissolution of the Visualization

This section of the six-session guru yoga is concluded by dissolving the visualization in front of you in one of three ways. You can imagine the guru as Buddha going to his natural abode, dissolving into the nature of light, or coming to the center of your forehead, dissolving inseparably into you. If your guru is still living, it is not appropriate to imagine the guru dissolving into the nature of light. Rather, imagine the guru becoming smaller and smaller and merging into your body. If your root guru has passed away, it is fine to imagine the guru dissolving into light and then into space.

Following the dissolution of the guru into yourself, imagine your mind becoming indivisible from the mind of the guru. Then imagine the arising of immutable bliss, and imagine the object of this subjective blissful awareness being emptiness.

5

Guru Yoga

The Need for Great Compassion

As the great Indian *paṇḍit* Śāntideva stated, the cultivation of great compassion is essential for bringing about the harvest of buddhahood. It is important at the beginning of the path, throughout the course of the path, and at the culmination of the path. At the beginning, it is like a seed. Just as there must be seed to have a crop, one must have great compassion to follow the Mahāyāna path. Along the course of the path, great compassion is to the practice what water and fertilizer are to the seed: there will be no harvest in their absence. Finally, upon the attainment of full enlightenment, great compassion is indispensable for serving the needs of sentient beings.

Indeed, great compassion is the very heart of the Mahāyāna path. Compassion initiates the path and is the gateway to the great profundity of the tantric path. For one lacking great compassion, it is difficult to enter the Mahāyāna path, and difficult even to speak of the tantric path. Even in the world at large, the absence of compassion and sympathy leaves beings without any protectors at all. Compassion acts as the condition for alleviating the suffering of others and bringing them happiness, because it is a state of awareness that cannot bear the fact that others suffer and are bereft of happiness. It is vital that we apply ourselves to the cultivation of great compassion.

To illustrate what happens to tantric practice without the presence of great compassion, there is a story from ancient India of a Hevajra practitioner who lacked great compassion. He succeeded only in attaining the Hīnayāna state of stream-enterer through his strong renunciation coupled with Hevajra tantric practice, but he could not attain Mahāyāna states because he lacked great compassion. One's practice may involve chosen deities, self-generation, and so forth, but without great compassion, it is not a Mahāyāna practice, and it does not culminate in the attainment of the three embodiments of a buddha.

According to Candrakīrti, the three essential factors of the path are great compassion, the spirit of awakening, and realization of emptiness. He points to great compassion as the root of the other two. It is very important to give special emphasis to the cultivation of great compassion and the spirit of awakening by applying ourselves to their development while engaging in the practice of guru yoga.

Guru Devotion

In guru yoga, one looks upon, or visualizes, the guru as being indivisible from one's chosen deity. Lama Je Tsongkhapa acknowledges this, but he says that the chief point of guru yoga is to apply oneself properly to guru devotion. One can accumulate a very profound store of merit by taking as the object of devotion one's own guru. It is common to this and other tantras such as Guhyasamāja, Cakrasaṃvara, and Yamāntaka, to invite the field of merit of one's own guru as indivisible from these chosen deities. Yet, it is even more profound to have the guru as the object of one's devotions. If one fails to do that and simply engages in visualization practices, then the practices are insignificant.

One may ask, "Is the guru's mind in one's own mind? Are the guru's mind and one's own mind actually of the same nature?" It is said that all animate and inanimate phenomena are displays of the innate mind. In this context, one's guru is, in a sense, an emanation of one's mind. However, as a result of ignorance, one may create a complete distinction between the guru and oneself because the guru appears as someone else and not as an emanation of one's own mind. For that reason, in all practices of guru yoga, there is the dissolution into emptiness of animate and inanimate phenomena. Then, meditating on emptiness, one generates the divine palace and so forth. The essential point of this practice is that the guru is an emanation of one's own mind. This is the purpose of the practices of generating oneself as the deity, with rays of light going out to all sentient beings to purify their unwholesome habitual propensities and obscurations. It is also the purpose of the practice of making offerings to the buddhas and then having the buddhas dissolve into oneself.

The fact that all phenomena are of the same nature as one's mind is obscure to us at the present time. Making an effort to eradicate such obscuration will eventually cause the innate mind to appear nakedly. When that happens, all animate and inanimate phenomena will appear as emanations of one's mind. As it says in the *Heart Sūtra*, having transcended the fallacious, one goes to nirvāṇa. At that point one's mind and the mind of the guru merge like water into water.

You may encounter the statement that mind pervades all animate and inanimate phenomena. Do not infer from this that there is only one mind. Rather, it implies that when one finally attains full enlightenment, one's mind and the guru's mind become of the same nature. It does not mean that they become identical. It would be impossible to make a distinction between the two if they were one mind. They are not one mind, but they are of the same nature. The continuum of the guru's mind and the continuum of one's own mind are distinct while still on the path, and they remain distinct upon the attainment of full enlightenment.

All the buddhas are equal in terms of their attainments and their virtues, in terms of what they have abandoned, and in their activities. However, from one supreme *nirmāṇakāya* to another, one may live longer than another, or one may have more disciples than another. In this sense there may be distinctions, which indicates that the buddhas are not one.

Because one's mind and that of the guru are of one nature at the culmination of the path, while engaging in tantric practice one cultivates that sense of the two being of the "same taste." In the Pāramitāyāna as well as Vajrayāna, the guru is the root of the path, and especially in tantric practice, proper devotion to the guru is essential.

There is a distinction between the Pāramitāyāna and the Vajrayāna, however. Although in the Pāramitāyāna one looks upon the guru as if he were a buddha, one does not look upon the guru as having the aspects of the body, speech, and mind of a buddha. In tantra, one not only looks upon the guru as a buddha and thinks of the guru as a buddha, but also regards the aspects of the guru as aspects of a buddha.

Is the ordinary appearance of the guru simply the guru's actual appearance or is it something created by one's own mind? The ordinary appearance is created by one's own defiled mind, which is blemished by mental afflictions. The story of Naropa illustrates this point. With great difficulty Guru Naropa sought out his teacher, Guru Tilopa. While on this quest, he met a man with a backpack. Naropa asked him, "Have you seen the master Tilopa?" The man said, "No, I have not seen Tilopa, but if you go over there by that mountain, you will find a person beating on his parents' heads." The person carrying the backpack was an emanation of Tilopa.

Naropa went to the mountain and saw a person bashing two heads. Naropa asked the person beating the heads, "Have you seen Tilopa?" The person said, "Yes, I have. I will show him to you, but before I do that, my parents have not treated me well, so you need to bash their heads, too." Naropa answered, "First, I am a prince; second, I am a fully ordained monk; and third I am a paṇḍit; and for these reasons I find it wrong to bash people's heads." Naropa reflected further and said, "I have been seeking out this teacher Tilopa in order to practice Dharma, and bashing people's heads is not Dharma, so I think I will be on my way." As soon as Naropa thought that, the person beating the heads and the people being beaten vanished. A voice from the sky said, "For the cultivation of great compassion it is necessary to realize emptiness. You must beat the head of self-grasping with the hammer of identitylessness."

The fact that the guru appears in an ordinary fashion is most often the result of the obscurations of one's mind. But the guru may appear in ordinary form for the sake of sentient beings. Also, in that very ordinary form of the guru, the buddha may dwell and teach Dharma. In order to cleanse impure appearances, one engages in the practice of guru yoga.

As discussed earlier, in one type of practice you imagine the guru becoming smaller and smaller and dissolving into your forehead. If the guru has passed away, it is appropriate to visualize the guru dissolving into light and going into your forehead. After dissolving the guru into the forehead, imagine your mind and the guru's mind becoming of the same taste. Since the guru's mind is of the nature of immutable bliss, upon the merging of these two minds, you should imagine that your mind is of the nature of immutable bliss, and that it is realizing emptiness. Abide in meditative equipoise, and from that state visualize the guru arising from the nature of immutable bliss.

THE FIELD FOR ACCUMULATING MERIT

Within the clear light of mahāmudrā free of conventional elaboration

The two phrases "clear light" and "free of conventional elaboration" are essentially synonymous. Conceptual elaboration in this sense refers to two things: grasping onto true existence and grasping onto the appearance of true existence. When those two are absent, there is the experience of emptiness. In the context of this practice, the immutable bliss that realizes emptiness is said to be free of conceptual elaboration (Tib. *spros bral*).

At present, our minds are constricted by conceptual elaborations. When the mind is free of such elaborations, the innate mind is able to manifest.

In terms of the Pāramitāyāna, the phrase "free of conceptual elaboration" refers to the absence of the appearance of true existence. In tantra, "free of conceptual elaboration" refers both to the subjective immutable bliss and to the objective emptiness that is realized by such immutable bliss. Similarly, in the Pāramitāyāna "clear light" refers to emptiness, whereas in tantra it refers both to the subject and the object, great immutable bliss and emptiness.

Moreover, both the grasping onto true existence and the appearance of true existence are called darkness. In the absence of such darkness, one's experience is called clear light. Conceptualization itself is also called darkness. The innate mind that is free of conceptual elaboration is also called clear light, and for that reason the innate mind is also called immutable bliss.

Mahāmudrā is so called because of its function. In general, a mudrā is something that is not transgressed. To transgress means to be apart from or to be outside. The innate mind, or awareness, is called mahāmudrā, or the great mudrā, because no phenomena transgress its nature.

When thinking of the clear light, do not think of actual light. When you have established meditative equipoise in the clear light, there are no dualistic appearances. The appearance of light is a dualistic appearance, which, therefore, would not arise.

Investigating the View

To understand the foregoing discussion, one must engage in the investigation of the view in which one does not seek to nullify the existence of something that does in fact exist, or look upon something that does in fact exist as being nonexistent. Rather, the task is to recognize that phenomena are already devoid of an inherent nature. This is the means for gaining realization of emptiness.

The refutation of true existence is simply the recognition of the absence of something that is already absent. Why negate that which is already nonexistent? The reason is that although there is no true existence, one has the sense that there is true existence. Because of that false imputation, one is not able to experience the lack of inherent existence of phenomena. One must recognize the manner in which one is falsely grasping onto the true existence of phenomena. The point is that phenomena both appear and are grasped as if they were present from their own side.

For example, it seems that the "I," or the self, is self-existent, already present. If the "I" existed in that way, it would exist immutably, that is, it would always abide in that same self-nature. But if the "I" exists in this fashion, does it exist within the body or the mind? We see that the body is regarded as "my body," so it cannot be equated with the self. Similarly, we regard the mind as "my mind," so it cannot be equated with the self. The body and the mind taken together cannot be equated with the self for the same reason, because again we speak of "my body and mind." If we ask, can such an "I" be understood apart from the body and mind? the answer is again no, because no such "I" can be found.

If we equate the self with the body, we have to recognize that, just as the body has many components, so would the "I" have exactly the same number of parts. Likewise, if we equate the self with the mind, just as the mind is comprised of many factors, so would the "I" have to have these parts as well. So, there would have to be many "I's," not just one.

By investigating in that way, one comes to the conclusion that such an "I" is utterly nonexistent, and one abides in the clarity of that realization. In that state the only thing that appears to the mind is the sheer absence of a self. Apart from that there is no other appearance of some other emptiness or anything else. Because this is the nature of the experience, that such an "I" does not exist, the experience is called inexpressible and inconceivable (Tib. *smra bsam brjod med*). Having ascertained the truth of identitylessness and imagining great bliss arising from the nature of such an experience, one visualizes the guru.

By having the realization of emptiness appear as the deity, all the appearances in the next stage of the meditation arise from the nature of that experience. Imagine the mind of clear light being like a television screen, and the images on it like the appearances arising from that domain of experience. That is what is meant by appearances arising as the displays of emptiness and bliss.

Visualizing the Merit Field

In the broad pathway of the immortal gods in front of me,
Is displayed an ocean of offering clouds of Samantabhadra,
Luminous like rainbows.
In their center, upon a jeweled throne supported by eight lions
Is a lovely lotus blossoming with a thousand petals.
On this are the discs of the moon, sun, rāhu, and kālāgni

The "broad pathway" or space in front refers to the emptiness or bliss of the mind. As you enter into this phase of the practice, imagine your subjective awareness being of the nature of immutable bliss and the object of your awareness being emptiness. Since the actual state of such an experience is utterly beyond all duality, imagine your mind to be like space.

The simile of the rainbow indicates that just as a rainbow appears in the sky, the guru and so forth appear in the space of bliss and emptiness. One visualizes a vast offering of jewels and precious substances of many kinds.

The jeweled throne is supported by eight lions, two on each of the four sides. Lions symbolize fearlessness, referring to the eight powers over which the Buddha has attained mastery. There are eight paranormal abilities, as well as various other powers of the Buddha.

As you do this and all the subsequent visualizations—of the sun and moon, the throne upon which the guru sits, and the form of the guru himself—imagine them all being produced from the nature of the awareness of immutable bliss realizing emptiness. This is a very important point, exclusive to the practice of tantra. It is indispensable to bear in mind that all these visualizations are creations of the mind of immutable bliss. It is very much like the appearance of the moon in the water. The water is likened to the mind of immutable bliss focused on emptiness; the reflection of the moon is likened to the visualizations that are created from the sphere of that mind.

In creating the visualizations according to your ability, imagine yourself being not in an ordinary environment but in a gorgeous, luscious green meadow or a meadow of the nature of jewels. If you can, imagine a lotus arising from space itself. If you have a hard time imagining a floating lotus, have the lotus arise from the meadow. The lotus has as many petals as you like. Upon that imagine a throne supported by eight lions. The throne is comprised of jewels and precious substances. Upon that imagine another lotus, an eight-petaled, variegated lotus. Upon that is a moon disc, a sun disc, the blue disc of rāhu, and a yellow disc of kālāgni. They are stacked upon each other like four pennies.

In the context of the outer, inner, and other Kālacakra, the moon, sun, rāhu, and kālāgni symbolize the outer celestial bodies. Inwardly, the thousand-petaled lotus symbolizes the mother's womb. The sun and the moon refer to the red and white bodhicitta. Rāhu and kālāgni symbolize the consciousness of the intermediate state.

If you relate this to the yogi's experience, then the lotus refers to the cakra at the genital region. The sun and moon symbolize the red and white bodhicitta as well as the right and left channels, and rāhu and kālāgni refer to the central channel. In the stage of generation these are symbolized by the different levels of the throne.

Upon them is the compassionate guru,
Indivisible from the Lord Kālacakra,
In whom are unified all the innumerable forms of refuge.

Seated on the lotus and discs is the guru "in whom are unified all the innumerable forms of refuge." This is a synthesis of all the buddhas in the form of Kālacakra, inseparable from the guru.

Bearing the brilliance of sapphire and blazing with glory,
He has one face and two hands holding a vajra and bell.
To symbolize the uncommon path of the union of method and wisdom,
He is in union with Viśvamātā, who is of the color of camphor
And holds a curved knife and skullcup.

"Bearing the brilliance of sapphire" indicates a blue color, and "blazing with glory" means that he radiates stainless light of the five colors. Very slender beams of light shine out in all directions like rays of sunshine.

The consort Viśvamātā (Tib. *sna tshogs yum*) is orange in color. In her right hand she holds a curved knife and in the left a skullcup. She is in the posture of embracing the deity Kālacakra around his neck. Kālacakra is embracing his consort under her arms while holding the vajra and bell.

With his right, red leg extended
And his left, white leg bent,
He dances in a hundred ways upon Māra and Rudra.

The right leg is red and outstretched; the left leg is white and bent. Beneath the two feet are Māra and Rudra. Māra probably refers to what is known in Tibetan as Garab Wangchuk (Tib. *dga' rab dbang phyug*), who looks very much like the Western Cupid. His hand implements are the five arrows of desire. Māra and Rudra, each with his own consort, are facing down and look a little bit depressed or worried. Maybe they do not like being stood upon.

The outstretched, red leg refers to the falling of the red bodhicitta, and the bent, white leg refers to the rising of the white bodhicitta from the genital region up the central channel.

The outstretched, red, right leg symbolizes the right channel. The bent, left, white leg symbolizes the left channel. The color blue represents the movement of the energy through the central channel upon blocking the left and right channels. The right and left channels symbolize both exercising the red and white bodhicitta and the attainment of immutable bliss. Therefore, the left and right channels also symbolize Kālacakra.

Their bodies, adorned with wondrous ornaments,
Like the expanse of space beautified by the constellations,
Stand in the midst of a blaze of five stainless lights.

These lines suggest the magnificence of Kālacakra. He wears the following bone ornaments: a circle at the crown of the head; two circles on the earrings; a necklace hanging down from the neck; and a sixteen-spoked wheel adornment hanging down from the necklace. There is a breast plate and a back plate, which are bound and crisscrossed in back and front.

There are also wrist ornaments, anklets, bracelets, and rings. On all these points—the upper arm, wrists, and ankles—are ornaments that seem to be vajras on each of the four sides, strung together with three bands.

Around the waist is a belt of three strands with an eight-spoked wheel in the front and vajras on either side. The belt looks more like a webbing of strands going around with vajra pendants hanging down.

The hanging folds of cloth are draped with a tiger skin. When the deity is in union with the consort, the tiger skin is somewhat loose and hangs down, as do the other raiments, and the deity is in a slightly wrathful mien.

There are five mudrās, namely, the ornaments at the head or crown, ears, neck, arms, and waist. A vajra garland hangs around the neck with something like a green scarf or ribbon dangling down. There is also a dangling lower garland.

The hair is wound up and piled on the head in two knots. On the crown of the head is Vajrasattva. At the base of the crown of tresses is an eight-spoked wheel. Five of the spokes have panels forming a crown. At the very peak of the front panel is a vajra jewel, like a crossed double vajra, in the form of a diamond. From the crown hang three ribbons on the right and three on the left. The consort has a similar crown. The vajra jewel is directly above the crown of the head. At the top of the crown of tresses is a variegated vajra, and upon that a half-moon.

The five-panel crown of both deity and consort suggests the five buddha classes. According to Kālacakra, the first point of the crown symbolizes Akṣobhya, to the right of that Amoghasiddhi, and to the left Amitābha. The back right side represents Ratnasambhava, and the left rear Vairocana. You can visualize the five points of the crown either as each having the seed syllable of those five buddhas or as actually being the five buddhas.

The "five stainless lights" are rays of white, yellow, red, green, and blue light emanating from the body of the deity, representing the five primordial wisdoms.

The three places of their bodies are graced
With the luminous forms of syllables
Of the divine nature of the three vajras.

These are the three vajras of the body, speech, and mind: the white *oṃ* in the center of the forehead, the red *āḥ* at the throat, and at the heart, the blue *hūṃ*. The text says three, but there are actually four. The fourth, the primordial wisdom vajra, is the yellow *ho* at the navel, which should also be visualized.

From the seed syllables at their hearts are emitted terrifying Vajravegas
Bearing various weapons, who draw in well a host of protectors dwelling

in countless realms;
And they become of one taste with the samayasattvas,
Thereby transforming into the great beings who comprise all the refuges.

The Vajravega is a wrathful deity, similar in appearance to Kālacakra, except that he has twenty-six rather than twenty-four hands.[9] From the syllable *hūṃ* at the deity's heart, visualize either one Vajravega being emitted or limitless Vajravegas going out in all directions. The Vajravegas draw in groups of protectors in the form of Kālacakra from their natural abode and bring them to merge with the *samayasattva* visualized in front.

The deity already visualized is known as the samayasattva, and those who are invited are the *jñānasattvas.* It is said that it does not really matter whether you invite them because they are already present. But it has some benefit for those who are concerned that the Buddha is not present in their visualization. To dispel that qualm you invite the buddhas, visualizing their presence and then imagining them becoming one with the deity.

The samayasattvas and the jñānasattvas become of the same nature, and one looks upon them as being the composite of all refuges.

The Seven-Limb Devotion

The seven-limb devotion, also called the seven-limb pūjā, relates to that which is to be purified. It is a counterpart to the accumulation of karma, which occurs naturally in terms of the bases,[10] and is a facsimile of an enlightened activity that corresponds to accumulating karma.

Homage

Reverent homage to the guru in whom the three embodiments are indivisible:
The dharmakāya of great bliss, primordially free of conceptual elaboration,
The sambhogakāya bearing the fivefold self-illumination of primordial wisdom
And the dance of nirmāṇakāyas in the oceans of realms of animate beings.

The first action of the seven-limb devotion is homage, which also acts as an antidote for pride. This is an expression of respect and reverence to the guru, who is of the nature of the dharmakāya, *sambhogakāya,* and nirmāṇakāya. The first line suggests the indivisibility of the three bodies of the Buddha. The expression "dharmakāya of great bliss, primordially free of conceptual elaboration," implies that the dharmakāya was never at any time truly existent. Immutable bliss is also called the dharmakāya. The dharmakāya is perceivable by other buddhas but not by those who are still practicing on the path. According to the Kālacakra system, the *svabhāvakāya* is a composite phenomenon.

The immutable bliss of the dharmakāya appears in the aspect of the sambhogakāya, which is observable only by āryabodhisattvas and not by ordinary beings. The sambhogakāya is said to have five definite attributes: time, location, nature, body, and aspect. There is a distinction in the explanation of the five definite attributes between this system and the Pāramitāyāna. In the Pāramitāyāna, the sambhogakāya is present until all sentient beings are enlightened. In the Kālacakra system, the attributes are as follows: (1) Time refers to the period until the ten signs have been brought to fulfillment; (2) location refers to the entrance of the vital energies into the central channel; (3) nature means the body of empty form, which is not comprised of composites of atoms and is not of a material nature at all—it is merely an appearance of the mind; (4) body refers to Vajrasattva's body; and (5) aspect indicates the embrace of the deity and consort. To trainees who perceive things in an ordinary fashion and therefore are unable to perceive the sambhogakāya, the deities appear in many ways, meeting the needs of all sentient beings.

"Reverent homage to the guru in whom the three embodiments are indivisible" means that the three bodies are of the same nature. Each pervades the other; that is, the mind is pervaded by the speech, the speech is pervaded by the body, and the body is pervaded by the mind. They are all mutually interpenetrating.

Offering

With a perspective free of the three spheres, without attachment or depression,
For the pleasure of the compassionate guru, the supreme field of merit,
I offer billowing clouds of outer, inner, and secret offerings
Actually presented and emerging from the play of samādhi

Visualizing the guru, making homage, and offering a maṇḍala are the means for keeping one of the pledges of Akṣobhya. This is to be done three times a day. By making offerings to the objects of refuge three times a day, one avoids the first of the forty-six secondary faults among the bodhisattva precepts.

One makes actual physical offerings, as well as imaginary offerings. In a tantric context it is inappropriate to make just ordinary offerings. Rather, such things as cookies and fruit must be dissolved into emptiness and transformed.

As in the previous visualization in front of oneself, so here, one begins by dissolving everything, especially the objects of offering, into emptiness. Having dissolved everything into emptiness, one cultivates immutable bliss and meditates on the emptiness of the offerings. Then one has the offerings arise from immutable bliss and offers them.

The offerings are made "without attachment," and also without the mind being discouraged or depressed. One has "a perspective free of the three spheres," meaning one is free from the conception that the objects of the offering, the offering itself, and the substance being offered exist inherently.

The text uses only a few words, but, as we can see, the common and uncommon offerings in reality are quite elaborate. One offers all of these to the supreme field of merit, the kind guru, and one should imagine the guru being very pleased to receive these offerings.

Among the different types of offerings, the outer offerings relate to the vase initiation. The inner offerings are connected to the secret initiation. The secret offering, the offering of the consort, is associated with the wisdom-gnosis initiation. The offering in which one visualizes great immutable bliss indivisible from empty form relates to the fourth initiation, which is the word initiation. The secret, wisdom-gnosis, and word initiations are among the higher and greatly higher initiations.

Outer Offerings

Six pairs of beautifully adorned, bliss-bestowing goddesses
Whose lotus-hands are graced with suitable offering substances,
As well as common and uncommon offerings,
Together with my body, possessions, and accumulations of virtue.

The offerings are held in the hands of twelve emanated offering goddesses, who are said to be more subtle and graceful than vines, and more beautiful than moonlight. They have eyes like the *utpāla* flowers. Their lips are naturally red, as if they were wearing lipstick. They have slender waists and broad hips, and they are full-breasted. They glance sideways out of their eyes, and they move very beautifully and gracefully.

One's offerings should be very fine and attractive. The offering goddesses themselves should be so attractive and beautiful that immediate happiness arises in the beings to whom the offerings are made.

The offering goddesses are in pairs. The first two, a dancer and a musician, are green. The offered music sounds as if it were created by a pair of hand drums. The first goddess is the dancer, performing various dances and holding clothing for offering. The clothes are like down in the sense that the material will compress and become quite small, yet when you let it loose, it gets as big as you want. The clothes are special because they are cool in hot weather and warm in cold weather.

Next are two black offering goddesses. One is holding offering water that is scented with camphor and sandalwood, both of which are cooling substances. In hot weather if you massage somebody on the heart with that, it is very cooling and refreshing. The other goddess holds flower garlands as well as petals, and she throws the petals and offers the flower leis, like the traditional Hawaiian greeting.

The goddess who offers incense and the one who offers lamps are red. The incense carrier has both natural and artificial incense substances. The other holds jeweled lamps that dispel the darkness.

Another offering goddess holds various types of food having the flavor of ambrosia. The other of the pair holds fruits that are delicious to taste and to smell. Both of these are white.

The next one is simply standing with her hands down. The other is smiling or laughing. They are yellow. The first one holds a crown in her hands, and the other holds a kind of jeweled garland that is worn down across the torso.

The last two are a singer, holding a vajra, and an embracer, holding a lotus. These offering goddesses are blue. The embracer serves as a consort.

These are all called the common, or outer, offerings.

Inner Offerings

We next emanate ten offering goddesses, who offer the following inner offerings:

1. Water, which is purified white bodhicitta
2. Fragrant water, which represents purified urine
3. Scent symbolizing purified bone marrow
4. Incense as purified excrement
5. Flowers representing purified flesh
6. Fruit as purified liver
7. Supreme fruit, offered as purified bile
8. A lamp symbolizing purified blood
9. Food representing purified intestines
10. Clothing as purified skin

In addition, there are thirty-seven uncommon offerings. In the Kālacakra stage of generation, there are body, speech, and mind maṇḍalas, each containing various offerings, as follows:

- Semen, or white bodhicitta, urine, excrement, blood, and flesh are offered in their purified aspects as the five mothers, or the five consorts. They reside in the maṇḍala of great bliss.
- The six senses and sense faculties are offered in the nature of the twelve bodhisattvas. The ears, nose, eyes, anus, tongue, and female sexual organ arise in their purified form as the six female bodhisattvas. The five senses and phenomena—form, sound, smell, taste, touch, and mental objects—arise in their purified form as the six male bodhisattvas. They reside in the mind maṇḍala.
- The eight substances of pus, phlegm, lice, organisms within the body, lymph, grease, pores, and hair arise as the eight *yoginis*. They reside in the speech maṇḍala, one in each of the four cardinal directions, and one in each of the four intermediate directions.
- The intestines, bile, bones, marrow, liver, lungs, channels, skin, heart, and fat arise as the ten wrathful deities *(krodhas)*. In the mind maṇḍala there are wrathful deities at each of the four doors, plus one above and one below, making six. In the body maṇḍala there are also four male and female wrathful deities at each of the doors, making ten.
- Eight more substances arise as ferocious beings (Tib. *gtum mo*). These are: tears, saliva, mucus, complexion, body odor, sweat, body grime, and teeth. Purified, they are the eight female ferocious beings, who dwell in cemeteries.

The visualization of these senses, faculties, and substances arising from the nature of immutable bliss and emptiness and taking on these appearances acts as a cause for transforming them into those deities.

Secret Offering

The secret offering entails the offering of a fully qualified, authentic consort, and offering union with that consort.

Maṇḍala Offering

> *The body, speech, and mind of myself and others, together with our possessions and virtues accumulated during the three times,*
> *As well as the excellent, precious maṇḍala with the mass of offerings of Samantabhadra,*
> *I raise up with my mind and offer to the guru, the chosen deity, and the Three Jewels.*
> *Please accept them out of compassion and grant me your blessings.*
> *Guru idaṃ ratnaṃ maṇḍalakaṃ niryātayāmi*

One also offers one's body and resources, that is, all one's possessions and so forth, as well as the roots of one's virtues of all three times. But one is not to offer one's bodies of the past, only those of the present and the future.

You offer your body to the guru in order to serve the needs of sentient beings. If you do not have that in mind when you offer your body to the guru, he would have to take care of it; and if he were to have many disciples, he would need a big expense account to take care of all the students' bodies.

Since an authentic guru has only one task, that of serving the needs of sentient beings, offering our own resources to the guru is a means of serving sentient beings. We should also practice informally. When eating, for example, we take the food with the aspiration to attain the highest possible awakening for the benefit of all creatures, and in order to do so, we take care of the body. Likewise in wearing clothes, think that we clothe the body for the sake of all sentient beings. We offer the body, speech, and mind of ourselves and others, as well as owned and unowned resources. Making these various offerings keeps the pledge of Amoghasiddhi.

The actual etymology of the Sanskrit term maṇḍala is *to take the essence.* When we offer the body, speech, mind, and resources, we offer their essence. We offer to the guru, the chosen deity, and so forth all the possessions with which we identify. The point here is not that the guru or the deity need these things, but that for the sake of our own merit, we ask that these be accepted with great compassion.

We ask, in effect, "May the blessing powerfully transform the ordinary body into the vajra body, the speech into the vajra speech, and the mind into the vajra mind." Also, we may ask for blessings (Tib. *byin rlabs*)[11] that our minds may be transformed into Dharma, our Dharma transformed into the path, and the path proceed without obstacles.

And finally, the last line "*Guru idaṃ ratnaṃ maṇḍalakaṃ niryātayāmi,*" means we take this circle of jewels and offer it to the guru.

Confession

From beginningless time, due to the untamed steed of my mind
Being intoxicated by the beer of the three poisons and negligence,
I have committed sins and downfalls and caused others to do so.
In particular I have disturbed the master's mind and disobeyed his instructions,
Broken the general and specific pledges of the five buddha classes,
And have failed to keep properly the twenty-five disciplines and so on.
Each of my mistaken deeds I disclose with intense remorse,
And I resolve to restrain myself in the future.

This is the confession of nonvirtuous deeds, which is to be done with the four remedial powers. Recite this, and again pause shortly to reflect.

This verse likens the mind that is subject to mental afflictions to a wild horse, "untamed" and "intoxicated by the beer of the three poisons and negligence." The point is that since beginningless time our minds have been untamed. They are subject to mental afflictions, such as the three poisons of desire, hatred, and ignorance, as well as negligence. The mind in such a state brings about only dangers and problems for ourselves and others. It perpetuates unwholesome actions and infractions, not only the ones done by us, but also the ones we have urged others to do in the past or present, and will urge others to do in the future. Here we disclose all such unwholesome actions and infractions of precepts that we have committed.

The phrase "I have disturbed the master's the mind" refers to not following the instructions of the vajra master. The text also mentions breaking "the general and specific pledges of the five buddha classes." There is a set of pledges relating to the five buddha classes, in addition to the fourteen root tantric downfalls and the eight secondary precepts (Tib. *sdom po*). The *Kālacakra Tantra* includes twenty-five disciplines. Infractions of any of these disciplines are to be confessed. The following are the specific pledges of each of the five buddha classes. One commits to engaging in each of the pledges associated with Vairocana and Ratnasambhava six times a day.

1. The six pledges associated with Vairocana are taking refuge in the Buddha, Dharma, and Saṅgha, and abiding by the three types of ethical discipline: keeping one's precepts, serving the needs of sentient beings, and applying oneself to virtue.
2. The four pledges associated with Ratnasambhava are the four types of generosity: material generosity, generosity of giving Dharma, generosity of giving loving kindness, and the generosity of giving fearlessness.
3. The three pledges associated with Amitābha are preserving the outer tantras (action and performance), the inner tantras (yoga and highest yoga), and the three vehicles or *yānas* (śrāvaka, *pratyekabuddha*, and bodhisattva).
4. The two pledges associated with Amoghasiddhi are keeping all the above pledges relating to all the other buddhas, and making offerings.
5. The four pledges associated with Akṣobhya are devoting oneself properly to one's spiritual mentor; the pledge of the mudrā; the pledge of the vajra; and the pledge of the bell. The last two actually mean bearing in mind the symbolic significance of the vajra and bell as one uses them. The vajra symbolizes great bliss and the bell symbolizes the realization of emptiness.

These are the nineteen individual pledges associated with the five classes of buddhas.

While reciting the line, "Each of my mistaken deeds I disclose with intense remorse, and I resolve to restrain myself in the future," we disclose our unwholesome actions with strong remorse and develop the intention to refrain from them in the future. If we do not have both regret for the unwholesome actions committed in the past and the intention to refrain from such action in the future, it is not possible for the habitual propensities from them to be purified.

If we feel very strong remorse for our unwholesome actions and infractions of precepts in the past, the power of those habitual propensities decreases, as if the seeds from these habitual propensities were rotting. If we do not have the intention to refrain from such action in the future, then of course the door will be open to repeating them, and again the mind will simply be polluted. The presence of both regret and restraint make the purification of the mind very strong.

To fully purify the habitual propensities of unwholesome actions, it is imperative to engage in all of the four remedial powers: (1) the power of disclosure, (2) the power of remorse, (3) the power of restraint, and (4) the power of purification.

The power of purification includes the power of applying the antidote and the power of reliance. These two seem to be implicit here. The power of reliance has two facets, namely, taking refuge and cultivating the spirit of awakening, together with the four immeasurables, including compassion and so forth. These two qualities were cultivated earlier in the practice. The power of applying antidotes entails reciting the purificatory mantra and meditating on emptiness, both of which are found in this practice.

At this point, in accordance with the leisure time that one has, it is good to recite other prayers of confession, such as *The General Confession* (Tib. *spyi bshags*) or various other confessional prayers.

Rejoicing

I rejoice in the oceans of good deeds done by myself and others,
From which rise a thousand bubbles of fine consequences.

The next part of the seven-limb devotion is rejoicing in virtue. These lines refer to the nature of wholesome actions that give rise to well-being.

Here we take delight in the deeds of the buddhas and bodhisattvas, of ourselves, and of other practitioners, such as the śrāvakas and the pratyekabuddhas. For example, we might take delight in someone's pleasant voice, which is a consequence of wholesome conduct in the past. Similarly, if we see a very attractive or affluent person, we may rejoice, thinking, "Oh, this is due to wholesome deeds in the past. How wonderful!"

There are many objects in which we may delight. There is great benefit and very little difficulty in doing so, and it acts as an antidote to jealousy.

Request to Turn the Wheel of Dharma

Please let fall the rain of Dharma of the three vehicles
In accordance with the interests and attitudes of inferior, middling, and superior disciples.

This is an entreaty that the wheel of Dharma be turned in order to eradicate the darkness of ignorance of sentient beings. The request counteracts the possibility of our being bereft of Dharma in the future, and it acts as a general antidote for the three poisons.

Supplication to Stay

May the coarse embodiments of the buddhas steadily continue to appear
To ordinary beings for hundreds of eons without being destroyed or changed.

This is the supplication that the awakened beings not pass into parinirvāṇa. It is also a prayer that the awakened beings and our spiritual mentors may live long lives. The essential point is to request the awakened beings and spiritual mentors to teach the Dharma. To do so, they must have long lives, so we make this supplication. In reality the buddhas are always present, but for the sake of people who are focused on this life alone—for the sake of short-sighted people who really rely solely on appearances—the request is that they do not withdraw their appearances.

Dedication

I dedicate my accumulation of virtue, such as this,
To be causes for the swift attainment of the state of union of Kālacakra.

Finally, this is the branch of dedicating the merit. Here we dedicate all our collections of virtue for quickly attaining the state of union of Kālacakra, the union of empty form and immutable bliss. The dedication of merit also acts as an antidote for the three poisons.

It seems that all four of the pledges of generosity associated with Ratnasambhava—giving Dharma, material things, loving kindness, and fearlessness—would be included in the dedication of merit. In terms of the gift of fearlessness, the main things to fear are the two obscurations, afflictive and cognitive. Dedicating the merit to attaining full awakening implicitly offers that fearlessness. Also, dedicating our collection of virtue to bring sentient beings to enlightenment is the giving of loving kindness. The other two types of generosity, of Dharma and material things, would also be included. Dedicating merit to the attainment of awakening implies that one would also meet with the necessary material circumstances, as well as the Dharma circumstances, to be able to pursue the path. The commonly cited analogy is that a drop of water added to the ocean will not vanish until the whole ocean disappears. Similarly, by dedicating our merit to the attainment of full awakening for all beings, the merit will not vanish until all sentient beings attain full awakening.

This concludes the seven-limb devotion. It is good to pause after each point of the devotion, especially after rejoicing in virtue and dedicating the merit, which are very powerful for enhancing the practice.

This also concludes the reflections and meditations of the common path.

6

Recollections and Practices

Śāntideva declares that the spirit of awakening is the ambrosia that dispels the affliction of suffering of sentient beings, and that nothing could possibly measure the merit of the spirit of awakening. He goes on to say that the spirit of awakening is the source of happiness for all sentient beings. How can we understand this? We can take contemporary figures, such as Mother Theresa, His Holiness the Dalai Lama, or persons from long ago, such as Jesus Christ, and we can see that these people are just like us in that they have bodies, sense faculties, and so forth. However, there is something special about these beings. When people think of them, many of them do so with great reverence. Just thinking of them brings happiness to the mind. Even when people are angry, such beings can soothe their minds and bring about happiness.

What is it about these beings that brings happiness to other people's minds? It is their kindness, the goodness of their hearts, for they have the wish to dispel the suffering of others and to bring about the well-being of others. This aspiration actually causes that result to occur.

It is the nature of the spirit of awakening to take upon oneself the responsibility for dispelling the suffering of others and bringing them to a state of lasting well-being. As the spirit of awakening arises, one pursues the path and engages in it to its culmination, the attainment of full awakening. Then one proceeds to engage in the activities of a fully awakened being, such as the three turnings of the wheel of Dharma, leading others out of suffering from its very source, and leading others to a lasting state of happiness as well as to perfect awakening.

Even under the present circumstances, insofar as we are able, we can reach out and, with a motivation of kindness, share Dharma with other people. We can give advice when others are having problems, and then, if they have sufficient confidence, help them put the teachings into practice. This can be a direct means of being of benefit to others.

Engaging in the practices and trainings of a bodhisattva is something that is right, and it is something we can do. If we can place ourselves in a position where we can be of service, establishing ourselves as friends to all sentient beings with the aim of relieving their suffering and bringing about their happiness, this is something very powerful because there is no limit to sentient beings. If we wish to engage in the practice of Kālacakra, it should be motivated by such kindness and compassion.

Recollection of the Three Roots

From this time until enlightenment
I shall develop the spirit of awakening
And the pure resolve,
And I shall cease grasping onto I and mine.

Now we should reflect again upon the three roots. The root of the two accumulations is ethical discipline. The root of ethical discipline is the spirit of awakening, and the root of that is compassion, loving kindness, and the superior resolve.

Compassion simply comes from the force of cultivating loving kindness. Correspondingly, loving kindness comes from the force of cultivating compassion. Compassion and loving kindness are intimately related. Saying that the root of the spirit of awakening is compassion implies that loving kindness is the root as well. As one relieves the suffering of others, their well-being is eventually established. Accordingly, if one brings about the well-being of others, their suffering will be dispelled, too.

The greater one's compassion, or feeling of not being able to bear the suffering of others, the greater one's loving kindness. In a person without much compassion, one who does not care much about the suffering of others, loving kindness will not fully arise.

The final line suggests that in order to abandon the concepts of *I* and *mine* as inherently existing, one meditates upon emptiness. As previously explained, if one's wisdom is not motivated by compassion, it cannot be called the accumulation of knowledge.

THE TEN PERFECTIONS

For the sake of the three accumulations
I shall practice the perfections of generosity, ethical discipline, patience, zeal, meditative stabilization, wisdom, method, prayer,
Power, and primordial wisdom.

The next stage of the practice is the reflection upon the ten perfections: generosity, ethical discipline, patience, zeal, meditative stabilization, wisdom, method, prayer, power, and primordial wisdom.

The three accumulations are merit, ethics, and knowledge. Ethics itself is the collection of ethical discipline. Generosity and patience constitute the collection of merit. The six final perfections—meditative stabilization, wisdom, method, prayer, power, and primordial wisdom—are all included in the collection of knowledge. Zeal, the fourth perfection, is required for all three collections of merit, ethics, and knowledge because zeal is an indispensable ingredient for all the other perfections.

Generosity is the mind of release. The mind that guards against unwholesome behavior is called ethical discipline. The mind that is unruffled, undisturbed, is known as patience. Zeal is delight in virtue. Lack of delight in virtue is called spiritual sloth. The mind that abides single-pointedly upon its object is called meditative stabilization. The mind that discriminates between different objects is known as wisdom. The object of the perfection of wisdom is emptiness, so wisdom is a mind that is able to discern emptiness.

The following is a review of the ten perfections according to tantra:

1. Freedom from conceptual elaborations is known as generosity.
2. Not losing one's regenerative fluids even when in union with a consort is known as ethical discipline.
3. The non-craving for the ordinary and the non-craving for true existence are called patience.
4. The gathering of the ten vital energies in the central channel is called zeal.
5. The mind that single-pointedly abides in immutable bliss is known as meditative stabilization.
6. The wisdom that is not overcome by conceptualization and that bears the speech of the buddha, which is perfectly suitable for those to whom it is directed, is known as wisdom.

7. Meditative stabilization is the means for retaining the drops while engaged with the three mudrās, namely, the action mudrā, primordial wisdom mudrā, and the empty form mahāmudrā.
8. Prayer is bringing oneself and others to fulfillment.
9. Power refers to the power of immutable bliss in which one gains liberation from the three states of existence.
10. Taking the bodhicitta from the tip of the jewel up to the crown of the head and experiencing immutable bliss is called primordial wisdom.

A very profound meaning is to be found in these explanations.

The Four Immeasurables

I shall cultivate loving kindness wishing that sentient beings be endowed with happiness,
Compassion wishing that they be free of suffering,
Delight in their dwelling forever in joy,
And the equanimity of impartiality.

This verse refers to the cultivation of the four immeasurables. The first three are wishing that sentient beings may experience happiness and freedom of suffering, and that they may abide in joy; the fourth is simply the equanimity of impartiality or even-mindedness.

Wishing for the happiness of others acts as an antidote for hatred. Wishing that sentient beings may be free of suffering acts as an antidote for cruelty. Wishing that sentient beings may abide continually in happiness is the antidote for jealousy. The cultivation of even-mindedness is the antidote for all the three poisons. Therefore, even-mindedness should be cultivated first.

Following the cultivation of even-mindedness, develop the wish that sentient beings who are bereft of happiness may experience happiness and well-being. Then let the yearning arise that sentient beings be free of suffering. Finally, for those sentient beings who have found well-being, yearn that they may remain in that state.

There is great benefit in continually reflecting upon each of these points: yearning that sentient beings be endowed with happiness, be free of suffering, and abide in happiness, and cultivating an even quality of mind. This brings about a real gentleness of mind. Whenever you see a sentient being, it is good to cultivate these thoughts.

The Four Means of Assembly

I shall beckon others well with generosity,
Engage in pleasant conversation,
Nurture them with meaningful behavior,
And give them great counsel according to their needs.

This verse concerns the four means of assembly. For a bodhisattva to serve the needs of sentient beings, it is appropriate to first show material generosity. Following that, one should speak pleasantly. Bodhisattvas should study and learn all kinds of things in order to meet the needs of various sentient beings. For those who are interested in carpentry, bodhisattvas learn carpentry. For those who are interested in theater, bodhisattvas study acting, and for those who are interested in business, bodhisattvas learn this field.

Just as we offer Dharma to others, so should we be practicing what we are teaching. Once we are practicing ourselves, we can encourage other people to do likewise. "If I have done it, then you can do it, too." This would be acting very skillfully. If we have developed extrasensory perception, we can see exactly what others need. If we do not have that, our task is somewhat more difficult.

The Ten Nonvirtues

I shall eliminate the ten nonvirtues:
The three kinds of bodily actions,
The four verbal ones,
And the three kinds of mental actions.

Now we come to the cultivation of mindfulness and introspection as means of abandoning the ten nonvirtues. The three physical nonvirtues are killing, sexual misconduct, and stealing. The four nonvirtuous verbal actions are lying, abuse, slander, and idle gossip. The three nonvirtuous mental actions are malice, avarice, and false views.

Whether one's actions of body, speech, and mind are virtuous or not depends on the mental processes involved. If one engages in action motivated by desire, hostility, or delusion, then the ensuing acts are nonvirtuous. As Nāgārjuna states, actions are virtuous if they are motivated by a lack of desire, lack of hatred, and lack of delusion with regard to actions and their results.

Desire and hatred refer chiefly to afflictive responses to events in this life. Otherwise it is difficult to understand. For example, if one engages in killing out of desire for the pleasures of this life, this would clearly be a nonvirtuous action of the body. But if one engages in killing for the sake of Dharma, this would clearly indicate the nonvirtuous mental action of holding to a false view.

The Five Hindrances

I shall eliminate the five hindrances
That obstruct the three trainings:
Remorse, lethargy, drowsiness,
Excitation, and doubt.

These five concern the eradication of the five hindrances. The first of these, remorse, is chiefly the regret of having to be separated from possessions and friends of this lifetime. It acts as a hindrance to the fulfillment of ethical discipline and is a serious obstacle to the cultivation of concentration. Lethargy, excitation, and drowsiness are also obstacles to concentration because both lethargy and drowsiness cloud the mind, and excitation agitates the mind. They interfere with the cultivation of concentration from both sides. Finally, doubt acts chiefly as a hindrance to the cultivation of wisdom. The kind of doubt involved here is having doubt about the nature of ultimate truth and the possibility of attaining liberation. Those five hindrances must be abandoned.

The *Kālacakra Tantra* provides another enumeration of the five hindrances, different from that which is set forth, for instance, in the *Suhṛllekha*, the *Friendly Letter to the King*, by Nāgārjuna. It is also different from the presentation of the five hindrances in the Vinaya. In other presentations, excitation and remorse are listed as one hindrance. Lethargy and drowsiness are also combined into one. Moreover, elsewhere, the remaining two are sensual desire and malice. In those presentations, sensual desire and malice are said to hinder chiefly the cultivation of ethical discipline.

As one engages in this practice, one should resolve to abandon those five hindrances.

The Four Afflictions

I shall eliminate the four afflictions
That are the root of cyclic existence:
Desire, hatred,
Delusion, and pride.

This verse brings to mind the four afflictions and cultivates the resolve to abandon them. Desire is a mental factor that sees contaminated phenomena as being attractive and yearns for them. Hatred is an aggressive state of mind that is focused upon and is averse to any of the three objects of anger, namely, illness, suffering, and the causes of suffering. Delusion refers to delusion regarding the relationship of actions and their results, or karma, and the mode of existence of phenomena. It can also be understood as a distorted intelligence that reifies any of the phenomena of saṃsāra or nirvāṇa. Pride is a mental factor that looks upon any event or quality related to oneself with a sense of conceit.

In other contexts, the teachings speak of six mental afflictions as the root of saṃsāra. The *Kālacakra Tantra* uniquely identifies these four afflictions—desire, hatred, delusion, and pride—as the root of cyclic existence.

Generally speaking, ignorance attends to the same objects that are apprehended with knowledge, but it does so in a way that is incompatible with actual knowledge. In the Kālacakra system, immutable bliss is called knowledge. That which is diametrically opposed to such knowledge is mutable desire, also known as ignorance. Another name for ignorance in the Kālacakra system is the habitual propensity for desire. As long as one has such propensities, one follows after desires.

It is quite evident that sentient beings, whether human, mammals, or even insects, naturally follow after the objects of desire, sexual desire in particular, without needing to be trained or educated. This is because they have habitual propensities for desire. Such desire is called mutable desire. On the same basis of desire, be it toward a man or a woman, male or female, aversion may also arise.

Sexual activity releases the white bodhicitta, the basis for joy. When the fluid is emitted, the joy that arises in dependence upon it also wanes. At that point it is said that one is free of desire because the pleasure arising from that has passed. The exhaustion that follows orgasm in both men and women and the decrease in the real vividness of awareness is called fainting. That causes the intelligence, or the power of the mind, to wane. Thus, that state is called stupor. Ignorance, which is to say mutable desire or the habitual propensity for desire, is said to be the root cause of cyclic existence.

This is a commentary on the point that desire, hatred, delusion, and pride are all roots of saṃsāra. In this way it becomes clear that this ignorance, which is the habitual propensity for desire, acts as the root of cyclic existence.

Following the post-orgasmic state, which is like fainting, there once again arises the sense of *I* with self-cherishing. The sequence is as follows: From the habitual propensity for desire arises desire. From desire occurs aversion. From aversion following orgasm there arises ignorance, and from that arises pride, a real sense of "I am." In this sense, the manner in which these four arise as the root of cyclic existence is clear.

This is a presentation unique to Kālacakra. However, bear in mind that grasping onto true existence, which is normally regarded as the root of existence, pervades all of these stages that have just been discussed. It is present at the time of the habitual propensity for desire and while desire is occurring. There is really no contradiction between this presentation and others on this point.

If the four so-called roots of saṃsāra did not arise in conjunction with the grasping onto true existence, then there would be no way to understand the four doors of liberation. It would not be comprehensible if one did not understand ignorance as being the false apprehension of reality. Ignorance refers here both to the habitual propensity for desire and the ignorance that falsely apprehends reality.

The antidotes for these afflictions are obvious. At the point in the completion stage when the regenerative fluid is about to be emitted, blocking the emission of the regenerative fluid acts as an antidote for mutable desire, and the realization of emptiness acts as an antidote for the ignorance that falsely apprehends the nature of reality. The basis for immutable bliss is the 1,800 drops of bodhicitta. In dependence upon each of those 1,800 drops there is immutable bliss, and when one experiences those 1,800 instances of immutable bliss, one becomes an ārya and an *arhat*. There seems to be agreement between this system and that of Cakrasaṃvara and Guhyasamāja that becoming an ārya and becoming an arhat are simultaneous, meaning here that one has gained a realization of the actual clear light.

In all of these three systems, Cakrasaṃvara, Guhyasamāja, and Kālacakra, one directly and nonconceptually realizes emptiness by means of the extremely subtle mind, and in so doing one eradicates all afflictive obscurations, both those that are inborn and those that are artificial.

The Four Contaminants

I shall eliminate the four contaminants
That are the cause of saṃsāra,
The contaminants of desire, of becoming,
Of ignorance, and of false views.

This verse relates to abandoning the four contaminants.[12] The term *contaminant* frequently refers to mental afflictions. The first contaminant is the desire for the sensual realm. This desire may be focused on any phenomena up to and including the *deva* realms within the sensual realm. The contaminant of becoming is the desire for the pleasures of the form and formless realms. The third of the four contaminants is ignorance. The final one refers to all types of distorted views, including the various classifications of 360 or twenty distorted views.

The Four Doors of Liberation

I shall accomplish perfect enlightenment
By means of the four doors of liberation:
Emptiness, signlessness,
Desirelessness, and nonactivity.

These are the four means of realizing emptiness, and the fourfold distinction is made in terms of the phenomena whose ultimate nature is emptiness:

1. The lack of inherent existence of an object is known as emptiness.
2. The lack of inherent existence of the cause of phenomena is called signlessness.
3. The lack of inherent existence of the result is known as desirelessness.
4. The lack of inherent existence of the actions of rising and passing is known as nonactivity.

According to the system of Kālacakra, the realization of emptiness acts as a substantial cause for the dharmakāya. The realization of signlessness acts as a substantial cause for the sambhogakāya. Realizing desirelessness acts as a substantial cause for the nirmāṇakāya. The realization of nonactivity acts as the substantial cause for the svabhāvakāya.

Supplication for Blessings

I pray to the compassionate guru, the synthesis of the three refuges,
Who, if relied upon, is the greatest wish-fulfilling
Source of all virtue and excellence within cyclic existence and peace:
Please bless my mindstream.

This verse compares one's spiritual mentor to a wish-fulfilling gem, for the guru grants all of one's wishes and, if relied upon, gives protection from the dangers of cyclic existence as well as the dangers of peace, which here refers to nirvāṇa.

This supplication is made while bearing in mind the excellent qualities and the kindness of one's spiritual mentor. Referring here to one's spiritual mentor as the composite of all three refuges means that the body of the guru can be regarded as the Saṅgha refuge, the speech of the guru can be regarded as the Dharma refuge, and the mind of the guru as the Buddha refuge. Another way of understanding it is that the guru is the Buddha refuge because one's spiritual mentor reveals the means to realize enlightenment. The abandonment of obscurations and the acquisition of positive qualities in the guru's mind can be regarded as the Dharma refuge. Thirdly, because the guru is appearing as the nirmāṇakāya, he or she can be regarded as the Saṅgha refuge.

Supplication is made to the guru who is the source of all of the virtues and goodness within cyclic existence and peace. Why are we making the supplication? So that any inappropriate aspects of our being may be blessed and transformed. Other supplications can include the prayers that one's own mind and that of the guru may be of the same nature, that one's mind may go to Dharma, one's Dharma may go to the path, and one's path may be free of obstacles.

To make this more elaborate in terms of one's guru devotion, reflect upon the benefits of guru devotion and the disadvantages of a lack of guru devotion or a poor relationship with the guru. Reflect upon the excellent qualities of the guru. Doing this keeps the tantric pledge related to guru yoga as described in the *Fifty Stanzas on the Guru* by Aśvaghoṣa. Reflecting upon the excellent qualities of the body, speech, and mind of the guru, one should make very earnest supplication.

The Name Mantra

Oṃ āḥ guru vajradhara mañjuśrī vagindra sumati jñāna śasanadhara samudra śrībhadra sarva siddhi hūṃ hūṃ

The name mantra should be recited with the attitude of prayerful supplication to the guru. It is good to visualize the name mantra as a circle at the heart of the guru and to engage in the visualization of the falling and entrance of nectar. The nectar flows from the heart of the guru on which you can visualize *hūṃ hūṃ* surrounded by the syllables of the name mantra. Imagine the nectar flowing from there and coming into your body, purifying it.

There are other ways of doing this visualization. You can simply visualize the four letters *oṃ, āḥ, hūṃ, ho,* and imagine the ambrosia flowing from those, or you can imagine the nectar flowing from the entire body of the guru. It does not make any difference.

You can visualize yourself alone or surrounded by all other sentient beings. As the nectar flows, imagine all unwholesome habitual propensities and obscurations being purified, both in yourself and in others. Imagine the purification of unwholesome habitual propensities to harming the guru's body, to acting contrary to the guru's advice, and thirdly, to disturbing the guru's mind. Imagine all of these habitual propensities being purified.

The above mantra is the name mantra of His Holiness the Dalai Lama in Sanskrit. In the mantra, the *oṃ āḥ* at the beginning and one of the *hūṃ hūṃ* at the end signify the body, speech, and mind of the buddha. The meanings of the other words in the mantra are as follows:

- *Guru* means spiritual mentor.
- In the term *Vajradhara, vajra* refers to the primordial wisdom of nonduality of bliss and emptiness. *Dhara* means to hold, for the guru has abandoned all impurities and holds the wisdom of nonduality of emptiness and bliss.
- *Mañjuśrī* is the embodiment of enlightened wisdom.

- *Vagindra* means the Lord of Speech.
- *Sumati* means excellent mind.
- *Jñāna* means primordial wisdom.
- *Śasanadhara* means holder of the teachings.
- *Samudra* means ocean.
- *Śrībhadra* means the gloriously good.
- *Sarva* means all.
- *Siddhi* means feats.
- One of the *hūṃ hūṃ* refers to the mind of the buddha, and the other signifies the request to please bestow all siddhis of the body, speech, and mind of the buddha, which are signified by *oṃ āḥ hūṃ hūṃ.*

Recite the name mantra as many times as you can.

Supplication for Initiation

Guru Kālacakra,
Please grant me the complete empowerments.
Bless me so that the four types of hindrances may be cleared away
And that the four embodiments may be achieved

Following the name mantra is the supplication for initiation. It is not appropriate to give an initiation that has not been requested. To avoid that fault, the supplication is included.

The supplication begins when one first visualizes the guru, Kālacakra. One begins the supplication by asking, "Guru Kālacakra, please grant me the complete empowerments." One says this to avoid requesting only the self-entry, or self-initiation, of a child (Tib. *byis pa bdag 'jug*) in the Kālacakra initiation and not the high or the very high initiations. So we are asking the guru to please not do that. Some people even give the self-entry of a child only partially. To try to keep that from happening, one asks the guru to please bestow the initiation completely.

Finally, it is called "of a child" because in this context the practitioner on the stage of generation is called a child, and the practitioner on the stage of completion is called an adult. The very terminology of what is called the self-entry of a child indicates that in order to fully practice the stage of completion, it is necessary to practice the stage of generation. You cannot become an adult without being a child first.

Why does one request initiation? To purify the four types of obscurations in order to achieve the four buddha embodiments. Just as one recites this verse three times in an actual initiation, so it is recited three times in this practice.

All of the preceding practices are said to correspond to the accumulation of karma in ordinary reality.

7

Receiving Initiation

Prerequisites

In order to practice tantra, it is necessary to have the basis of some understanding of emptiness. Another indispensable prerequisite is the cultivation of the spirit of awakening. Therefore, the spirit of awakening and some understanding of the view are regarded as basic for receiving initiation. To authentically receive initiation, one must be able to reflect upon emptiness and have some understanding of the wisdom that realizes emptiness, and also the experience of the spirit of awakening. If one does not have any understanding of emptiness and does not have experience of the spirit of awakening, it is still possible to go for initiation, but it is highly questionable whether one will actually receive it.

In the threefold division of outer, inner, and other in the *Kālacakra Tantra*, the outer and the inner are known as that which is to be purified. They are the basis to be purified. The path that is the purifier, or the purifying agent, of the basis to be purified consists of the initiations, the stage of generation, and the stage of completion. The results of purification are the qualities of buddhahood, such as the three or four bodies of the buddha.

Stated another way, the basis is that which is to be purified—one's psychophysical aggregates, elements, and sense bases. The path is the practice of generating them in their divine form. In the resultant purification, the purified aspects of the aggregates, elements, and sense bases manifest in their divine form.

If one fails to understand these fundamental points, one's practice of highest yoga tantra is utterly without meaning.

Some people say that the practice of generating oneself as a deity is the stage of generation, and meditation on emptiness is the stage of completion.

However, that shows an insufficient understanding of the process. One of the absurd consequences of the view that merely meditating on emptiness constitutes the stage of completion is that people practicing Hīnayāna and Pāramitāyāna would be practicing the stage of completion even though they do not imagine themselves being deities. One must understand the three factors of the basis to be purified, the purifying path, and the result of purification.

Understanding Emptiness

The Amdo Guru, Choney Guru Rinpoche, said, "If one realizes all the appearing phenomena as mere apparitions of thought, then the emptiness that is the absence of conceptual elaborations can arise without dependence." There are two interpretations of the manner in which we conceptually grasp onto true existence. One explanation is from tantra and the other is from sūtra.

The tantras explain that an experience similar to a nonconceptual realization of emptiness occurs simultaneously with the manifestation of the subtle mind. One has to say that it is an experience *similar* to the nonconceptual realization of emptiness. Otherwise, if one says that by the manifestation of the innate mind one has gained an actual nonconceptual realization of emptiness, this would imply that as soon as that mind had manifested one would become an ārya. This would be a false consequence. For example, the very subtle innate mind does manifest during the death process. However, most people do not realize emptiness at that time.

At the time of the basis, that is, in the experience of ordinary persons rather than highly realized yogis, there are experiences that are comparable to the realization of emptiness. At the point of death, the extremely subtle primordial mind manifests, but we as ordinary beings are not able to recognize it. What kind of experience is it subjectively? It is like fainting. Similarly, in the state of very deep sleep there is a facsimile of the manifestation of the innate mind. Likewise, while engaging in sexual intercourse, a facsimile of the manifestation of the innate mind also occurs. But again, it is difficult to ascertain. An analogy we might use is that when the father is present, the son is not, and when the son is present, the father is not. This experience relates to all three: death, deep sleep, and sexual intercourse. In these cases, most people are not able to ascertain the innate mind. Once that experience has passed, the opportunity has passed. Then conceptualization comes crowding in and precludes the ascertainment of that mind.

References are made to the clear light of sleep, of death, and of sexual intercourse even though we have difficulty ascertaining such clear light. The point of such practices as mahāmudrā and Dzogchen is to ascertain the nature of this innate mind and then to maintain this realization.

In the state of deep sleep, only that state of deep sleep appears to the mind, and most people are not able to ascertain it. In this state of nonconceptuality, we cannot ascertain it as emptiness, that is, we do not ascertain that this is the mind that is realizing emptiness. This experience is said to be one in which dualistic appearance has vanished. What is the nature of this innate mind? It is free of conceptual elaborations, and no dualistic appearances are present.

All the aspects of ourselves and our environment—of mountains, forests, buildings, and so forth—are conceptually apprehended by identifying this as opposed to that. That very conceptualization itself arises from the innate mind. When we realize that all inner and outer phenomena are nothing more than conceptual elaborations, then we realize that, apart from those elaborations, no such phenomena exist.

It says in the Cakrasaṃvara sādhana that all phenomena are simply illusion-like conceptual elaborations. The *Guhyasamāja Tantra* states that practice in this system leads to definite liberation from all conceptualizations. From these statements, we can reason that the innate mind manifests eternally upon the attainment of full awakening, and from the moment of attaining full awakening there is no occasion in which conceptualization could arise for a buddha.

That is the tantric interpretation of the manner in which phenomena are apprehended by means of conceptualization.

The sūtras explain that the assertion that all phenomena are simply conceptual designations implies it is impossible to assert their true existence. If, for example, one is looking at an illusion of horses and elephants, and one apprehends that they are of an illusory nature, that understanding refutes the notion that they are truly existent.

Understanding the Aspects of Purification

Two terms are pertinent here: accordant behavior (Tib. *chos mthun sbyar ba*) and behavior that accords with the basis to be purified (Tib. *sbyang gzhi dang chos mthun sbyar ba*). If one wishes to have a fine ordinary rebirth in the future, one engages in wholesome actions to accumulate the karma that leads to that result. That is an example of accordant behavior. One engages in behavior that accords with the basis to be purified by undertaking the practices to accumulate merit previously described, such as developing the spirit of awakening and so forth, which lead to the attainment of the bodies of a buddha.

In addition, there are three aspects: the basis to be purified, the purifier, and the result of purification.

An example of the basis to be purified is death. What is the purifier? Meditation on emptiness, in which one generates the pride of being the dharmakāya. This practice acts as the purifier for death. The practice of meditating on emptiness with the pride of dharmakāya is the path of purification in the stage of generation. The experience of realizing immutable bliss is the purifier in the stage of completion. The result of purification is the dharmakāya.

The Four Drops

The four principal aspects of the basis to be purified are the four specific types of drops[13] located in the forehead, throat, heart, and navel cakras.

The drop found at the navel cakra and the one at the forehead cakra are of the same type. The drop at the throat is of the same type as the one at the genital cakra. Roughly halfway along the shaft of the male organ or beneath the female organ is a drop of the same type as that at the heart. At the very tip of the jewel, or vajra—that is, at the tip of the male organ—there is a drop of the same type as that at the navel cakra; this drop would be in a comparable channel in the female organ, but this is not clearly stated in the tantra.

The meaning of the drops is as follows:

- The drop at the forehead cakra corresponds to the waking state. It has the ability to bring forth the various appearances of the environment and so forth to the mind. In the basis state, meaning before one practices, this drop has the ability to bring forth the impure appearances of objects. As one engages in the process of purification, the impure appearances vanish and are replaced by pure appearances, which also stem from, or are empowered by, that drop.

- The drop at the throat cakra produces the dream state. It also brings forth expression, or articulation, so it has the capability of producing delusive speech. When purified, it has the capacity to bring forth the unvanquishable speech.
- The drop at the heart cakra creates the deep sleep state. Moreover, it has the dual capacity to bring forth delusion, or darkness, of the mind on the one hand, and nonconceptualization on the other. The darkness aspect is gradually purified and its capacity for nonconceptual awareness is enhanced. This culminates in the nonconceptual, primordial wisdom of a buddha.
- The drop at the navel cakra has the capacity of producing sexual joy. It is called the sexual joy of emission, or it might be called orgasm, literally meaning to drip down. The result of purification of this drop is immutable bliss.

In the impure state these are called the four drops. At the time of fruition they are called the four bodies of the buddha. The drop at the forehead, as it is purified, becomes the body vajra. The drop at the throat becomes the speech vajra. The drop at the heart becomes the mind vajra, and the drop at the navel becomes the primordial wisdom vajra.

In terms of the path of purification, during the completion stage one purifies these by means of meditation focused on the different drops. In the stage of generation one does so by generating them as deities. They are also generated as deities during the initiation.

The following suggests the existence of these four drops: In the state of deep sleep most of the vital energies in the body converge in the drops at the heart and in the sexual organ. But when these energies start to move from the state of deep sleep, they may converge at the navel cakra and at the throat, which brings one to the dream state. Then when the energies move from the drop at the throat up to the forehead, one wakes up.

Then there is something called the fourth occasion, which refers to orgasm. In this case, the energies converge at the navel cakra and at the sexual organ, and they have the capacity to bring forth bliss.

Each of these drops is said to be a mixture of red and white bodhicitta and is about the size of a sesame seed. It is said that in each of these drops there is an aspect of the extremely subtle energy-mind. Sentient beings who are born from the womb and who are endowed with the four elements and the red and white bodhicitta are endowed with these four drops.

There is no reason why animals would not have these four drops, but most references to them pertain to human existence.

At death as well as in the *bardo,* or intermediate state, the four drops are nonexistent. At that time, the innate mind still has the habitual propensities of those four drops.

The foregoing is the explanation of the basis to be purified as it is understood in the Kālacakra system. Generally speaking, though, there are the other bases to be purified, such as the aggregates, elements, the sense bases, and so forth.

Other Bases to Be Purified

The five elements with which we are endowed—earth, water, fire, air, and space—become the five consorts upon purification at the time of fruition. The five aggregates—form, feelings, recognition, compositional factors, and consciousness—which are the bases of purification, transform into the five classes of buddhas. The ten forms of vital energy (Tib. *rlung bcu*) are also bases to be purified, which, at the time of fruition, become the ten śaktīs. A śakti is a female embodiment of power, specifically the power to bring forth bliss. The consorts in their purified aspect at the time of fruition refer to the realization of emptiness.

Additional bases of purification are the right and left channels. At the time of fruition, they transform into the main deity with consort. Other bases to be purified are the six subjective sense bases—eyes, ears, nose, tongue, body, and the mental sense—as well as the six objective sense bases—visual form, sound, odors, tastes, touch, and mental phenomena. At the time of fruition, they become the six male bodhisattvas and the six female bodhisattvas.

There are said to be six faculties for action (Tib. *las kyi dbang po drug*): the mouth, anus, urine orifice, hands, feet, and regenerative organ. Those are bases to be purified, which, upon fruition, become the six male wrathful beings called krodhas.

The six corresponding activities (Tib. *bya ba drug*) of articulation from the mouth, activities of the hands, movement with the feet, emission of excrement from the anus, emission of urine, and emission of semen, are also bases to be purified. At the time of fruition, they become the six female krodhas.

Upon purification, the aggregate of primordial wisdom and the element of primordial wisdom transform into Vajrasattva and Prajñāpāramitā respectively. The *Prajñāpāramitā Sūtras* are frequently referred to with the term *mother*, for they bear āryas just as a mother bears sons and daughters.

The twelve shifting energies (Tib. *'pho ba*) and the 21,600 energies throughout the day are all transformed in the context of Kālacakra into deities at the time of fruition.

The Cultivation of Pure Appearance

The *Kālacakra Root Tantra* states that the entire inner and outer Kālacakras appear in the purified form of the maṇḍala. The outer and inner Kālacakras consist of the bases to be purified. The purified form of the maṇḍala refers to the purified state of fruition.

Actually, anything that is true of Kālacakra refers in fact to the fruitional Kālacakra. References to the processes on the path of the outer, inner, and other Kālacakra are called Kālacakra, but in reality they only lead to the true Kālacakra.

How does it happen that the outer and inner Kālacakras appear as the pure maṇḍala? First of all, one dissolves one's body, resources, environment, and so forth into the nature of emptiness. From emptiness one imagines these to arise in the aspect of immutable bliss. If the mind is not happy, immutable bliss is out of the question, so we have to rely on the power of imagination.

How can we bring about some facsimile of immutable bliss? At this point in the meditation we bring to mind something that makes us happy. It may be an event, an aspect of Dharma, or a wholesome activity in which we participated in the past, anything that will bring forth some degree of happiness. The recollection creates a good feeling, and we imagine that to be of the nature of immutable bliss, and with that bliss we then focus on emptiness. In this way, we will get a glimpse of the facsimile of the actual state we are trying to realize.

Alternatively, if we have access to states of mental and physical well-being resulting from our meditation, we can tap into these states. In that case, before focusing on emptiness, we engage in our meditation practice to bring forth that mental and physical well-being, and as soon as that arises, we focus on emptiness. From this experience of immutable bliss and emptiness we create the palace with the various deities, the male and female bodhisattvas, the male and female wrathful beings known as krodhas, the chosen deities, the consorts, and so forth.

It is very important to continue in the practice of the stage of generation between meditation sessions. Although we are not in a position to bring an end to ordinary appearances, in our mind's eye we should still imagine our environment, other beings, and so on to be of the nature of the palace and the deities. Although we cannot really stop ordinary appearances arising to the senses, we should cultivate the sense of living in the palace of the deity and being surrounded by deities.

It is said that once we have become very familiar with this practice, the habitual propensities in the mind that cause us to grasp onto ordinary appearances wane. When that happens, we actually see the environment as the palace. It becomes less imagination and more of a perception. Is our sensory perception altered by such an experience? Our mental experience of our environment is so powerful that we actually apprehend the palace. At the same time the appearances to the senses remain ordinary. We perceive them as mere appearances, without reifying them.

Here is a way to understand this. There are three different cooperative conditions for perception, namely: (1) the objective condition (Tib. *dmigs rkyen*), (2) the immediately preceding condition (Tib. *de ma thag rkyen*), and (3) the dominant condition (Tib. *bdag rkyen*). In this case, what is altered is the immediately preceding condition, which refers to the state of the mind itself, together with its habitual propensities. When that happens, the nature of one's mental experience of events is altered. The immediately preceding mind is the condition for the subsequently altered moment of awareness.

The following analogy may shed light on this. If one is utterly enchanted by some lovely music, one does not ascertain what is appearing to one's visual sense, for one is absorbed in the awareness of the sound. Similarly, if one is absorbed in some visual event, one may be unable to ascertain sounds that are appearing to the auditory faculty. This is analogous to what happens in the stage of generation, in which the ordinary appearances are overwhelmed by the power of one's imagination.

To illustrate this, some time ago in Tibet there was a yogi who had attained quite a high degree of realization in the practice of Yamāntaka. In his practice, during and between sessions, he had a very clear vision of the many-armed form of Yamāntaka. This yogi was from Kham and once journeyed to Lhasa to attend the Great Prayer Festival at the beginning of the Tibetan new year. Such a new monk coming to that festival is obliged to do one of two things. Either he could make many offerings to the monks who were already there, or else he could simply join in and do the work, like any of the other resident monks. This monk was in fact a great yogi. He chose the latter route. The task he was given was to help serve the tea with a big kettle that one has to hold with both hands. But he had such a clear vision of himself as Yamāntaka that he kept on asking people, "With which pair of hands should I hold the kettle?" Finally the visiting monk addressed his question to the monk in charge, who told him, "Just use your two mitts." The point is that this yogi had such a vivid experience of his form as Yamāntaka that it overwhelmed the ordinary appearance of his hands.

There was another man who continually meditated upon his own form as having two great long horns coming out of his head. He simply decided to imagine that he had horns! Whenever he came to a doorway, he complained that he could not get through. To the mind's eye, when one becomes very familiar with such a visualization, these are the types of results that ensue.

Between sessions, whenever we encounter another being, we simply imagine, "This is Kālacakra." Similarly, when we are looking at inanimate objects like trees and so forth, we continue to remind ourselves, "This is of the nature of primordial wisdom." This practice will establish very powerful habitual propensities in the mind that will lead gradually to the overwhelming of ordinary appearance. In addition, when you hear ordinary sounds, it is appropriate to imagine that you are hearing *oṃ, āḥ, hūṃ*, superimposing that over the ordinary sound. In this way we actually transform that experience as well.

We do the same for all the purely mental events that appear to the mind. If we look upon these mental events as being of the nature of emptiness and bliss, this will gradually transform the mind so that they are actually experienced in that way.

The principal teacher of my chief teacher, Shako Khen Rinpoche, or Gen Nyima, was a great Tibetan yogi by the name of Tongpön Rinpoche. It was said that when Tongpön Rinpoche was present in a monastic assembly with the tantric master, he saw all the monks as Vajradharas. These are the types of appearances that occur when one gains a high degree of realization in the stage of generation.

The statement that all the entire inner and outer Kālacakras appear in the purified form of the divine palace, or maṇḍala, also refers to vajra yoga, entailing the six phases of the yoga that leads to the fulfillment of immutable bliss in the stage of completion. In the Kālacakra system, the six-phase yoga is often known as vajra yoga, which refers to immutable bliss. Because the practices of the six-phase yoga in the stage of completion directly bring about such immutable bliss, they are called vajra yoga.

The above statement refers to the attainment of the body and mind of a buddha. The first two phases of the six-phase yoga, that of retraction and meditative stabilization, are designed to directly bring forth empty form. Vajra speech is brought forth by the middle two of the six phases, namely prāṇayāma and retention. The two final phases of recollection and samādhi bring forth immutable bliss, or the mind of the buddha.

Now we move on to the practice to the actual process of the initiation.

The Initiation Process

From the heart of Kālacakra are emitted sugatas with their consorts
As well as the circle of the maṇḍala; the empowering deities
Bestow the empowerments of water, crown, crown ribbon, vajra and bell,
Conduct, name, and permission.

The *sugatas* are the tathāgatas, that is, the buddhas of the five classes—Akṣobhya and so forth—and their consorts. The chief deity Kālacakra is also with his consort. Keep in mind that it is the guru you are visualizing in front of you.

In the guru yoga text in Tibetan, the senior tutor of His Holiness the Dalai Guru, Kyabje Ling Rinpoche, mentioned the tathāgatas first, but it might be somewhat easier to imagine "the heart of Kālacakra" emitting the circle of the maṇḍala and all of the deities of the maṇḍala. In either case, you are inviting twelve deities: Kālacakra with his consort and the five tathāgatas with their five consorts.

In this visualization, you bring to mind the four-sided palace of the maṇḍala. In the center of the maṇḍala is an eight-petaled lotus, and upon the center of that lotus stands the principal deity Kālacakra and his consort. Upon each of the eight petals of the lotus are the eight śaktīs. The petals are like a drawing on the floor of the palace. Imagine around that a square. In each of the four directions there is a tathāgata, and on each of the corners in between the cardinal directions you visualize the consorts of those four tathāgatas.

Among the five tathāgatas, you imagine Akṣobhya as being of the same nature as the principal deity, Kālacakra. You visualize the consort of Akṣobhya, Prajñāpāramitā, as being of the same nature as Viśvamātā. Here is a further elaboration. The four tathāgatas in the four cardinal directions, on the sides of that square, face inward toward the principal deity. Each of those four tathāgatas is embracing his respective consort who is facing away from the principal deity. In the intermediate directions, that is, on the corners of the square, the four consorts are facing toward the principal deity. They, too, are embraced by their respective tathāgata consorts who are facing outward.

Around them are the six male and six female bodhisattvas, making a total of twelve deities. There are two on the eastern side, which is the front side, and two on all the other sides, south, north, and west. Then there is one on each of the corners of this square. They are totally separate, and do not even hold hands. As before, they are all in a dual aspect, giving us twelve pairs. Since they are all in pairs, we have twenty-four deities.

At each of the doors are the krodhas, and each of those is embracing a wrathful female being. Above and below are two other krodhas, each embracing a consort.

The initiating deities are appearing in the aspect of these deities of the maṇḍala. Among these deities in the maṇḍala, the five consorts of the tathāgatas bestow the water initiation. The five tathāgatas bestow the initiation of the crown. The eight śaktīs bestow the crown ribbon initiation. The chief deities of the maṇḍala, Kālacakra and Viśvamātā, bestow the initiation of the vajra and bell. The male and the female bodhisattvas bestow the conduct initiation. They wear on their thumbs something like a vajra ring, which is one of the implements of initiation. The wrathful beings, or krodhas, bestow the initiation of the name. The implement of that initiation is a type of vajra bracelet, or vajra wristband.

You may recall that when you received the Kālacakra initiation, at one point a flower was dropped to determine the buddha class to which the initiates belong. At that time in a proper initiation, the guru gives a kind of blessing, stating that this will be our secret name and that we will bear this name until we attain full enlightenment. There may be some prophetic aspect to it. In any case, this is associated with the name initiation, and the deities who bestow this are the male and female krodhas.

Vajrasattva with his consort bestow the initiation of permission. We should think of Vajrasattva as being nondual from the principal deity. The principal deity Kālacakra, Akṣobhya, and Vajrasattva are all of the same nature. The consort of Vajrasattva is Vajradhātvīśvarī, and she is of the same nature as Viśvamātā. The consort of Akṣobhya, Prajñāpāramitā, is also of the same nature as Viśvamātā.

The different implements of initiation of Vajrasattva with his consort correspond to different types of disciples, as determined by the dropping of the flower. These various implements of initiation are the following:

- A wheel associated with Vairocana
- A jewel associated with Ratnasambhava
- A lotus associated with Amitābha
- A sword associated with Amoghasiddhi
- A vajra associated with Akṣobhya

In using these implements of initiation, the deity and consort are encouraging the students to eventually turn the wheel of Dharma in accordance with the propensities of disciples relating to those five classes.

The water and the crown initiations purify the drop at the forehead related to the waking state. The crown ribbon initiation and the vajra and bell initiation are for the purification of the drop at the throat associated with the dream state. The conduct initiation and the name initiation are for purifying the drop at the heart related to the deep sleep state. Finally, the initiation of permission purifies the drop at the navel cakra associated with what is simply called the fourth occasion.

They likewise grant the four pairs of the higher and greatly higher empowerments
As well as the supreme empowerment of the vajra master.

These are the eight further initiations, namely, the four higher initiations and the four greatly higher initiations. There are two sets of four. Also, there is the initiation of the vajra master. Sometimes the initiation of the vajra master is included in the initiation of permission.

As a result, the channels and vital energies of the body become functional,
And I am empowered to cultivate the two stages.

Here the text speaks explicitly of making functional the physical channels and vital energies. In fact, the initiations are specifically designed to remove the impurities of the four drops. This particular sādhana, however, is especially designed to purify the channels and the energies. Therefore, it refers to these explicitly.

Making the channels and energies serviceable means removing any obstacles or interferences in their proper functioning, thereby facilitating your meditation practice. In this case, the 21,600 karmic energies and the material factors of the body are purified by bringing these energies into the central channel.

Furthermore, by receiving these initiations, one is empowered to cultivate the two stages, namely the stages of generation and completion.

I come to have the fortune of actualizing in this lifetime
The sevenfold state of Kālacakra,
In which the 21,600 karmic vital energies
And all the material elements of the body are consumed.

The "sevenfold state of Kālacakra" is comprised of the following:

1. The embrace, the union of deity with consort, both being in the nature of empty form. The Tibetan term for this is *kha sbyor,* literally, the joining of the mouths as in a kiss, but it refers more generally to

the embrace. The interpretative meaning is the embrace itself, while the definitive meaning is the union of emptiness and bliss.

2. The fulfillment of enjoyment.
3. Great bliss, referring here to immutable great bliss.
4. The lack of inherent existence. This can be understood in two ways: (a) the object of immutable bliss is the very absence of inherent nature, and (b) the immutable bliss itself is devoid of intrinsic nature. The latter is perhaps preferable in this context.
5. Being of the nature of great compassion.
6. The eternal, unceasing stream of enlightened action.
7. The nature of being unceasing. The meaning here is that awakened beings do not simply abide in nirvāṇa, which is regarded as the extreme of quietism.

These are simply seven names for different aspects of a fully awakened being.

The Meaning of Initiation

The Tibetan term translated here as initiation (Tib. *dbang*) literally means empowerment. The ceremony is so called because it empowers, or authorizes, the disciple to engage in the practice of Vajrayāna. If one has not received the initiation, one does not have the authority to do so. In this sense the Tibetan term could also be translated as authorization. But it is not nearly as glamorous to say, "I am going to an authorization."

In the process of initiation there are three phases:

- Purification of the four drops.
- Transformation. In dependence upon the previous purification, the four drops are so transformed that at the time of fruition they become of the nature of the four bodies of a buddha.
- Activity. The essential meaning of this is that through the process of initiation one is empowered to engage in the practice of the two stages.

Both the basis to be purified and the process of purification refer to the four drops. The first seven initiations—water, crown, crown ribbon, vajra and bell, conduct, name, and permission—are all self-entries of a child. All of these together are also called water initiation, because in each case there is a bestowing of an anointment, which is the literal meaning of *abhiṣeka*, the Sanskrit term for initiation.

By receiving the seven self-entries of a child, one is authorized to engage in the practice of the stage of generation. In other tantric systems, such as Cakrasaṃvara and Guhyasamāja, one receives the vase initiation. The function of the vase initiation is similarly to authorize one to engage in the stage of generation. The difference is one of terminology. In the other systems this is called the vase initiation, and in this it is called the water initiation.

To illustrate this point, recall that among the bases to be purified is the drop at the forehead associated with the waking state. During the process of purification in the stage of generation, one visualizes that drop as the vajra body, which begins the process of purification of that drop. Moreover, the same process in the stage of generation is acting as a ripener of one's being, of one's continuum, for the stage of completion. At that point in practice, the disciple generates himself or herself as the vajra body.

Entering the Maṇḍala

It is stated that it is not permissible to give the Kālacakra initiation unless one is using a sand maṇḍala. However, if the master is a very highly realized vajra master and the students are highly realized students, it is possible to give the initiation in a maṇḍala of primordial wisdom.

There are two ways this may happen. One is that the guru may instantaneously generate the entire maṇḍala with his mind. The disciple is then right in the midst of the guru's visualization. Another possibility is that the doors of the heart of the guru, as it were, open up and there is the maṇḍala at the heart of the guru, and the disciples enter into this maṇḍala. If you are able to enter into such a maṇḍala, you fully experience great bliss.

Two of the foremost tantric practitioners of the past were King Indrabhūti, the chief disciple of the Guhyasamāja Tantra, and King Sucandra of Śambhala, who was the chief disciple for the Kālacakra Tantra. Both of them received their respective initiations, Guhyasamāja and Kālacakra, from the Buddha himself. In those cases, the type of maṇḍala they entered to receive the initiation was instantaneously created by the Buddha. They instantaneously saw the maṇḍala and actually experienced being in it.

In the more mundane cases, one must have a sand maṇḍala to give the initiation. The guru meditatively dissolves the sand maṇḍala into emptiness, and from emptiness the guru generates the Kālacakra maṇḍala where the sand maṇḍala is located. Then the initiation is bestowed within that maṇḍala. In this case, all this is done by the power of visualization. It is not directly experienced as in the previous cases.

On the occasion of the initiation, the disciples should also imagine dissolving the entire environment into emptiness, and then from emptiness visualize the maṇḍala.

The Kālacakra maṇḍala has four entryways. In clockwise direction, the colors on top of the doors of the palace are black, red, yellow, and white. These colors correspond to the colors of the faces of Kālacakra facing each of those directions. The black at the bottom is east, the yellow at the top is west, the white at right is north, and the red at left is south.

The process of entering the maṇḍala is associated with the use of the blindfold. When wearing the blindfold, we imagine ourselves being outside the maṇḍala, and at the point in the initiation when we remove the blindfold, we should imagine having entered the maṇḍala. The purpose of this is to avoid any obstacles to the practice. Also, it is while standing blindfolded outside the east door of the divine palace that one takes the various precepts, including the tantric precepts. We then remove the blindfold and enter the palace through the east door, proceeding on to the north, to the white face of Kālacakra.

8

The Seven Self-Entries of a Child

Initiation to Achieve the Vajra Body

Prior to receiving the water initiation, the first of the seven self-entries of a child, we visualize light emanating from Guru Kālacakra's heart, striking us, and then drawing us into the mouth and then into the heart of the deity. We transform into a drop and in that form go from the heart down into the *bhaga* (womb) of the consort. We imagine ourselves as a drop in the bhaga of the consort and dissolve into emptiness.

The chief person meditating on emptiness here is the guru, but the disciples do as well. It is at this point that the quality of our own mind becomes of the same nature as the guru and chosen deity's mind.

From that emptiness arises the syllable *oṃ* and from that arises the vajra body. The vajra body is white, having three faces and six hands. The central face is white, the right face is black, and the left face is red. Here Amitābha is white, and the vajra body is of the nature of Amitābha. The hand implements of the vajra body are as follows: The right hands, top to bottom, hold (1) a hammer, (2) a spear, and (3) a trident. The left hands, top to bottom, hold (1) a white, eight-petaled lotus, (2) a wheel, and (3) a rosary.

Paṇḍārī, consort of Amitābha, is red and holds the following hand implements: On the right, (1) a triple arrow, (2) a vajra hook, and (3) a resounding *ḍāmaru*. On the left, (1) a bow, (2) a vajra noose, and (3) a nine-faceted jewel.

Water Initiation

In the process of the water initiation (see chart 2), rays of light are emanated from the guru's heart, inviting all the buddhas in the form of the vajra bodies and dissolving them into himself. The initiation deities are invited, and the guru requests them to bestow initiation. Upon such supplication, all the initiation deities with consorts go into union, and from their sexual bliss, drops descend and enter the crown of Kālacakra's head. They flow down the central channel into the bhaga of the consort and dissolve into ourselves, thereby bestowing initiation. When inviting the initiation deities, we should imagine the whole Kālacakra maṇḍala with all the deities and consorts.

Keep in mind that in this stage of the process of purification, one is purifying the drop at the forehead associated with the waking state. One is transforming that drop into the vajra body of the buddha. One receives this phase of the initiation with the deity facing north. We are generated as the vajra body, and the place where this initiation is received is in the maṇḍala of the vajra body. This maṇḍala is visualized as the primordial wisdom maṇḍala.

The water initiation purifies the five elements. For each of the consorts with the tathāgata, there is an entire initiation process in which we visualize and invite the buddhas in the form of vajra bodies. Together with their consorts, they dissolve into us. Then there is the invitation to the initiation deities to bestow the initiation. This process recurs for each of these five elements, as follows:

- The space element of one's body and the water that is used during this phase of the initiation are generated in the form of Vajradhātvīśvarī at the crown. She has three faces and six hands, and she is embracing Vajrasattva.
- The air element of one's body and the initiating water are generated in the form of Tārā at the navel. She is embracing Vairocana.
- The fire element of one's body and the initiating water are generated in the form of Paṇḍārī at the forehead, and she is embracing Amitābha.
- The water element of one's body plus the initiating water are generated in the form of Māmaki at the throat. She is embracing Ratnasambhava.
- The earth element of one's body and the initiating water are generated in the form of the consort Locanā at the heart, and she is embracing Amoghasiddhi.

Each of the consorts—Vajradhātvīśvarī, Tārā, Māmaki, Paṇḍārī, and Locanā—dissolves into light and becomes of the nature of the initiating water. With the water and the vase, they bestow upon us the initiations while we are at the northern door of the palace.

By this process of initiation, any defilements of the five elements are purified, and one is empowered to attain the siddhis of the five consorts. Seeds for eventually actualizing the five consorts are placed in one's being. One is authorized to cultivate the path of the consorts and to attain the siddhis related to them during the stage of generation. This initiation also places in one's being the capacity for attaining the first bodhisattva ground. Replicas of the five consorts dissolve into oneself, and then one arises in the nature of the five consorts. Later on, one generates these five consorts in the maṇḍala and meditates upon them. This is a unique and profound aspect of the Kālacakra system.

The people with whom one has received tantric initiation are called one's tantric siblings. The reason for that is evident here. We are generated, in this case, as the body vajra in the bhaga of the consort and have in a sense been conceived there. Everybody who is receiving initiation together is going through the same process, so it is as if we were born from the same womb at the same time.

If we can get a real understanding of this now, it might be possible for us to actually receive the initiation the next time it is offered. However, if we do not have any idea of what is going on, it is difficult to receive initiation.

Crown Initiation

Following the water initiation is the initiation of the crown (see chart 3). The crown initiation is designed to purify the five aggregates. At this phase of the practice we have already generated ourselves as the vajra body. Although it is not very clear in the teachings on Kālacakra, I surmise that this phase of the initiation is done by generating the body maṇḍala, which means that the visualization is done inside our own body.

The crown initiation has five phases, and it is given by the five tathāgatas. In the actual process of the crown initiation we generate two sets of deities. We generate our own aggregates as the deities with their consorts, and we also generate the crowns as the same deities. Where are these crowns, the outer implements of initiation? They are by the principal deity with his consort. We visualize them in an initiation using a sand maṇḍala. If you receive initiation in a primordial wisdom maṇḍala, you do not need to do the visualization because the crowns are already there.

- The green crown and one's aggregate of consciousness are generated in the form of green Akṣobhya at the crown cakra. Akṣobhya is embracing his consort, blue Prajñāpāramitā. Bear in mind that Prajñāpāramitā, Viśvamātā, and Vajradhātvīśvarī are all of the same nature.
- The white crown and one's aggregate of recognition are generated in the form of white Amitābha at the forehead cakra. He is embracing his consort, white Paṇḍārī.
- The red crown and one's aggregate of feeling are generated in the form of red Ratnasambhava at the throat cakra. Ratnasambhava is embracing his consort, white Māmaki.
- The blue crown and one's aggregate of compositional factors are generated in the form of black Amoghasiddhi at the heart cakra. Amoghasiddhi is embracing his consort, yellow Locanā. (Note that in the *Guhyasamāja Tantra,* Amoghasiddhi is generated at the genital cakra, while in this case he is generated at the heart cakra.)
- The yellow crown and one's aggregate of form are generated in the form of yellow Vairocana at the navel cakra. He is embracing his consort, black Tārā.

All the above deities are endowed with crowns and all the pertinent ornaments. They have three faces and six hands holding various implements.

The visualization is sequential. In the water initiation we visualize the consorts, then in the later crown initiation we visualize the deities. Both times they are in union. Actually, both times we visualize everyone, but their positions are different. For example, in the water initiation the consort at the crown of the head is Prajñāpāramitā, facing the main deity Kālacakra, and she is in union with Akṣobhya, facing to the back. Later on in the crown initiation, we visualize Akṣobhya facing Kālacakra, and the consort Prajñāpāramitā is facing to the back. In the water initiation, at the forehead we have Paṇḍārī facing Kālacakra, in union with her consort, Amitābha, facing backward. Later, in the crown initiation, we visualize Amitābha facing Kālacakra, with Paṇḍārī facing backward.

In the water initiation, Māmaki is at the throat, facing Kālacakra, in union with her consort, Ratnasambhava, who faces backward. Later, in the crown initiation, Ratnasambhava faces forward, and Māmaki backward.

During the water initiation, we visualize Locanā at the heart facing Kālacakra, in union with her consort, Amoghasiddhi, who faces backward. In the crown initiation, Amoghasiddhi faces forward while in union with his consort, Locanā, who is facing backward.

We first visualize Tārā in the water initiation at the navel cakra facing Kālacakra, in union with Vairocana, who is facing backward. During the crown initiation, Vairocana is facing forward in union with Tārā, who faces backward.

Now the five crowns and the five aggregates are all generated in the forms of the five classes of buddhas. The central deity, Kālacakra, sends rays of light from his heart, inviting the five classes of buddhas, who then dissolve into the crowns as well as into oneself. After that, from the heart of Kālacakra rays of light are emitted, inviting the initiating deities. In this case, the initiation is bestowed upon the crowns, not upon ourselves, in the following way: After the crowns are generated in the form of the respective buddhas—Akṣobhya and so forth—the initiation is bestowed on them. These respective deities, having been initiated, dissolve into light, and then the light takes on the form of the respective crowns—green, black, and so forth. Once they have transformed into light and have taken on the form of the different crowns, the five classes of buddhas come one by one, pick up the crown, and place it upon our heads, and thus we receive the crown initiation. This is a process of initiation that is unique to the Kālacakra system.

Keep in mind that at this point you have already generated yourself as the vajra body in which you have generated the five classes of buddhas. You imagine the five aggregates (which you have been visualizing as these five buddhas) as "now having actually become the five buddhas." A replica of each of the five buddhas in the maṇḍala is emanated from their bodies and dissolves into your own. Then the initiating deities also dissolve into the five buddhas within your own body.

In terms of a parallel in ordinary life, the initiation of the water corresponds to the mother bathing her infant in water.

There is an Indian custom whereby an infant's hair is left to fall free, but at some point in early childhood the hair is tied up in a knot. Tying up the child's hair is the parallel for the crown initiation. This is an Indian custom, and there is something somewhat similar in the Tibetan tradition. Until a child is six or seven, the hair is left to hang down, but from the age of about seven or so onward the hair is braided. This custom applies to both boys and girls.

The crown initiations purify the defilements of the five aggregates and also empower one to attain the state of the five buddhas. The seeds of the five buddhas are established in one's continuum, and the capacity for attaining the second bodhisattva ground is also established. Both the water and crown initiations are bestowed in the northern direction of the maṇḍala, which is associated with the drop at the forehead.

The parallel for both of the first two initiations is that while still in the mothers womb, the five aggregates and the five elements of one's being are established. Similarly, in the initiation process, first the five elements are purified, and then the five aggregates are purified. In this way the five elements are purified so that they are fit to be transformed into the five female tathāgatas, namely, the five consorts. The five aggregates have been purified of all defilements so that they can transform into the nature of the five male tathāgatas. Both of these initiations are chiefly designed to dispel defilements of the body. The seed of the vajra body is established, and one is authorized to attain the siddhi of the vajra body.

This concludes the section of the initiation that empowers one to achieve the vajra body by means of purifying the drop at the forehead associated with the waking state.

Initiation to Achieve the Vajra Speech

The next initiation concerns the purification of the defilements of the drop at the throat associated with the dream state. It is known as the inner initiation. Recall that in the preceding stages of the initiation the guru is facing the northern door. Now imagine the central deity taking you, the disciple, with his right hand and bringing you over to his left. The north would be to the guru's left, so he takes you with his right hand and brings you around to the opposite side, to the southern door. The southern door, which is on the left of the maṇḍala, is red. It corresponds to the color of the face in that direction, and it is said to be the face of the speech.

The guru is facing the southern door, and rays of light are emitted from the guru's heart, drawing you inward. You go into the mouth, then down and into the consort's bhaga. The initiation is known as inner because you are taken inside. You dissolve into emptiness and from the emptiness are generated as the vajra speech.

The vajra speech is red, with three faces and six hands. Ratnasambhava is also red, and the vajra speech is of the same nature as Ratnasambhava. The consort is white Māmaki, who also has three faces and six hands.

As before, rays of light are emitted from the guru's heart, and he thereby invites the jñānasattvas. These jñānasattvas dissolve into yourself, inside the bhaga of the consort. Following that, the initiating deities are invited by sending rays of light out from the principal deity's heart. They go into union, and from the union drops descend through the crown of the principal deity's head. They come down through the same passage and initiate you as the vajra speech.

Then you are, in a sense, born. You emerge from the womb of the consort and abide by the southern door of the palace. This phase of the practice is preliminary to the actual stage of generation.

The crown ribbon and vajra and bell initiations both pertain to the vajra speech. The basis to be purified in these initiations is comprised of the ten vital energies and the two side channels, the right and the left channels. Recall that at the time of the basis, that is, at the time we are starting out, the cakra at the heart is imagined as an eight-petaled lotus. This corresponds to eight directions, and we have an energy associated with each of these eight directions, as well as an energy going upward, and another one going downward. Thus, there are ten vital energies. The last eight energies are associated with the four cardinal and four intermediate directions. In the Kālacakra system, you are facing things from one direction to another. Once you have come to the south, leap over to the north—don't keep on going clockwise.

1. Life-sustaining energy originates and is chiefly located in the central channel above the heart, but it also courses through the other parts of the body in various channels.

2. Descending energy originates in the central channel from the heart down, and is a downward-evacuating energy.
3. Fire-accompanying energy is associated with the channel going to the east, or straight forward.
4. Turtle energy is associated with the channel to the southeast, veering off to the deity's right.
5. Ascending energy moves south to the deity's right.
6. Lizard energy is to the southwest, going off to the deity's right side in the back.
7. Pervasive energy moves in the channel to the north, to the deity's left side.
8. *Devadatta* energy is the energy to the northeast, on the deity's left, front side. When a man and woman pray for a child, and the woman conceives, the child is often called Devadatta, or "a gift from the gods."
9. Nāga energy moves in the channel to the west, behind the deity.
10. *Dhanaṃjaya* energy moves to the deity's northwest.

Later, in the self-generation phase of the practice, we visualize an eight-petaled lotus, which symbolizes these various channels with the corresponding energies. The eight śaktīs are also symbolized by the eight energies going in the cardinal and intermediate directions.

Vajradhātvīśvarī symbolizes the life-sustaining energy that moves through the central channel from the heart upward. Viśvamātā symbolizes the descending energy, moving from the heart down and also through the central channel. Recall that Vajradhātvīśvarī and Viśvamātā are of the same nature, and that they are associated with the central channel. It is, of course, one central channel, connecting from below the heart to above the heart.

As previously mentioned, the eight petals of the lotus symbolize the eight channels of the corresponding energies. The center of the lotus symbolizes the central channel. Moreover, through the whole meditation process we imagine the eight śaktīs and the two consorts above and below in our visualizations. All of these are the purifying agents for those energies.

Generally speaking, the eight-petaled lotus that provides the base for the chosen deities is variegated in color. However, in the elaborate sādhana of Kālacakra, the eight-petaled lotus that forms the base for the śaktīs is entirely green. In this phase of the practice, the color of the lotus is not stated, so we may imagine it as green. However, if we visualize the petals of the lotus corresponding to the colors associated with the various energies, the colors are as follows:

- ❖ East and southeast are black.
- ❖ South and southwest are red.
- ❖ North and northeast are white.
- ❖ West and northwest are yellow.

If we would like to have a correspondence among the bases to be purified, the agent of purification, and that which is purified, then it would be good to visualize in this way. In the stage of generation, we visualize the bases to be purified, namely, the ten energies in the forms of the eight śaktīs and two consorts. We visualize the eight subsidiary channels as the eight petals of the lotus.

Crown Ribbon Initiation

We are now at the stage of the crown ribbon initiation (see chart 4). There are two sets of tassels, or ribbons, five on the left and five on the right, hanging down from the crown. We visualize these ten tassels in the form of the ten śaktīs. Sometimes the text refers to eight śaktīs, but here we have ten śaktīs, which include Vajradhātvīśvarī and Viśvamātā.

Recall that you are the vajra speech, abiding in the southern direction of the maṇḍala. At this point of the initiation, dissolve your own ten energies and the ten crown ribbons into emptiness. Then generate your ten energies and the ten tassels in the form of the ten śaktīs:

1. The fire-accompanying energy in the east and one of the black crown ribbons are dissolved into emptiness, and we generate them in the form of the goddess Kṛṣṇadīptā (Tib. *nag mo 'bar ma*).
2. The turtle energy in the southeast and the other black crown ribbon are dissolved into emptiness, from which we imagine the goddess Dhūmā (Tib. *du ba ma*).
3. The ascending energy in the south and one of the two red crown ribbons are generated in the form of red Raktadīptā (Tib. *dmar mo 'bar ma*).
4. The lizard energy in the southwest and the other red ribbon are generated as the red goddess Marīci (Tib. *smig sgyu ma*).

5. The pervasive energy in the north and one of the white crown ribbons are generated as Śvetādīptā (Tib. *dkar mo 'bar ma*).
6. The Devadatta energy, located in the northeast, and the second white crown ribbon are generated as Khagamanā (Tib. *mkha' snang ma*).
7. The Nāga energy and one of the yellow crown ribbons in the west are generated in the form of Pītadīptā (Tib. *ser mo 'bar ma*).
8. The Dhanaṃjaya energy, located in the northwest, and the other yellow crown ribbon are generated in the form of Pradīpā (Tib. *mar me ma*).
9. The life-sustaining energy and one of the blue crown ribbons are generated in the form of the goddess Vajradhātvīśvarī.
10. The descending energy and a green crown ribbon are generated in the form of the goddess Viśvamātā.

All the goddesses have four faces and eight hands. Each of the goddesses in the four intermediate directions carries a yak-tail fan used to cool the central deity. The one to the southeast holds a black fan, the one to the southwest holds a red fan, the one to the northwest a yellow fan, and the one to the northeast a white fan. The goddesses in the cardinal directions hold different hand implements.

The Kālacakra system speaks of ten signs that occur in the stage of completion, starting with retraction. The ten signs correspond to the insertion of the ten energies into the central channel. The above goddesses symbolize the signs that appear as the energies enter into the central channel, such as smoke, mirage, and an appearance of space.

These various goddesses, associated with the different directions, are generated in two places: at the crown ribbon of the principal deity and at our heart. The internal visualization is quite straightforward because it is associated with these energies, and everything has its place; there is a logic to it.

As before, rays of light are emanated from the principal deity's heart, inviting the jñānasattvas, who merge into the deities who are present where the crown ribbons were, and with the deities who have been generated inwardly. Again, light is emanated from the heart, inviting the initiating deities, who initiate only the deities where the crown ribbons were. These goddesses receive initiation, dissolve into the nature of light, and then transform into the form of crown ribbons. After that, the ten śaktīs in the maṇḍala take hold of the ten crown ribbons, bring them to us, and give us the empowerment of the crown ribbon.

In this system as well as in other systems of tantra, when these various initiations are bestowed, the initiating implements—the crown ribbon and so forth—are touched briefly on five spots: the forehead, throat, heart, and left and right shoulders. In the Guhyasamāja initiation, the crown ribbons go together with the crown. The sequential process here, with the crown first and the crown ribbons second, is unique to Kālacakra.

The parallel of this stage of the initiation in ordinary life is piercing the ears of the child. This is still a common tradition in India and among Tibetans. The process purifies one's own ten energies, making them fit to enter into the central channel.

The involvement of the ten śaktīs in this process of initiation empowers us to attain the common siddhis. Indirectly, the stage of generation leads to the uncommon siddhi of full enlightenment, so that would also be implicitly involved in this stage of initiation.

By this process, the capacity for the ten perfections is also established in one's being. The ten śaktīs are also called the ten *pāramitās,* so the capacity for attaining those is established. The result is the attainment of the third bodhisattva ground.

Vajra and Bell Initiation

We remain in the form of the vajra speech in the southern direction of the maṇḍala during the next phase of the initiation, the vajra and bell initiation (see chart 5). Recall that Kālacakra is holding the vajra and bell and embracing Viśvamātā, who is holding a curved knife and skullcup.

In this phase of the initiation you simultaneously dissolve into emptiness, and from emptiness imagine the following:

- Your right channel becomes Kālacakra with his consort, with one face and two hands.
- The vajra held by Kālacakra also becomes Kālacakra with his consort, with one face and two hands.
- Your left channel transforms into Viśvamātā embracing Kālacakra.
- The bell held by Kālacakra also becomes Viśvamātā embracing Kālacakra.

Blood courses in the right channel, known as the wisdom channel, and regenerative fluid courses in the left channel, known as the method channel.

Rays of light are emanated from the heart of Kālacakra and invite both the jñānasattvas and the initiating deities. The jñānasattvas, in the form of Kālacakra with consort, dissolve into the two sets of Kālacakra with consort in front of you. They dissolve into the Kālacakra with consort on your right, the Kālacakra with consort on your left, as well as the two forms of Viśvamātā.

The initiation deities bestow initiation upon the two sets of Kālacakra with consort in front of you, appearing where the vajra and bell had been present. They go into sexual union, dissolve into the nature of emptiness and bliss, and then dissolve into the vajra and bell. Then the principal deity with consort bestows the vajra and bell initiation upon you by touching the initiating implements to the five points.

The parallel of this stage of the initiation in ordinary life is the laughter and speech of a child. It is said that the root of speech is the vital energy. A child's speech is induced by the power of such energy. The two chief channels through which the energy courses are the left and the right, which are purified and correspond to the laughter and speech of the child. The defilements of the left and right channels are thus cleansed. This establishes in you the capacity for joining these two side channels with the central channel.

The vajra initiation aspect of the vajra and bell initiation empowers you to attain immutable bliss, and the bell aspect of this initiation empowers you to attain the speech of the buddha bearing all excellent qualities (Tib. *gsung rnam pa thams cad pa*), that is, the all-faceted speech of the buddha in which with one utterance he is able to serve the needs of all sentient beings. There is no place where the speech of the buddha does not reach; it is omnipresent.

In dependence upon the chief deity with consort, one is empowered to attain siddhis. The energies moving through the sun and moon channels, referring to the right and left channels, are simultaneously purified. The special capacity that comes from this occasion is the attainment of the fourth bodhisattva ground.

Both of the foregoing initiations are given in the southern direction of the maṇḍala, and are designed to purify speech. Simultaneously, they purify the drop at the throat that produces the dream state, and they also purify the defilements of speech.

The first two initiations, the water and the crown initiations, are analogous in ordinary life to the formation of the elements and the aggregates of the child in the womb. These initiations are designed to purify the defilements of the elements and the aggregates.

As a synthesis of the second two initiations, the crown ribbon and the vajra and bell initiation, the parallel in ordinary life is the formation in the womb of the ten channels and the ten energies that course through those channels. They are the basis to be purified for these two aspects of initiation. These two initiations are designed to cleanse the impurities of the channels and the energies. They authorize you to engage in the actions of the vajra speech and establish the seeds of the vajra speech, and you are empowered to attain siddhis by means of the vajra speech.

Initiation to Achieve the Vajra Mind

The conduct initiation and the name initiation are designed to establish the vajra mind. Recall that the previous two initiations were given in the southern direction of the maṇḍala, with the guru facing in that direction. As we move to the next initiation, imagine being brought 270 degrees clockwise from the southern direction over to the eastern direction.

As in the previous cases, light is emanated from the guru's heart, striking you, and drawing you into his mouth. You proceed down through his vajra, into the bhaga of the consort, where you are generated in the form of the vajra mind.

As before, rays of light emanate from the guru's heart, inviting the jñānasattvas in the form of Kālacakra with consort. They come and dissolve into you. The initiating deities are invited, and they go into union, which causes the drops to flow down into the crown of the Kālacakra deity and on down to you, through his vajra into the bhaga, where they initiate you. Then you emerge from the womb of the consort in the form of the vajra mind at the eastern door of the maṇḍala.

The vajra mind is similar in aspect to black Amoghasiddhi. There are three faces—black in the center, white to the right, and red to the left—and he has six hands. In the right hands, top to bottom, are (1) a sword, (2) a curved knife, and (3) a trident. In the left hands, top to bottom, are (1) a shield, (2) a skullcup, and (3) a *khaṭvāṅga.* A khaṭvāṅga is a long staff with bracelets on it.

Amoghasiddhi is embracing the consort Locanā, who is yellow. She has three faces: yellow in the center, white to the right, and black to the left. Her three right hands hold (1) a wheel, (2) a club, and (3) a vajra in wrathful aspect, which means that it has open prongs. In her three left hands are (1) a spear, (2) a vajra, and (3) an iron chain.

The two are embracing each other. The male deity, the vajra mind, embraces the consort under her arms, and she embraces him around his neck.

Conduct Initiation

The next of the seven initiations is the conduct initiation, bestowed by the male and female bodhisattvas (see chart 6). The function of this initiation is to purify all defilements of the twelve sense bases, which are the following:

- The six subjective sense bases, or sense faculties (Tib. *nang gi skye mched drug*), comprising the five sensory faculties—the eyes, ears, nose, tongue, body—and the mental faculty.
- The six objective sense bases (Tib. *phyi'i skye mched drug*), comprising the five sensory objects—form, sounds, smell, taste, and touch—and mental objects.

The implement of the conduct initiation is a thumb vajra, which is a vajra ring that goes on the thumb. In this initiation, you generate the various sense faculties in the form of the male bodhisattvas. Then you dissolve the six objects as well as the implement of initiation, the thumb vajra, into emptiness. These are generated in the form of the female bodhisattvas.

The sense bases and their respective deities are as follows:

- The visual faculty becomes red Kṣitigarbha and consort, white Rūpavajrā. Visual form becomes white Rūpavajrā and consort, red Kṣitigarbha. At each of the eyes we have Kṣitigarbha with consort as well as Rūpavajrā with consort. There are two pairs of deities at each of the eyes.
- The auditory faculty becomes green Vajrapāṇi and consort, blue Śabdavajrā. Sound becomes blue Śabdavajrā and consort, green

Vajrapāṇi. At each ear we also have two pairs of deities, Vajrapāṇi with consort and Śabdavajrā with consort.

- The olfactory faculty becomes black Ākāśagarbha and consort, yellow Gandhavajrā. The smell sense object becomes yellow Gandhavajrā and consort, black Ākāśagarbha. At the nose we have two pairs, Ākāśagarbha with consort and Gandhavajrā with consort.
- The gustatory faculty becomes white Avalokiteśvara and consort, red Rasavajrā. Taste becomes red Rasavajrā and consort, white Avalokiteśvara. At the tongue we have two pairs of deities, Avalokiteśvara with consort and Rasavajrā with consort.
- The tactile faculty (in the genital region) becomes black Viṣkambhī and consort, yellow Sparśavajrā. Touch becomes yellow Sparśavajrā and consort, black Viṣkambhī. At the genital region, we again have two pairs, Viṣkambhī with consort and Sparśavajrā with consort, each in union with his respective consort.
- The mental faculty (located in the heart) becomes blue Samantabhadra and consort, green Dharmadhātuvajrā. Phenomena, or mental objects, become green Dharmadhātuvajrā and consort, blue Samantabhadra. At the heart are blue Samantabhadra with consort, and green Dharmadhātuvajrā with consort.

There are two thumb vajras for each of these pairs, and each thumb vajra has six facets. We generate each of the six facets of each of the two thumb vajras in the form of the above twelve deities, corresponding to the twelve sense bases.

As before, the jñānasattvas and the initiating deities are invited, and the initiating deities dissolve both into those various facets of the thumb vajras as well as into the deities generated in your own body. Then the initiating deities who have been invited bestow the initiation upon the implements of initiation. The deities who have been generated from the implements of initiation, the thumb vajras, go into union, melt into the nature of great bliss, and then transform into the nature of the implements of initiation. The male and female bodhisattvas of the maṇḍala bestow the initiation using these implements of initiation.

This initiation purifies the faults of the six faculties and their six objects, and transforms them into the six male bodhisattvas and six female bodhisattvas. Replicas of the six male and six female bodhisattvas of the maṇḍala are emanated from their bodies and dissolve into the respective deities in your own body. Then the initiating deities dissolve into yourself.

The parallel of this in ordinary life is the actual birth of the child, not its conception, and this pertains to the infant's experience of the various sensory objects.

This purifies all defilements of the six faculties and their six objects. One is thereby authorized to attain the siddhis of the six male and six female bodhisattvas. By realizing the nature of the five sense objects, one is empowered to enjoy them, and one is also empowered to attain the vajra sense base. The result of this particular phase of the initiation establishes the capacity for the attainment of the fifth bodhisattva ground.

Name Initiation

In the next initiation, the initiation of the name, the implements of initiation are bracelets and anklets (see chart 7). The faculties of action and the activities are purified:

- The six faculties of mouth, arm, leg, defecation, and urination, and the supreme faculty of regenerative fluid emission.
- The six activities of talking, taking, going, defecating, urinating, and emitting regenerative fluid.

These are generated in the forms of the six male and female wrathful deities, called the krodhas, making six pairs of male and female krodhas.

- Green Uṣṇīṣacakravārtin is generated at the orifice for urination. Normally this deity is generated at the *uṣṇīṣa* (crown protuberance), but here method and wisdom are reversed, so we generate the deity, together with the implement of initiation, at the urethra. Atinīlā is his consort, and she is blue. The activity of urination is generated as blue Atinīlā, and her consort is green Uṣṇīṣacakravārtin.
- At the faculty of the mouth is black Vighnāntaka. The mouth faculty as well as the implement of initiation, a bracelet, are generated as that deity. His consort is yellow Stambhanī. The activity of speech is generated as yellow Stambhanī, and her consort is the deity black Vighnāntaka.
- The faculty of the hands and one facet of the implements of initiation

are generated in the form of red Prajñāntaka and his consort, white Māninī. The activity of taking with the hands is generated in the form of white Māninī, who is embracing her consort, red Prajñāntaka.

- The faculty of the feet and one facet of the implements of initiation are generated as the deity white Padmāntaka, embracing his consort, red Ḍombinī. The activity of walking is generated in the form of red Ḍombinī, whose consort is white Padmāntaka.
- The faculty of the anus and one facet of the implement of initiation is generated as the deity yellow Yamāntaka, whose consort is black Ativīryā. The activity expelling excrement is generated in the form of black Ativīryā and her consort, yellow Yamāntaka.
- The so-called supreme faculty is the orifice for the regenerative fluid. The regenerative fluid and the implement of initiation are generated in the form of blue Sumbharāja. His consort is green Raudrākṣī. The activity of the emission of regenerative fluid is generated as green Raudrākṣī and her consort, blue Sumbharāja.

The male deities represent the faculties, and the female consorts symbolize the activities. When the activities are highlighted, instead of speaking of male deities with their consorts, we speak of goddesses with their male deity consorts.

Rays of light are emitted from the principal deity's heart, inviting the jñānasattvas, who merge into these twelve deities who have been generated from the implements of initiation, as well as those who are generated within one's own body.

The initiating deities bestow the initiation upon the deities generated from the implements of initiation, who enter into union and then dissolve. They take on the form of the implements of initiation. Then the male and female krodhas take the implements of initiation in hand and bestow the initiation simultaneously while telling the disciple, "You will attain buddhahood in the form of such and such a tathāgata." They tell us which name and which class is associated with that phase of the initiation when we drop the flower.

By means of this initiation, the various actions and activities are generated in the form of the male and female krodhas, who produce replicas of themselves and dissolve into the corresponding male and female beings in one's own body. Following that, the initiating deities also dissolve into these deities within oneself.

The parallel in common life is giving a child its name after it is born. This initiation purifies all defilements of the faculties of action and the corresponding activities. It empowers one to attain the siddhis of the male and female krodhas. The result of the initiation establishes the capacity for attaining the sixth bodhisattva ground.

The preceding two initiations of conduct and name are given in the eastern direction of the maṇḍala, associated with the vajra mind. They act to purify all defilements of the drop at the heart, associated with the deep sleep state.

Just as the faculties and activities emerge while in the womb, so do the karmic impurities of the mind associated with the various types of actions and functions emerge at that time. The experiences of the various sense objects and the mental defilements associated with them are purified by this process. The capacity for the vajra mind is established and one is empowered to attain the siddhi of the vajra mind. This leads to the meditation in the stage of generation in which one generates the male and female bodhisattvas as well as the male and female krodhas. At the time of fruition, or enlightenment, these various elements in one's body and the faculties for action and their associated activities are established as the male and female bodhisattvas and as the male and female krodhas.

It is important to understand how the elements, faculties, and activities relate to the process of initiation, how they lead to the different aspects of generating the seeds in the stage of generation, how they lead to the corresponding aspects in the stage of completion, and how they lead to various attainments at the time of fruition. To receive an authentic initiation in accordance with the tantras themselves, the disciple must understand the interrelationship of the process of initiation with the stages of generation, completion, and fruition. Further, one should understand how they pertain to the bases to be purified, the path, and the result.

Initiation to Achieve the Vajra Primordial Wisdom

At this point, we, the disciples, are taken by the hand and brought 180 degrees clockwise around from the eastern direction in front to the western direction in back, which is associated with the vajra primordial wisdom.

As before, rays of light are emitted from the heart of the principal deity from the western direction. They strike us, and draw us into the mouth of the deity, down to the level of the throat. With the arising of joy at the heart, great desire flames up. We melt, go through the vajra of the principal deity into the bhaga of the consort, and there we dissolve into emptiness.

From emptiness we arise in the form of the vajra primordial wisdom, similar in aspect to Vairocana—yellow, with three faces and six hands. The three faces are yellow, white, and black. In the right hands are, top to bottom, (1) a wheel, (2) a club, and (3) a wrathful vajra (literally, a "fear-inciter"). In the three left hands, top to bottom, we hold (1) a conch, (2) a vajra chain, and (3) a ringing bell. Our consort is black Tārā. Her three faces are black, red, and white. She has six hands; the right hands hold (1) a sword, (2) a curved knife, and (3) a trident. The left hands hold (1) a shield, (2) a skull, and (3) a khaṭvāṅga.[14] The consort and deity are embracing.

Rays of light are emitted from the heart of the principal deity, inviting the jñānasattvas, who dissolve into us. Then the invited initiation deities go into sexual union, and the drops that enter through the crown of the principal deity bestow initiation on us in the bhaga of the consort.

Initiation of Permission

Of these seven initiations, the initiation of permission entails the purification process of the drop associated with the fourth occasion (see chart 8). The implements of initiation are a wheel, a vajra, a sword, a jewel, a lotus, and another wheel.

In the permission initiation, the aggregate of primordial wisdom (Tib. *ye shes kyi phung po*) and the element of consciousness are generated as blue Vajrasattva and blue Prajñāpāramitā, respectively. The implements of the initiation are generated as blue Vajrasattva and blue Prajñāpāramitā. Blue Vajrasattva is embraced by green Vajradhātvīśvarī, and blue Prajñāpāramitā is embraced by green Akṣobhya.

As before, rays of light are emitted from the principal deity. They invite the jñānasattvas, who merge into both sets of deities, the internal deities and those as whom the implements have been imagined. Then the initiating deities are invited, and they bestow initiation upon the deities who have emerged from the implements of initiation. The initiation deities, Vajrasattva and Prajñāpāramitā, take the implements of initiation and bestow initiation upon us. In each case they incite us to turn the wheel of Dharma associated with that implement of initiation, the implement having previously been determined by the dropping of the flower.

- The initiation with the wheel symbolizes our turning the wheel of Dharma in the future.
- The initiation with the vajra symbolizes turning of the wheel of Dharma of the vajra class.
- The initiation with the sword symbolizes turning the wheel of Dharma of the sword class.
- The initiation with the jewel symbolizes turning the wheel of Dharma of the jewel class.
- The initiation with the lotus symbolizes turning the wheel of Dharma of the lotus class.
- The final initiation with the second wheel symbolizes turning of the wheel of Dharma of the wheel class.

One's aggregates of primordial wisdom and consciousness are both transformed into the form of Vajrasattva with consort. Vajrasattva and his consort emit replicas of themselves, which merge into the Vajrasattva with consort in one's being. Then the initiating deities dissolve into the Vajrasattva with consort in one's being.

Vajra Master Initiation

The wheel process of initiation is bestowed with the injunction to take upon ourselves the task of being a vajrācārya, or vajra master. We are given a conch, a volume of scriptures, and a bell, which symbolize the lack of inherent existence of all phenomena. That is followed by the permission of the mantra.

In this vajra master initiation, three pledges are given. They are the vajra mind pledge, the bell speech pledge, and the mudrā body pledge. Both you and the vajra dissolve into emptiness, and from emptiness both arise as Vajrasattva. The bell is generated as Prajñāpāramitā, who is your own consort in this case. This symbolizes that the disciple should continually cultivate the great bliss symbolized by the vajra, the realization of emptiness symbolized by the bell, and do these in union, which is made possible by the practice with the mudrā.

The seventh initiation has two facets. One is called the initiation of the mantra, and the other, the initiation of the vajra master. Usually, one is included in the other. Here they are sequential.

The parallel in ordinary life, especially of the initiation of the mantra, is the instruction, the child being read to by the parents.

It is said that while the embryo is still in the womb, its vital energies do not yet move. They start moving only at birth. With the first breath immediately following birth, the primordial wisdom energy begins to move, and that first breath is through the central channel. The breath in the left and right channel, or the left and right nostrils, is of even magnitude. Normally it is not even, but it is said to be even at this point in time.

This initiation purifies the defilements of the aggregate of primordial wisdom. The so-called aggregate of primordial wisdom is the bliss of orgasm in men and in women. This establishes the seed for actualizing Vajrasattva and purifies the defilements of the element of consciousness. This phase of the initiation leads to the attainment of the seventh bodhisattva ground.

Summary of the Seven Initiations

There are four maṇḍalas: the maṇḍala of meditative stabilization, the body maṇḍala, the cloth maṇḍala, and the colored sand maṇḍala. The seven initiations must be granted in dependence upon the colored sand maṇḍala. Each of these seven initiations involves the use of water, so they are called water initiations. The Kālacakra system does not use the term "seven vase initiations," but rather "the seven initiations of the self-entry of a child," or "the seven water initiations."

The initiation generally purifies unwholesome habitual propensities of body, speech, and mind. It authorizes meditation on the stage of generation, and it empowers one to attain the mundane siddhis. It also establishes in one the capacity for accumulating merit, and it authorizes one to engage in the various types of activities associated with the stage of generation. One thereby becomes what is called an *upāsaka.*

It is said that if in this life one practices the stage of generation and brings it to its culmination, one attains the degree of merit corresponding to the merit of a bodhisattva on the seventh bodhisattva ground. However, if one authentically receives the initiation and does not practice the stage of generation but very assiduously abandons the ten nonvirtues, it is said that within seven lifetimes one will attain the seventh āryabodhisattva ground. If one practices the Pāramitāyāna alone, such an attainment takes two countless eons. On this path, one could reach the same attainment in roughly 700 years (taking as a maximum lifespan for each life one hundred years). But within those seven lifetimes, one might eventually apply oneself diligently to this practice and thus reach that attainment before seven lifetimes have passed.

Here is a brief review of the seven initiations (see also chart 9):

1. The water initiation is conducted with a vase, is given by the five consorts, and purifies the five elements.
2. In the crown initiation, the five parts of the crown are generated as the five tathāgatas, thereby purifying the five aggregates. The first two initiations purify the defilements of the drop at the forehead associated with the waking state. They purify impurities of the elements and the aggregates and establish the capacity for attaining the vajra body.
3. The crown ribbon initiation is associated with the ten śaktīs. They purify the ten energies.
4. In the vajra and bell initiation, the vajra and bell transform into Kālacakra and consort. They purify the two side channels, right and left, drawing the energies into the central channel. Both the crown ribbon and the vajra and bell initiations are designed to remove the impurities of the drop at the throat associated with the dream state. They also purify any impurities of the speech, such as deceptive speech, and they establish the capacity for attaining the vajra speech.
5. The conduct initiation is associated with the six male and the six female bodhisattvas. They purify the six sense bases and the six sensory faculties.
6. The name initiation is associated with the six male and female krodhas. They purify the six action faculties and the six activities. The conduct and name initiations are designed to remove impurities associated with the drop at the heart that produces the deep sleep state.

They establish the capacity for attaining the vajra mind.

7. The permission initiation removes the impurities of the drop associated with the fourth occasion. Vajrasattva and his consort Prajñāpāramitā, bearing the symbols of the five types of buddhas, bestow this initiation, thereby purifying the defilements of the aggregate of primordial wisdom and the consciousness element.

The result in the fruition stage is that these seven initiations bring forth the vajra body, vajra speech, vajra mind, and vajra primordial wisdom. At this point, the initiating deities who have been invited to the palace in front of oneself, including Kālacakra with consort and the eight śaktīs, are all dissolved into oneself. Vajrasattva appears on the crown of one's head, and Akṣobhya arises from the crown of the head of each of the eight śaktīs around oneself as well as one's consort.

If we were receiving only the seven initiations of the self-entry of a child, we would dissolve those invited initiating deities who were in the space in front. If we are also receiving the high and the greatly higher initiations, we do not dissolve them yet.

9

The Higher and Greatly Higher Initiations

Śāntideva says, "All the joy in the world comes from the desire for others' happiness, and all the suffering in the world comes from the desire for one's own happiness." And he continues, "Enough of much talk! Note the difference between the fool who seeks his own benefit and the sage who works for the benefit of others."

Generally, it is said that all phenomena are mere appearances to the mind, and the preceding comments by Śāntideva illustrate that point. For example, in relating to such appearances, if one yearns for the well-being of all sentient beings and acts accordingly, the well-being comes back to oneself. If, however, one wishes to harm sentient beings, the harm comes back to oneself. Whether one experiences harm or well-being is not dependent upon some utterly objective event. One's experience is created by the mind.

In a sense, we emanate our own nature out into the world. What we emanate is what we get back. If we emanate hostility, which is not in accord with our buddha nature, suffering comes back. If we look upon others with an altruistic motivation, what we send out is actually in accordance with our own essential nature, our buddha nature, and what comes back is similarly in accordance with our own nature.

If we discard the well-being of others and devote ourselves exclusively to our own well-being, this at best can lead only to our own individual liberation, a Hīnayāna attainment, but it cannot lead to full awakening. It means that we are not able to fully manifest our own buddha nature. In the Mahāyāna context, we take upon ourselves the responsibility for the well-being of all sentient beings and the eradication of suffering of all sentient beings, enabling us to fully reveal our own nature.

In the Vajrayāna context, one regards the entire environment of animate and inanimate phenomena to be in the nature of bliss, which is in accord with one's own nature. It is said that when one attains full awakening in this practice, one realizes the actual nature of all sentient beings. It is with primordial wisdom that one realizes the actual nature of sentient beings, and at the point of enlightenment, one realizes the innate mind of every sentient being.

When we hear incitements to cultivate an altruistic motivation or engage in wholesome activity, the speaker is not simply being moralistic or arbitrarily telling people what to do. Rather, these words relate to a very profound aspect of reality itself. Emanating hostility and aggression brings about a bit of harm out in the objective world, but that emanation chiefly comes back to oneself, disturbing the equanimity of the mind and bringing suffering to oneself. Therefore, training in an altruistic motivation is extremely important. Not only is this training for the sake of other sentient beings, it is also for one's own benefit.

The actual nature of the seven water initiations, or the seven self-entries of a child, as well as the four higher and the four greatly higher initiations, is the emergence of great bliss and the resultant realization of emptiness. This is the very nature of each of the initiations.

A sentient being born from the womb and endowed with the four elements and the white and red drops is brought forth by orgasm following the emission of the regenerative fluids of the two parents and their "being overcome with joy" (Tib. *bde bas brgyal*). On that occasion, when the male and female are fainting with joy, the very subtle mind manifests. Normally, people are not able to recognize the arising of that very subtle mind. But if one were able to recognize it, one would experience something like a realization of emptiness.

The consciousness of the fetus that is about to be conceived enters into the midst of these red and white drops of the regenerative fluid. The mind that enters that union of the fluids is the very subtle mind. At that time, three very subtle minds are conjoined, namely, those of the two parents and that of the being who is entering the womb. There is a conjoining of the three subtle minds as well as the red and white fluids.

In other tantric systems such as the Guhyasamāja, the conjunction of the red and white constituents forms the nucleus at the heart around which the fetus grows. In the Kālacakra system, one surmises on the basis of the formation of the channels that the red and white constituents would be at the navel of the embryo that is about to be formed. The reason for this is that Kālacakra and consort are generated at the navel cakra, and the experience of immutable bliss arises from them.

According to both Guhyasamāja and Kālacakra, the basis for the extremely subtle consciousness is the red and white indestructible drops, which are in the central channel at the heart. At the point of death, these red and white drops separate. The white drop descends, and the red drop ascends. At the point of the separation of these two drops, the very subtle consciousness departs.

The yogi who is practicing highest yoga tantra and who has achieved control over the white and red bodhicitta can cause the red drop to move from the navel and the white drop to move from the crown. This is done by bringing forth the *tummo* flame at the navel cakra and melting the white bodhicitta at the crown of the head.

According to the Guhyasamāja and Cakrasaṃvara systems, it is not possible to bring forth the very subtle consciousness to the same extent that occurs naturally at the time of death unless one engages in practice with a karma mudrā, that is, a consort. In the Kālacakra system, engagement with a karma mudrā is not needed in order for the subtle mind to manifest.

The chief reason for engaging in consort practice is not for the sexual bliss that arises, but rather to bring about the full manifestation of primordial wisdom. For that reason, a practitioner seeks out a fully qualified karma mudrā, and gradually practices with such a karma mudrā in order to fully manifest the very subtle innate mind.

In terms of the female consort, not just any woman will do. It is best if the consort is an emanation of a ḍākinī. If one cannot find an emanation of a ḍākinī, then the next best thing is to find a karma mudrā who has realization on the stage of completion. If one is not available, then one seeks out a karma mudrā who has realization on the stage of generation. If one cannot find such a karma mudrā either, then one seeks out one who is well trained and has practiced well on the common path, who has fully and authentically received initiation, and who is keeping the vows and pledges very strictly.

According to the Kālacakra system, it is still appropriate if the consort is an older woman (with no specified age limit), whereas in the Guhyasamāja and Cakrasaṃvara systems, it is said that an older woman is not appropriate as a consort. In the scriptures on the tantras in general, the ages of the consorts most appropriate for karma mudrā practice are stated. Generally speaking, it is good when the tummo fire has not diminished too much. If you are dealing with an emanation of a ḍākinī, however, it does not matter if she is old.

For these reasons, it is said that not just any karma mudrā is appropriate. The karma mudrā has to have some specific qualities. But it is also true that if the male yogi is highly realized and can control the movement of the drops, then the qualities of the karma mudrā are not so significant.

In terms of the activities of the principal deity with consort, there is a danger that these explanations can give rise to misconceptions or doubts. The story of a Tibetan nomad of the Abuhor tribe, who was on a pilgrimage, illustrates this danger. In many temples, the Abuhor saw representations of deities in union with consorts. After gazing at these for a while, he said that if that is all it takes to attain enlightenment, he must be enlightened already! He did not understand the significance of these representations.

The Four Higher Initiations

There are eight more initiations, namely, four higher and four greatly higher initiations. In an authentic initiation, these are received by going into union with an actual consort, a karma mudrā. This practice is in accord with certain facets of reality, although it is not done nowadays.

The names of the four higher initiations are: vase initiation, secret initiation, wisdom-gnosis initiation, and word initiation. The four greatly higher initiations are given the same names, that is, vase, secret, wisdom-gnosis, and word.

Generally speaking, the greater the bliss there is in the mind, the more subtle the mind, and the more subtle the mind, the more conceptualization is diminished. The more subtle the mind that realizes emptiness, the more powerful an antidote it is for the mental afflictions. This accounts for the fact that in the tantric practice, one uses sensual objects such as food, drink, and so forth, and tries to bring forth as much bliss and joy from these as possible.

In the tantras it is said that there is no greater nonvirtue than abandoning sensual desire. The reason for this is that experiencing pleasurable sensual objects causes joy to arise, which may lead to the manifestation of a subtle mind, which is then used to penetrate the nature of emptiness. This is very effective in terms of overcoming the obscurations of the mind. On the other hand, if one simply abandons the objects of desire and desire itself, one closes off the access to such practice.

In the context of tantric practice, if one engages in sensual pleasures in the ordinary, mundane way—without realizing their lack of inherent existence and without bringing forth the qualities of joy and the subtle mind—then the disadvantages of that would be greater than those of transgressing the four primary vows of a Buddhist monk.

The Indian tantric sage Kṛṣṇa-pa commented that if one lacks the realization of yoga but still engages in tantric union with a consort, the practice leads not to wisdom but to hell. Actual primordial wisdom does not arise. What does happen as a result of this mere parody is that one takes birth in a hell realm. Therefore, it is crucial to either do this practice correctly or not do it at all. If we engage in such practice and we do it correctly, it has a great benefit. If we engage in such practice incorrectly, it results in disaster.

The Higher Vase Initiation

For the vase initiation of the four higher initiations, one is in the northern direction and generates oneself as a vajra body. Then one offers to the guru Kālacakra, in the sense of offering a maṇḍala, a fully qualified consort, or *vidyā,* so called because the innate mind manifests in dependence upon her.

Kālacakra accepts the offered consort and, with the deities of the maṇḍala as witnesses, gives the consort back, saying, "I give this consort back to you for the sake of your experience of the union of bliss and emptiness." Bearing in mind that we are already generated in the form of the vajra body, the consort is generated in the form of the śakti Viśvamātā.

At this point, in the form of the vajra body, one holds and caresses the breasts of the consort and embraces her, resulting in great desire. In dependence upon that, the white bodhicitta melts, and the experience of bliss arises. With that bliss one focuses on emptiness, and with this experience of bliss and emptiness, one receives the vase initiation.

Although in this initiation no vase is actually used, it is nevertheless called a vase initiation because the breast of the consort is likened to a vase, for it is called "a container of white milk."

It is said that the vase initiation purifies the desire to smile and laugh. Recall the four kinds of pleasure, one of which was smiling and laughter. It also removes the defilements of the drop at the forehead associated with the waking state, and it empowers one to attain the resultant vajra body.

This concludes the vase initiation.

The Higher Secret Initiation

For the higher secret initiation, the disciple is brought around to the right to the southern side of the palace and is generated in the form of the vajra speech. The guru and the consort go into union, and rays of light emitted from the guru's heart bring in all the deities of the maṇḍala, including Kālacakra with consort. These come into the mouth of the guru and are dissolved by the great desire at the heart. Although it is not clear in the text, they also go into the mouth of the consort, because both the red and the white regenerative fluids are involved.

Then they arrive at the tip of the jewel of the vajra, and this symbolizes the primordial wisdom of nondual bliss and emptiness. The guru first takes one drop of the white bodhicitta and places it in the mouth of the disciple. Then the consort also takes one drop of the red bodhicitta from the lotus and places it in the mouth of the disciple. One experiences the secret substances of the deity and the consort and gazes at the lotus of the consort, thereby arousing great desire. With great desire and the concomitant great joy, the white bodhicitta melts, giving rise to bliss, which is then focused upon emptiness. With that experience, the secret initiation is received.

This purifies the defilements of the drop associated with the dream state and establishes the capacity for one to attain the vajra speech and the ninth bodhisattva ground.

The Higher Wisdom-Gnosis Initiation

For the higher wisdom-gnosis initiation, one is taken by the hand, moving clockwise to the front, to the eastern direction. In the form of the vajra mind, one stands before the eastern face of the deity. This is for the sake of removing any defilements of the drop that brings forth the deep sleep state.

The wisdom-gnosis initiation is so called because one enters into union with wisdom, referring to the consort. Because the initiation is produced by melting one's own bodhicitta, it is said that one receives initiation in the maṇḍala of the relative spirit of awakening.

The disciple is already generated in the form of the vajra mind. The consort, specifically the one who was previously offered to the deity, is generated in the form of Viśvamātā. One enters into union with the three attitudes: (1) regarding one's body as divine, by visualizing the bodies of both the consort and oneself in divine forms; (2) regarding one's speech as mantra, by visualizing the *phaṭ* syllable as in the two instances explained below; and (3) regarding one's mind as being reality itself, by meditating on emptiness.

Then as the principle deity you dissolve your own vajra—the male organ—into the nature of light, and from the light arises the syllable *hūṃ*. From the *hūṃ* arises a vajra. Think of the central channel as running along the long axis of the vajra. To prevent the white bodhicitta from emerging from the vajra, you imagine it being blocked with a yellow *phaṭ* syllable at the tip. The reason for visualizing that yellow *phaṭ* syllable is to arrest the power of the descending energy that propels the white bodhicitta outward. In your mind's eye you do not think of an ordinary male organ. Instead, you visualize a vajra. But now, with pleasure arising from contact in sexual union, imagine a five-pointed vajra with the prongs on the side. This visualization is very awkward. The following is not in the text, but it is in the oral tradition. To make it conform better to what is actually being sensorially experienced without bringing in ordinary appearances, imagine this five-pointed vajra with the central shaft and the *phaṭ* at the tip as if it were enclosed by a very smooth, round, pleasant glass container, but not of ordinary glass. Its smooth exterior, its rounded shape, is composed of tiny vajras, minuscule particles of smooth glass so small that they give the appearance of a smooth form. In this way you can conform this meditation to experience without bringing in ordinary appearances.

Then you dissolve the lotus—the ordinary female organ of the consort—into light. From that light you generate the lotus in the form of a red three-petaled lotus with an empty center. The center of that is the central channel, and you imagine this being blocked by the yellow syllable *phaṭ* as well.

With the three attitudes you enter into union. As the white bodhicitta drops from the crown to the genital cakra, you experience great bliss. With the mind of great bliss you meditate on emptiness. That experience is called the wisdom initiation.

This purifies defilements of the mind, establishes in one's being the drop related to the vajra mind, and authorizes one to attain the vajra mind. It also establishes the capacity for attaining the tenth bodhisattva ground.

The Higher Word Initiation

For the fourth higher initiation, the word initiation, one is led by the hand clockwise to the back, which is in the western direction. Facing the primordial wisdom face of the deity, one generates oneself in the form of vajra primordial wisdom and one's consort as Viśvamātā. As before, one goes into union.

In this fourth initiation, one goes into union, experiences bliss, and the white bodhicitta descends this time to the tip of the jewel, whereas previously it went down only to the level of the genital cakra. Bliss arises, and one meditates on emptiness. This is called the provisional fourth initiation. The experience of bliss and emptiness introduces one to this initiation.

This initiation purifies the defilements of the drop that produces the fourth occasion. It establishes the capacity to attain the vajra primordial wisdom, and it also establishes the capacity for attaining the eleventh bodhisattva ground.

Because this is an initiation that is introduced by words, it is called the word initiation. Because this initiation is attained in dependence upon the union of the two truths, which is the definitive meaning, it is said to be attained in dependence upon the ultimate spirit of awakening.

With these four initiations—the vase initiation, secret initiation, wisdom-gnosis initiation, and word initiation—the capacity is established to attain the eighth, ninth, tenth, and eleventh bodhisattva grounds.

The Four Greatly Higher Initiations

The bases to be purified are the same for the four higher initiations and the four greatly higher initiations, but the processes of purification are different. I have not been able to identify the difference in function between the two, but one could infer that the distinction is a matter of degree: the higher initiations may purify certain defilements on a gross level, and the greatly higher initiations may do so on a more subtle level.

For the four greatly higher initiations, the disciple is brought to the respective quarters of the maṇḍala, as before.

The Greatly Higher Vase Initiation

The first of the greatly higher initiations is the vase initiation, given in the northern direction. One is generated in the vajra body form. At this point the disciple has ten consorts, whose attributes are described in the scriptures. These are generated in the form of the ten śaktīs.

The process of initiation is quite similar to the preceding. The vase initiation begins as before with the fondling of the breasts, the embrace, and resultant arousal of great desire. The white bodhicitta melts from the crown of the head to the forehead. At the forehead there arises bliss, from that bliss one focuses on emptiness, and with that experience one receives the vase initiation.

The functions, the seeds it establishes, what it empowers one to do, and the capacity established by the initiation are the same as in the earlier vase initiation, and it is called by the same name and has the same etymology.

The Greatly Higher Secret Initiation

The disciple is now led around to the southern side of the maṇḍala, corresponding to the vajra speech, and one generates oneself as vajra speech.

According to the Gelug tradition, there are two different presentations of this secret initiation. One is by Gyeltsab Je, one of two principle disciples of Lama Je Tsongkhapa, in his presentation on the stage of completion. There are also notes taken from Je Tsongkhapa's teachings on the stage of completion by an unknown disciple. These two accounts are in agreement. They state that in this secret initiation the principal deity goes into union with the consort, and then the secret substances are given to the disciple.

According to Khedrub Je, the other of the two chief disciples of Je Tsongkhapa, it is the disciple, not the principal deity, who goes into union with the consort. Furthermore, the white bodhicitta descends into the heart cakra, not to the throat.

The interpretation of Gyeltsab Je and Je Tsongkhapa's note-taker seems to be more reasonable, for this is called the secret initiation, which refers to the bestowal of the secret substances.

Following that interpretation, the principal deity goes into union with nine of the ten consorts. In union with these consorts, rays of light are emitted from the heart of the principal deity, inviting all the buddhas. They may come either to the crown of the head or into the mouth—it does not make any difference—then they come down to the level of the heart, melting into light. Next, great desire arises in the principal deity, the white bodhicitta comes to the tip of the jewel of the vajra, and similarly the red bodhicitta of the consort comes down to the tip of the lotus. A drop of the white and of the red bodhicitta is forced onto the ring finger and given to the disciple. Upon tasting the two secret substances, the disciple gazes upon the lotuses of the nine consorts. Consequently, great desire arises, and the bodhicitta melts and drops down to the level of the heart. With this great desire one focuses upon emptiness, and at that point the secret initiation is received.

Although the principal deity goes into union with the nine consorts, because the fluid is not emitted, the bliss does not decline. It is said that if the fluid is emitted it leads to death, but if it is retained it leads to the siddhi of immortality. Moreover, it is said that if one familiarizes oneself with this practice of retaining the fluid, the body takes on a more and more youthful appearance. It becomes very supple and strong, and eventually one's appearance approaches that of a sixteen-year old.

The explanation of this initiation in terms of the drops, authorization, and so forth is exactly as previously described for the higher secret initiation.

The Greatly Higher Wisdom-Gnosis Initiation

For the wisdom-gnosis initiation, the disciple is led around clockwise to the eastern direction in front of the maṇḍala, facing the vajra-mind face of the deity. As described before, the disciple and the nine consorts enter into union with the three attitudes explained before.

In union with these consorts, the drops descend from the level of the heart to the genital cakra. Bliss is experienced at that point, and one meditates upon emptiness. With that experience, one is introduced to the third greatly higher initiation, the wisdom-gnosis initiation. The etymology and all the results of the initiation are similar to the preceding presentation of the higher initiation.

When the white bodhicitta goes from the genitals to the tip of the jewel, it indicates bliss and emptiness. That is of the nature of the wisdom-gnosis initiation. It is called the "mere fourth initiation" (Tib. *dbang bzhi pa tsam*), but is of the nature of the wisdom-gnosis initiation.

At this point, Gyeltsab Je and Khedrub Je differ in their explanations. One says that on the occasion of the wisdom-gnosis initiation, the white bodhicitta goes directly to the tip of the jewel. The other says simply that it goes to the genital cakra, and then when it goes to the tip of the jewel, it is called the *mere* fourth initiation, to distinguish it from the *actual* fourth initiation. The latter interpretation is probably more reasonable, for it corresponds more closely to the basis to be purified.

The Greatly Higher Word Initiation

When the white bodhicitta is at the tip of the jewel, one generates oneself and the consort as deities of empty form. At that point, one's mind arises in great bliss, and one ascertains emptiness. Then the union of body and mind appears to the mind's eye. By that experience one is introduced to the union of the body and mind that occurs at the time of fruition, and that is called the word initiation, or fourth initiation.

The purification of the various elements of purification that occurs during this initiation is similar to that described in the higher word initiation.

An exclusive quality of this greatly higher word initiation is that the capacity for attaining the twelfth incomparable ground is established. The other aspects, including the etymology and so forth, are the same as in the higher initiation.

Pledges

Bear in mind that during the initiation you are told of the pledges that you must keep and the downfalls that you must guard against. You are given an introduction to the discipline. You are also told that you must abide by the twenty-five types of conduct within the Kālacakra discipline. Moreover, note that there are some differences between the fourteen root tantric downfalls in the general presentation of tantra and those in the Kālacakra system.

Summary of the Initiations

For the first seven initiations, you are introduced to the various bases to be purified, the four drops, and the process of purification. The agents of purification are the various implements of initiation, corresponding to each of the initiations described previously.

For the higher and the greatly higher initiations, the bases to be purified are the four drops, whose defilements are removed, and the processes of initiation are the four higher and the four greatly higher initiations themselves. The results of purification are the four bodies of the buddha.

While practicing the stage of generation, the basis to be purified is comprised of the four drops. The processes of purification are the generation of oneself as the four buddhas: the vajra body, the vajra speech, the vajra mind, and the vajra primordial wisdom. This is one aspect of the process of purification. Another is visualizing the various deities in the maṇḍala.

Due to the meditation processes on the stage of generation, the vital energies and the channels are blessed. During the stage of completion, due to the direct action upon the channels and energies that have been blessed, immutable bliss arises, and one is able to transform those energies into the deities, which were merely imagined during the stage of generation. Then at the time of fruition, the maṇḍala of Kālacakra and all of its inhabitants are actually manifested.

In order to arrive at the stage of fruition, it is necessary to cultivate the mind of immutable bliss and to generate the empty form. The six-phase yoga in the stage of completion is the means for accomplishing that. To make these channels and the energies serviceable, the practice of the completion stage by itself is not sufficient—it needs to be blessed by the practice of the generation stage. Furthermore, if one has not cultivated the pure vision and divine pride in oneself as the deity during the generation stage, in the first of the six phases on the completion stage, namely, retraction, it is said that the deity with consort will not appear.

Because it is impermissible to meditate on the stage of generation without previously having received the initiation, the initiation precedes such meditation, and the initiation establishes in one's mindstream the seeds of the deities that one visualizes later on. Moreover, it is said that if one is not utterly devoted to the well-being of others, one is not allowed to receive the initiation.

Therefore, prior to the actual initiation, the disciple comes in front of the palace of the maṇḍala, and the guru calls out from the maṇḍala, "Who are you?" You must answer, "I am a fortunate bodhisattva." If you do not respond in this way, he will tell you, "Go away."

If you gave the correct answer to this question, the deity then asks, "What do you want?" Now the appropriate response is "In dependence upon the experience of sensual objects, I seek great bliss." If you give that answer, the principal deity will say, "Come right in."

10

The Purification of Death

It is said that compassion is the one virtue that brings forth all others. The mind that is unable to bear the suffering of others gives rise to the yearning to alleviate their suffering and bring them to a state of well-being. We realize that in our present condition, we do not have the means to completely alleviate the suffering of other sentient beings, or the means to bring them to a lasting state of happiness. We understand that we cannot achieve our aspirations. If we focus on being of material service to others, at best we can alleviate sentient beings' suffering only temporarily. We cannot bring about circumstances that are lasting or essential. Moreover, it is not even certain that such material efforts will actually bring any happiness. They may, in fact, accomplish the opposite of our intentions.

When one becomes accustomed to the cultivation of compassion, one is able to sacrifice any type of resource or possession in order to alleviate the suffering of others. As compassion increases, one is able to sacrifice even one's body for the sake of others if the need arises. Therefore, it is evident that compassion is a great, powerful force. The cultivation of compassion culminates in the state of full awakening in which one has a manifest ability to serve the needs of all sentient beings.

In order to totally eradicate the root of suffering of others, it is necessary to dispel all forms of delusion. For this reason bodhisattvas engage in all sorts of trainings. They become fully adept in the complete training of the śrāvakas, they are well-versed in the training of the pratyekabuddhas, and of course they become well-versed in the training of the Mahāyāna path. This is the manner in which the arousal of great compassion leads to all other excellent qualities.

Review of the Path

I come to have the fortune of actualizing in this lifetime
The sevenfold state of Kālacakra,
In which the 21,600 karmic vital energies
And all the material elements of the body are consumed.

At this point, if you are so inclined, you can recite a short text called *The Foundation of All Excellence* (Tib. *yon tan gzhir gyur ma*). It is helpful to reflect upon it and engage in the integrated meditation on the whole path to enlightenment.

Even if you cannot meditate on the entire path from beginning to end, it would be good to recollect the three principles of the path: the spirit of emergence, the spirit of awakening, and the perfect view. This reflection creates an appropriate motivation for the next phase of the practice, the stage of generation and completion. The author emphasizes the benefits of reviewing the common path, perhaps especially for beginning practitioners, to show that it is a prerequisite for the tantric practices. If one does not train well in the common path and instead goes directly to the highest yoga tantra, it could not be anything more than Hīnayāna practice anyway.

Supplication to Vajradhara

When I earnestly, reverently pray to you,
Guru Vajradhara,
Embodiment of all the infinite refuges,
Please bless my mindstream.

You then begin the recitation, which is a supplication to Vajradhara. This request is not made casually but with a heartfelt understanding of the nature of saṃsāra and of the miserable states of existence, as they pertain to oneself and to all sentient beings. The supplication is made with a profound, heartfelt yearning for freedom. If one cannot truly feel the suffering of oneself and all sentient beings in this cycle of existence, then engaging in this supplication and subsequent practice will merely be an imitation. It will not be an authentic practice.

The purpose of the supplication is to ask for the blessing of one's mindstream, to ripen one's own being in order to ripen the minds of others. That is why it is made first.

Blessing One's Mindstream

Due to the power of such fervent prayer,
My primary Guru Kālacakra
Comes to the crown of my head
And joyfully dissolves, becoming of one taste with me.

Having made this supplication, we should imagine the guru being very pleased. If we have visualized him sitting on a lotus throne, we can imagine it dissolving into him. But it does not matter whether we invite the guru with the complete throne, the sun, and the lotus, and so forth, or whether we have them first dissolve into the guru.

The guru comes to the crown of the head, and we imagine ourselves being purified by ambrosia descending from the guru's body. We imagine ambrosia flowing down from the crown of our head, purifying all obscurations, unwholesome habitual propensities, and mental afflictions. This is good for the mind. By engaging in this preliminary step of doing the purification just before the guru dissolves into us, we create a sense of purity. Otherwise, if we think of our body or body-mind as being defiled, we would not want to invite our guru to be inseparable with us. Following that, the guru comes down, dissolves into ourselves, and literally we become of the same taste, or the same nature, as the guru.

In the practice of Kālacakra we do not transform the three bodies into the path. In other words, we are not transforming death, the intermediate stage, and birth. There are just two phases in Kālacakra, transforming death and transforming birth. The intermediate stage is not present in the Kālacakra system. This is the purification of death.

Causes, Effects, and Conceptualization

All phenomena—causes, effects, nature, and actions—
Are primordially empty of intrinsic nature,
Like illusions and dreams.

We can understand the causes of phenomena in two ways, namely, the causes that compel us to continue in the cycle of existence and the causes that lead us to the attainment of full awakening.

The causes for the perpetuation of the cycle of existence are karma and mental afflictions. In this context, the causes for attaining spiritual awakening are the practices of the stage of generation and the stage of completion, motivated by the spirit of awakening. Effects can also be interpreted in two ways, namely, the effects of the truth of the source of suffering and the cycle of rebirth, and the effects of the attainment of awakening. Then the text refers to the general nature of phenomena without regard to the cause or effect of any specific phenomenon.

The term "actions" in the above verse refers to the activities of creation and cessation. This can refer to the manner in which the truth of the source of suffering brings forth misery, or it can refer to the manner in which a former saṃsāric life brings forth a later one. In terms of enlightenment, it may also refer to the manner in which the stages of generation and completion bring forth such things as the empty form body and so forth.

In this context, "phenomena" includes not only composite but also non-composite, or permanent, phenomena. Because all phenomena are mere appearances devoid of true, or intrinsic, existence, they are said to be "like illusions and dreams."

In considering the lack of intrinsic nature of causes, effects, and nature, the one that is easiest to understand is the lack of intrinsic nature of phenomena themselves. With regard to seeking out the lack of inherent existence of the nature of a phenomenon, one could seek the designated object with respect to an object such as a pen, or with respect to oneself. For example, with regard to oneself, one can ask whether the body alone is "I," and it obviously is not. The mind is obviously not "I," the body and mind together are not "I," nor is something else apart from those "I." This is fairly straightforward. Nevertheless, a qualm may arise as one reflects back on previous lives and thinks, "But wasn't the cause for my existence a previous life? And would that not imply that I do truly exist?" Similarly, in terms of the attainments or effects that one looks to in the future, the qualm might arise, "If those things that I am striving for don't truly exist, if they are just like illusions, then what is the point?"

To counter those two qualms, one first goes back to the lack of true existence of the cause. One recognizes that the very fact that a thing or event is a cause is true merely in dependence upon a conceptual designation; that item or event does not exist inherently. It, too, is an illusion and lacks intrinsic nature. Likewise, the results that one is striving for are simply conceptually designated and lack intrinsic nature. In dependence upon a merely designated cause, there arises a merely designated result. The cause that has a capacity for producing a merely designated result is not truly existent.

The lack of inherent existence of a cause is said to be its signless quality, which suggests that there is no sign of its having the capacity to truly exist as a cause. In terms of the lack of intrinsic nature of results, because there is no capacity to attain any truly existent result, therefore, the results are said to have a quality of desirelessness. Similarly, the activities themselves are brought forth by conceptual designation, and they lack inherent existence or true existence as well. Being a mere conceptual designation precludes the possibility of there being a truly existent causal relationship between any causes and effects, including actions and their consequences.

One should carefully examine the way in which one designates specific phenomena. For example, one can ask, "What determines that a seed precedes a sprout?" What occurs is that one designates something as a sprout. This is a basis that appears, and with regard to that basis one says, "This is a sprout." Bear in mind that two appearances are involved. One is the appearance that one designates as a sprout, and the other is the appearance of the location of the sprout. The third appearance, which one designates as the seed, is at the same location as the sprout before it has arisen.

One must conceptually ascertain the sequential nature of those appearances. By the power of that conceptual apprehension, one ascertains the sprout as being the result of the seed and the seed being the cause of the sprout. The progression of these events occurs by the power of the conceptual designation. It does not arise purely from the objective side of those events themselves, unrelated to conceptual designation. Even though there may be a grain in the ground that one designates as a seed, there is no certainty that it will in fact give rise to a sprout. Moreover, someone who is unaware of the relationship between the sprout and the preceding location of the seed would not be able to establish that there is a causal relationship between the sprout and the seed. The presentation of causes and effects is established by the ascertainment of the sequential relationship of causes and effects, and that comes by the force of conceptual designation.

Take, for example, a class attended by a group of people, each of whom always sits in the same place in the classroom. We can apprehend this situation and say that there is an order in which they always sit. One day someone new attends the class, and on that particular day everyone sits in a new place. The people who have been attending the class would say that people are not sitting in their proper order, but the new person would not see anything out of order. Whether the order is mixed up or not is something only in one's own mind.

One can ask, "Are causes and effects actually sequential or are they simultaneous?" Let us imagine some point at which the label "sprout" has not yet been designated, and later on it is so designated. When one designates something as a sprout, one is not explicitly designating other things as being its causes—such as the seed, the fertilizer, moisture, heat, and so forth. Nevertheless, the very moment one says, "This is a sprout," these other factors are implicitly designated as the causes for the sprout.

This is true for one who has established the causal relationship between sprout, seed, fertilizer, and so forth. When people designate something as a sprout, although they are not explicitly designating the cause, this is done implicitly by the sequence of appearances that relate to the appearance of the sprout.

If one does not understand this process, it is very difficult to establish how anything comes into existence. On the one hand, one may assert that everything lacks inherent existence, and, on the other hand, one asserts that things really do have functions. It is hard to juxtapose those two assertions. For instance, if we consider a group of people in a particular room, for example, we may think they are all more or less the same, insofar as all are human beings. This is a kind of general supposition. But when we start to investigate, we find that we have hardly anything in common. We can start from the gross and go to the subtle, and we find very few things in common. When we start to investigate in detail and go down to the components of which the body is made, we find again that everything is truly unique! We don't find much real commonality. Even if we go down to the smallest particles of which the body is formed, these too are not exactly identical from one body to the next. They give rise to different results and they arise from different causes. They are unique. The statement that all phenomena are delusive refers to this point.

Transforming Death Into the Path

When the text states that phenomena are "primordially empty of intrinsic nature," it refers to transforming the dharmakāya into the path through the dying process. The dying process is the basis to be purified, and the dharmakāya is the fruitional state. At this point, the meditation on emptiness is for transforming the dharmakāya into the path by way of the dying process.

How does one transform the fruition into the path? By recognizing the similarity between the dharmakāya and death. Recall that in the dying process the innate mind manifests, and there is an experience similar to realizing emptiness. In the fruitional state of the dharmakāya, the innate mind is fully manifested, and there is an actual realization of emptiness.

Now in terms of the practice, one meditates on emptiness, then imagines that the innate mind manifests and that one is nonconceptually experiencing emptiness. At that point one cultivates the sense of divine pride, "I am the dharmakāya." That is how one transforms the dharmakāya into the path in relation to the dying process. The union of wisdom and bliss, with which one imagines directly realizing emptiness, is identified as dharmakāya, and one identifies with that by thinking, "I am the dharmakāya."

In pursuing this practice there is a risk that if one is fully focused on the thought, "I am the dharmakāya," one's mind may get caught up in conventional reality. So there is another interpretation of this stage of the meditation. Some people say that when one is imagining bliss and emptiness, directly realizing emptiness, and abiding in this meditative equipoise, the pride of being the dharmakāya is implicitly present even without thinking, "I am the dharmakāya."

Khedrub Je, one of the foremost disciples of Lama Tsongkhapa, says that in dependence upon ordinary pride in saṃsāric life we establish our own body and mind, we accumulate karma, and we cycle around in existence. Taking that as a parallel, he says that as one imagines the manifestation of the innate mind and further imagines emptiness and bliss, divine pride arises, and one consequently engages in various virtuous actions.

Here is my critique of the interpretation that says that the pride of dharmakāya is implicitly present, even though it does not appear to one's mind's eye: Even though one is imagining that the innate mind is manifesting with emptiness and bliss, one is simply focused on emptiness—nothing else. This does not entail the pride of being the dharmakāya, so such pride does not enter into the situation. To counter that insufficiency, while the main force of your awareness is imagining the innate mind and focusing on emptiness, with one small fraction of your awareness, you cultivate the thought, "I am the dharmakāya." Then everything is complete. It is also very difficult to do!

As mentioned earlier, it is said that in the Kālacakra system there is no explicit transformation of the sambhogakāya into the path in relationship to the intermediate state. The question may arise, "Is the intermediate state not purified in the Kālacakra practice?" The answer is that it is purified because there is no intermediate state utterly apart from the processes of death and rebirth. By thoroughly purifying death and rebirth, the intermediate state is implicitly purified as well.

The way to understand this point is as follows: One's body of empty form cannot be separated from this gross body, which is composed of material particles, until we abandon all obscurations—in other words, until buddhahood. In order to attain full awakening, the agents of purification are the 21,600 immutable blisses, and the bases to be purified are the 21,600 red and white drops. In order to actualize that, it is necessary to be a sentient being who is born from the womb and has the four elements and the white and the red constituents. A bardo being, a being in the intermediate state, cannot do this because such a being is not born from a womb and does not have the four elements and the white and red constituents. One cannot cultivate the path on the basis of being a bardo being.

Once again, this is the point at which one should meditate on emptiness, imagining the manifestation of the innate mind, focusing on emptiness, and with a fraction of one's mind cultivating the thought, "I am the dharmakāya."

Kyabje Trijang Rinpoche states, probably based upon an assertion by Kyabje Phabongka Rinpoche, that just prior to engaging in the meditation on emptiness in which you transform the dharmakāya into the path in relationship to death, you should think, "As the dharmakāya I am inaccessible to sentient beings, which is not satisfactory. Therefore, I will emanate as a sambhogakāya." Then, think, "A sambhogakāya is still inaccessible to most sentient beings, so I will emanate as a nirmāṇakāya." One should follow that line of thought prior to the meditation. In the Kālacakra system, however, we do not explicitly transform the sambhogakāya into the path in relationship to the intermediate state, so we can skip that and go straight to the nirmāṇakāya.

Not only do we precede the practice with this anticipation but we also continue it in the practice, such that at the end of the dharmakāya practice we think of the three phases: "As the dharmakāya, I am inaccessible to sentient beings; therefore I will arise as sambhogakāya," and at the end of that we can reflect, "As a sambhogakāya, I am inaccessible to most sentient beings; therefore, I will arise as a nirmāṇakāya." We should also cultivate the motivation to serve the needs of all sentient beings by means of the three *kāyas.*

Dissolution of the Elements and Appearance of the Ten Signs

In the meditative practice, one imagines that one's water element subdues the element of fire. With the absence of the fire, the earth element is unable to persist, so it dissolves into water. The air element dries up the water element and then dissolves into consciousness, and consciousness dissolves into space. Then all phenomena of the environment and one's body—everything that is composed of material particles—dissolve into emptiness. The object, emptiness, and the subject, primordial wisdom, become inseparable.

In other systems such as Cakrasaṃvara and Guhyasamāja, the dissolution of the four elements of (1) earth, (2) water, (3) fire, and (4) air correspond in a one-to-one sequential fashion to the four signs of (1) smoke, (2) a mirage, (3) a firefly, and (4) a butter lamp. In contrast, in the Kālacakra system, first all the elements dissolve, then those various signs appear sequentially. The *Kālacakra Root Tantra* states how these different elements dissolve one into the other, how everything dissolves into emptiness, and then how the various signs appear.

In the Cakrasaṃvara and Guhyasamāja systems, the first element to dissolve is earth into water. In those systems, the first sign to appear is a mirage, not smoke. In the Kālacakra system, the first one is smoke. The reason for this difference is said to be that in the Guhyasamāja and

Cakrasaṃvara systems, the sign prior to the mirage, namely, the sign of smoke, is concealed, though in fact it does occur. So in reality the smoke sign is first.

From that experience of meditative equipoise in the dharmakāya arises a smoke-like appearance. People seem to have different experiences of this smoke-like appearance. Some experience it like the drifting of smoke in the room, and others have an experience more like smoke coming out of a chimney.

The mirage-like experience is common to our ordinary experience of a mirage, having a kind of wavering quality.

There seem to be two types of firefly-like experience. One is like seeing fireflies flying around in the dark, and the other is more like flashing lights, which also resemble fireflies.

Likewise, for the lamp-like experience there seem to be two types of appearances that may occur. One is a vision like a flame that does not flicker. Another possibility is like a flame that has a translucent shade around it, concealing the actual flame itself. It is more diffuse.

The Kālacakra system speaks of ten signs. The first four of the ten signs are said to be the four night signs. In the practice on the stage of completion, the corresponding meditation has to be practiced in the dark. The signs correspond to the night, and while one does not necessarily have to practice at night, one must practice in the dark.

The four night signs, already described, are the following:

1. A smoke-like appearance.
2. A mirage-like experience.
3. A firefly-like experience.
4. A lamp-like experience.

The next six signs are daytime signs. They are to be imagined in the corresponding meditation that gives rise to those signs. This practice is to be done in the light. The six daytime signs are as follows:

5. The blazing of fire. Some people may have a vision of seeing not only the blazing of fire, but even something being consumed, like wood going up in flames.
6. The experience of the round disc of a full moon.
7. A disc of the sun.

8. Rāhu in the shape of a blue disc. Normally it is green, but in this case it is blue.
9. A vision of forked lightning.
10. A drop, or a seed. This too is a blue disc, with a kind of black design in it.

For the first four signs, as the smoke and so forth appear sequentially, we should cultivate divine pride. For example, as the smoke appears, we should imagine, "Now I have attained enlightenment in the form of Dhūmā." The next one is Marīci, then Khagamanā, the firefly goddess, and finally Marmema, the lamp goddess. We imagine in each of these cases, "I have attained enlightenment" in that form.

As each of the next four signs appears—the flame, the moon, the sun, and rāhu—we imagine ourselves as having attained enlightenment in the form of the four blazing goddesses: the śaktīs Kṛṣṇadīptā in the east, Raktādīptā in the south, Śvetādīptā in the north, and Pītādīptā in the west. These four goddesses are associated with the first four of the six daytime signs. When the lightning sign appears, one should imagine oneself as having attained the enlightenment of Vajradhātvīśvarī. When the seed appears, imagine having attained enlightenment in the form of Viśvamātā.

In the preceding stage of transforming the dharmakāya into the path in relation to death, one dissolves both oneself and one's entire environment into the nature of emptiness. I have already explained briefly the manner in which the dissolution of the body occurs.

Dissolution and Creation of the Universe

In the dissolution of the rest of the world, first the power of the earth element dissolves into that of water, then the water element dries up and dissolves into fire, then fire dissolves into air, and air dissolves into space. Then one cultivates the pride of the primordial wisdom of great bliss, in which all dualistic appearances of subject and object have vanished. This, in short, is called transforming the dharmakāya into the path in relation to death.

It is said that upon the complete dissolution of the entire world with all animate and inanimate entities within it, the only thing remaining is the mind of clear light, the innate mind. It seems that when one dies, the environment, together with the inhabitants that one experiences, also vanishes. It is said further that when the innate mind brings forth thoughts, the very subtle energy brings forth energies that are conjoined with those conceptualizations as well. Those energies are conjoined with conceptual states of awareness. There are said to be twelve energies. For the conceptualizations and the energies of conceptualization, there are said to be twelve subjective and objective energies. When it is explained in this way, it almost seems as if awareness itself is energy.

In considering the twelve subjective and objective energies,[15] we see that the six objective energies appear to the six senses as the various sensory objects. The six subjective energies bring forth the clarity, or the awareness, of those objects. When those twelve objective and subjective energies are purified, the fruitional primordial wisdom of great bliss manifests.

Recall that in the explanation of the conduct initiation, we generated the twelve sense bases as the six male bodhisattvas and six female bodhisattvas to purify the mind. In the Kālacakra system, those twelve subjective and objective energies are of the nature of the six elements. There are no composite phenomena that are not included among the six elements. The energy of earth manifests as the earth element. Similarly the energy of water manifests as water, the energy of fire as fire, and the energy of air as air. The energy of space appears in the aspect of space. The energies manifest as various shapes and colors. The innate mind gives rise to those conceptual energies. Then, depending on which energy is predominant, they give rise to various elements, forms, shapes, and colors.

When one becomes a highly realized yogi or yoginī, it is possible to counteract the power of the various elements so that fire does not burn. Similarly for the other elements, the yogi is not subject to their ordinary qualities.

This is how the entire universe, together with animate and inanimate entities, arises from the energy-mind. It is also stated in the tantras that the great energy that is free of conceptualization pervades all of existence. It is free of the knower and the known; it is divorced from all duality.

From the impure energy and mind, there arises this world of apparently tangible phenomena having limitations and borders that we experience right now. The world of animate and inanimate phenomena that arises from pure energy-mind is a world of phenomena that is itself a manifestation of primordial wisdom that realizes emptiness. This realization of emptiness by primordial wisdom is to be understood in the context of buddhahood.

If an actual form of the buddha's body were to appear to us, even if it appeared very small, it would be impossible for us to see its borders. An illustration of this point is the uṣṇīṣa (crown protuberance) of Buddha Śākyamuni. There is a story of a bodhisattva, whose name in Tibetan was Shugs 'chang. Shugs 'chang had great paranormal abilities and he wanted to find out where the uṣṇīṣa of the Buddha stopped, how high it would go. With his supernatural powers he zoomed into the sky, but he could never find the top of it.

Another mark of the Buddha was a coiled hair at the point between the eyebrows. Śāriputra wanted to see how long it was, so he started pulling on it. He just kept on pulling and pulling, but he never reached the end. And Maudgalyāyana wanted to know how far you had to go before you could not hear the Buddha's speech any more. Using his paranormal abilities, he went extremely far away, but he found that no matter how far he went, the volume and clarity of the speech were the same.

In our practice, we dissolve the offerings into emptiness and generate them in the nature of the primordial wisdom of bliss and emptiness. By so doing, we generate them in a way that is inexhaustible for both the buddhas and sentient beings.

Here is another story. The great Tibetan Yogi Drukpa Kunlek, who lived only about six generations ago, once came to the great monastery Tashi-lhunpo in Shigatse where there were about 3,300 monks in residence. He told the administrators that he wanted to make an offering of tea to all the monks there. This was the grand tea offering, which is a Tibetan custom. He was told, "That is fine, we'll accept gladly. How much butter do you have and how much tea do you have?" The amount of butter he had was enough to fit into one finger of a glove. Similarly, he had about one finger-full of tea. He said, "This is what I have to offer." They told him to stop fooling around. He said, "Just start pouring and you will see that it will suffice." They started pouring the tea, and it served all of the monks, and there was still some left. It turned out to be an inexhaustible supply of Tibetan tea. When one can generate one's offerings in the nature of the primordial wisdom of bliss and emptiness, the offerings take on an inexhaustible aspect.

The world is brought forth by energy-mind. Without understanding all this, the meditative process of visualizing the palace or maṇḍala can seem quite pointless. However, when one dissolves the impure universe into emptiness, meditates on emptiness, then generates the palace together with the whole maṇḍala out of the primordial wisdom of emptiness and bliss, one sees how this corresponds to the natural evolution of the universe.

This process of the creation of the pure and impure cosmos will not be discovered by scientists using physical instruments. If you want to discover this, you must do it by means of meditation. As you gain a more and more profound realization of emptiness through the process of meditation, the clearer this whole evolutionary process becomes. So if some western cosmologists would like a really precise understanding of the evolution of the cosmos, they should first gain a realization of emptiness, develop the spirit of awakening, then practice the stage of generation and the stage of completion, and they will be completely satisfied.

Returning to the stage of generation, there are three different ways in which the deities of the maṇḍala are generated. The first is called instantaneous arising, in which the whole maṇḍala arises all at once out of emptiness. The second is called the three process generation, or the threefold process: out of emptiness one first generates the seed syllable, then the implement, and then the deity. In the case of Vajrasattva, one generates first the *hūṃ* upon a lotus, the *hūṃ* transforms into a vajra upon a lotus, and this transforms into Vajrasattva. The third process is the generation through the five purifications.[16] This entails transforming the dharmakāya into the path in relation to death. In that phase, one meditates upon emptiness free from dualistic appearances of subject and object.

The Certainty of Death

There is a verse by the Tibetan sage Ngulchu Dharma Bhadra (Tib. *dngul chu dharma bhadra*) that says it is certain that the great adversary, death, will come for people like us. It states that it is possible that the Lord of Death will come today. The point is that there is absolutely no certainty as to the time of death. There is no way to know whether death will come in the near future or in the distant future. When we are compelled to leave all the affairs of this life behind and go on to the next life, then everything in the world—all our possessions, concerns, friends, and resources—has to be left behind. None of these are of any benefit to us whatsoever. Even this body, which we cherish so dearly, has to be left behind. The final line of the verse says, "Bless me that I may accomplish that which is of true benefit." The point is that, at the time of death, the only thing that is of benefit is one's practice of Dharma.

If we consider the five billion people on this planet in light of the possibility of sudden death and the certainty of death, we realize that even though there appear to be a lot of people in this world, they are actually in a constant state of change. Like the layered skins of an onion, one generation dies and is replaced by the next. We are one of the skins of the onion. When our layer of skin gets peeled off, there is only one place to go, and that is to future lives. In this regard there is only one thing that is of benefit, and that is Dharma.

Future lives simply go on without end. Since, in this lifetime, we are attracted to the practice of Dharma and are able to practice it, we have a good chance to perpetuate this opportunity for spiritual practice. By this process of devotion to Dharma it is possible to establish a continuity of Dharma practice from one life to another. In this process, one's spiritual insights increase further and further. Eventually this leads to the point where we are no longer compelled to take rebirth in the cycle of existence.

When we are no longer compelled to take rebirth but have freedom of choice, we will have abandoned all suffering. There are great benefits in this. So it is important to assiduously devote ourselves to the practice of Dharma, specifically to the transformation of our own minds. Mental afflictions such as desire, hatred, and delusion bring unhappiness to us, not only in future lives but in this lifetime as well. It is very important to regard these mental afflictions as adversaries and to counter even the very subtle arisings of these afflictions of the mind.

Conversely, it is important to recognize the wholesome factors of the mind such as loving kindness and compassion, recognizing that these bring well-being not only in future lives but also in this lifetime. We should apply ourselves diligently to the cultivation of these wholesome qualities.

11

Generating Oneself as Kālacakra

The Process of Birth

From the sphere of emptiness, like the emergence of a bubble,
The moon, sun, rāhu, and kālāgni
Appear in the center of a lotus in blossom.

The primordial wisdom of emptiness and bliss is likened to bubbles coming forth from water. Just as bubbles arising from water are of the very nature of water, so are the deity, the throne, the clothing, and the offerings of the very nature of primordial wisdom.

The stage of generation suppresses ordinary appearances and ordinary conceptual grasping. We normally experience the world as something that is tangibly firm, and composed of matter, and we suppress these ordinary appearances and our grasping onto true existence by imagining that the appearances are of the nature of primordial wisdom. Meditating upon emptiness counters the grasping onto the true existence of phenomena, and imagining what appears to the mind as being of the nature of primordial wisdom counters ordinary appearances. Grasping onto the true existence of phenomena is the basis for actions that lead to the experience of suffering, whereas by relying on insight into the lack of inherent existence of phenomena, we engage in actions that lead to happiness and well-being.

The moon, sun, rāhu, and kālāgni, arising from the sphere of emptiness, appear on a lotus. Think of the lotus as being of the nature of wisdom. There are eight opened petals. Generally speaking, the lotus throne in the maṇḍala is green and it is in the mind maṇḍala of Kālacakra. In other tantric systems, the eight-petaled lotus that forms the seat for the principal deity in the maṇḍala is of different colors. In those systems, the petals in the four cardinal directions are red, those in the southeastern and the northwestern directions are yellow, the petal in the southwest is green, and the petal in the northeast is black. The significance of the formation and the colors of the petals of the lotus relates to the subsidiary channels and the process of the purification of the energies therein.

In the Kālacakra system, the mind maṇḍala is green. Since there is not just one right way to give this teaching, we can choose how to visualize the lotus. The following is the visualization that seems most viable. Visualize the eastern and southeastern petals as black, the southern and the southwestern petals as red, the northern and northeastern petals as white, and the western and northwestern petals as yellow. Then imagine the top of the center of the lotus as green and the bottom side of the center as blue. This accounts for all the ten energies.

The lotus with its eight petals symbolizes the primary and subsidiary channels together with the central channel in the middle. The goddesses that we generate upon these petals, as will be explained later, symbolize the energies that course through these channels.

Upon that lotus we visualize the moon, sun, rāhu, and kālāgni, one stacked on the other. The moon represents the left channel; the sun, the right channel; rāhu, the portion of the central channel from the heart up; and kālāgni, the central channel from the heart down. These four platforms symbolize the four drops in the following way: the moon symbolizes the drop at the forehead that produces the waking state; the sun symbolizes the drop at the throat that produces the dream state; rāhu symbolizes the drop at the heart that produces the deep sleep state; and kālāgni symbolizes the drop at the navel that produces the fourth occasion.

Whichever of these symbolic interpretations we want to use, the point is that the four drops, the channels, and the energies are the bases to be purified. The agents of purification are exactly what you visualize in the eight-petaled lotus with its center: the goddesses who are located on these petals.

Upon them are the moon and sun, of the nature of the white and red elements,
Adorned with a garland of vowels and consonants, of the nature of the signs and symbols of a buddha.

This white moon disc rests upon the moon, sun, rāhu, and kālāgni discs already visualized, and it symbolizes the white bodhicitta that was received from one's father. The sun disc is beneath the moon disc and symbolizes the red bodhicitta received from one's mother.

To symbolize the future attainment of the thirty-two signs of a buddha, one visualizes around the periphery of the second moon disc two sets of the sixteen vowels of the Sanskrit alphabet. Both sets come from the back and meet in front, one set clockwise and the other set counterclockwise. The short vowels *a i ṛ u ḷ* and *a e ar o al ha ya ra va la anusvāra aṃ* go counterclockwise from the back to the front. Clockwise from back to front are *lā vā rā yā hā āl au ār ai ā ḷ ū r ī ā āḥ.*

Beneath the moon disc we visualize a second sun disc, symbolizing the red bodhicitta received from the mother. This represents the eventual attainment of the eighty symbols of a buddha. For that reason we visualize twice the forty consonants of the Sanskrit alphabet.

The first set of forty consonants goes clockwise from back to front. Each consonant has a long vowel: *lā vā yā ḍā ḍhā / llā vvā ḍḍā ḍhḍhā llā / vvā rrā yyā ssā ffppā / śśā xxkkā ttā ththā ddā dhdhā nnā / ppā phphā bbā bhbhā mmā / ṭṭā ṭhṭhā ḍḍā ḍhḍhā ṇṇā / ccā chchā jjā jhjhā ṇṇā / kkā khkhā ggā ghghā ṅṅā.*

The second set of forty consonants goes counterclockwise from the back to the front. Each consonant has a short vowel: *ṇa gha ga kha ka / ña jha ja cha ca / ṇa ḍha ḍa ṭha ṭa / ma bha ba pha pa / na dha da tha ta / xka śa ṣa fpa sa / ha ya ra va la / ḍha ḍa ya va la.*

The moon disc also symbolizes the mirror-like primordial wisdom produced by the purification of the form aggregate. It is said that one generates Kālacakra by means of the five purifications, of which this is one. The sun symbolizes the primordial wisdom of equality, which is produced by the purification of the aggregate of feeling. In both cases this purification takes place by means of the stage of completion.

> *In the center are the syllables of vital energy,* hūṃ *and* hi, *which become unified in the form of the syllable* haṃ.
>
> *This transforms into myself as Kālacakra.*

Embedded in those two final discs of the sun and moon are two syllables, both standing upright and facing forward. There is a *hūṃ,* and right in front of that is a *hi.* They do not protrude above the moon disc; they are just embedded in the two discs. The moon disc and the sun disc are like two pennies, one on top of the other, and the *hūṃ* is embedded in both of them, as is the *hi*, which is right in front. The *hūṃ* symbolizes the energy that is the mount of awareness, and the *hi* symbolizes the awareness that rides upon energy.

This symbolizes the entrance of the energy-mind into the conjunction of the red and white bodhicitta at conception. The moon and the sun symbolize the two fluids. The embedding of the *hūṃ* and the *hi* symbolizes the entrance of the energy-mind into that mixture.

The *hūṃ* symbolizes the primordial wisdom of discernment, which is produced by the purification of the recognition aggregate in the process of the stage of completion. The *hi* symbolizes the primordial wisdom of accomplishment, which arises from the purification of the aggregate of compositional factors and is purified in the stage of completion.

Then the preceding four—the top moon disc, the sun disc beneath that, the *hūṃ,* and the *hi*—all mix together, and from them arises the syllable *haṃ.* The *haṃ* appears visually as the syllable *ha* with a crescent moon and a little circle above it, symbolizing the primordial wisdom of the absolute nature of reality. This arises through the purification of the aggregate of consciousness, brought about by the state of completion.

From the *haṃ* then arises Kālacakra with four faces and twenty-four arms, together with consort (see chart 10).

To give a more detailed explanation of the symbolism of the *haṃ*, the *h* portion of that syllable symbolizes the consciousness of a bardo being. In order for this to be articulated, it has to be conjoined with the *a*, and then we have *ha*, a consonant. Consonants in Tibetan, Sanskrit, and Pāli include the vowel *a.* The *a* part of the *ha* symbolizes the energy of a bardo being, the energy that forms the mount for the bardo consciousness. The crescent moon sign above the *ha* symbolizes the red constituent that one receives from the mother, and the little drop above that symbolizes the white constituent.

The whole syllable *haṃ* symbolizes the body, speech, and mind of the bardo being who enters into the union of the male and female regenerative substances. The red and white constituents suggest the body, and the *h* part of the *ha* symbolizes the consciousness of the bardo being. The *a* part of the *ha* relates to the energy that symbolizes speech.

In the stage of completion, the moon sign symbolizes the tummo fire, and the drop above it symbolizes the white constituent that melts from the crown of the head. The *ha*, comprised of the *h* and the *a*, symbolizes the generation of the energy-mind into the nature of great bliss. In terms of its symbolic significance for the fruition of the path, the entire *haṃ* symbolizes Kālacakra.

In terms of ordinary life, Kālacakra arising from the *haṃ* symbolizes conception, or entering into the mother's womb, and is a facsimile of the process of birth.

That one syllable *haṃ* has four different symbolic interpretations, which relate to the basis to be purified, the state of generation, the stage of completion, and the fruitional stage.

Kālacakra's Form

For the practice of Kālacakra, we are very fortunate in this age to have the television, which shows forms coming together, transforming into other forms, with one image being superimposed upon another. This is analogous to the types of imagery that you generate in Kālacakra practice. When the very subtle energy-mind manifests, it is actually possible to transform one's body instantly into different shapes.

The Body, Four Faces, and Six Mudrās

Bearing the brilliance of sapphire and blazing with glory,
I have four faces and twenty-four hands, the first two embracing my consort
And holding vajra and bell symbolizing the vajra of supreme, immutable bliss
And the reality of emptiness of a nature free of conceptual elaboration.
The remaining right and left lotus hands
Are graced with such hand symbols as a sword and shield.

"The brilliance of sapphire" refers to the blue color of Kālacakra's body, and "blazing with glory" refers to an aura of light around him. It is blue, but like the radiance of the sun, it is ablaze with light. There are four faces. The front face is black; the right, red; the back, yellow; and the left, white. The front face is slightly wrathful, and the teeth are showing somewhat. The right (red) face shows a little desire. The back (yellow) face is abiding in samādhi, and the left (white) face is very serene. Each face has three eyes.

It is said that Kālacakra wears a crown of tresses. On the crown of his head is an eight-spoked wheel, which touches the skin. The hair comes through the spokes and is drawn upward. The ends of the hair are brought back into the center and tied into bunches. This is what is called a crown of tresses.

In the center of this eight-spoked wheel is the lord of the class, Vajrasattva. Of the eight spokes, five of them point to the front and to the sides. At the tip of each of the five spokes pointing to the front is a panel, forming a five-paneled crown.

At the very top of that crown of tresses is a precious vajra jewel. Right in front of the crown of tresses, on top of the head, is a variegated crossed vajra. The four prongs of the variegated crossed vajra match the colors of the four faces—that is, the prongs are black, red, yellow, and white, going clockwise from the front.

The variegated crossed vajra is vertical. The black protrusion points down, and the yellow up, just like in the vertical maṇḍala. The red protrusion goes to the right, and the white protrusion goes to the left. It is not embedded in his head, but rather stands on the top of the head.

Kālacakra wears vajra earrings, which are little circlets, or rings. For each of the ornamental rings at the various places on his body, there are generally said to be eight spokes. Some people say that the wheel ornament at the throat has sixteen spokes.

There are various bracelets, armlets, and anklets. The bracelets are on the wrists, and the armlets are on the upper arms. There are anklets, one on each ankle. Some people say there are rings that go around the thighs, but that is not certain. In some depictions, there are two bracelets on each wrist with vajras at the top, bottom, and the two sides, making four vajras per wrist. There is also an ornament at the chest that has eight spokes. There is a belt ornament with a wheel in the front, a wheel in the back, and vajras on the left and right sides. The belt also has some webbing with tassels hanging down.

There are six mudrās, or ornaments. Some say that these are the head ornaments, the ear and throat ornaments, and all of the limb ornaments, including those on the wrists, upper arms, and ankles. All the limb ornaments are counted as one. On the chest is a breast plate with a crossed band. This makes five types of ornaments. The sixth is made in the following way: One takes a human bone, burns it, and makes it into a powder; then puts three fingers into it and marks the body in different places. That is the sixth mudrā. Other people do not count the breastplate as one of the six, but do count the belt. There are different ways of enumerating the mudrās.

There is this distinction: the father deity has six mudrās, including these three finger markings. The mother deity, the consort, does not have the three finger markings because the markings symbolize the white bodhicitta.

Kālacakra is wearing a vajra scarf, green and about twelve feet long, and a vajra rosary. He is also wearing what appears to be a tiger skin kilt. It has a fold coming down in the front and in the back, and it is held together with a ring around the waist. It falls in loose folds.

The Twenty-Four Arms and Hands

Kālacakra has three throats and six shoulders, three on each side. The front two shoulders are blue, the middle two are red, and the back two are white. These bifurcate into the twelve humeri, six on each side. Well up on the upper arm is a further bifurcation into twenty-four arms, twelve on each side. For example, the blue shoulder bifurcates into two humeri, and at the level of the upper arm these bifurcate into four arms. The same thing happens to the arms of the other colors on both sides.

For all the hands, the thumb is yellow, the index finger is white, the middle finger is red, the ring finger is black, and the small finger is green. Those are the colors on the back of the hand. For each of the fingers, the inner side is black from the base of the finger to the first joint. It is not just the joint but the whole section of the finger that is black. The second segment of the finger is red, and the third white. In addition, Kālacakra is wearing rings radiant with light.

Some people say that the thumb is completely yellow; the index finger, white; the middle finger, red; the ring finger, black; and the small finger, green. That is, the fingers are the same color on the palm and the back side of the hand. According to the second interpretation, it is not the segment of the finger that is black, red, or white—just the joints. One joint is black, the next is red, and the third is white.

The term "lotus hands" refers to the hands from the wrists to the tips of the fingers, and they are holding various implements. On the right side, going from bottom to top, the three sets of four hands hold the following implements:

- The blue hands hold (1) a vajra while embracing the consort, (2) a sword, (3) a trident, and (4) a curved knife.
- The red hands hold (1) three fire arrows, (2) a vajra hook on the back of which is a vajra, (3) a rattling ḍāmaru, and (4) a hammer with two vajras, one on the top part and one along the handle. The three arrows are called fire arrows but they are not blazing. Fire often symbolically refers to the number three; remember, for example, the triangle that transforms into the fire maṇḍala.
- The white hands hold (1) a wheel, (2) a spear, (3) a club, and (4) an axe.

On the left side, from bottom to top, the three sets of four hands hold these implements:

- The blue hands hold (1) a bell with a vajra top, (2) a shield, (3) a khaṭvāṅga with a vajra on the top of the prong, and (4) a skullcup filled with blood. The prongs of the vajra on top of the khaṭvāṅga are somewhat open. On the bottom part of the top section of the khaṭvāṅga is a vajra, on top of that is a yellow vase, and on top of that is a variegated crossed vajra. Then there are three heads. The first one is a freshly cut blue head. The second head is red, and it is half-dried. The third one is white and it is so dried up that it is just a skull. The heads are in three stages: fresh, somewhat decayed, and well-dried. On top of that is a five-pointed vajra. The heads symbolize the mind, speech, and body of the buddha, in that order. At the base of the vase on the khaṭvāṅga is a ḍāmaru and a bell, with three folds of cloth dangling down.
- The red hands hold (1) a bow, (2) a vajra lasso with a hook on one end and a vajra on the other, (3) a jewel, and (4) a white lotus.
- The white hands hold (1) a sea shell in which a certain kind of creature takes birth five times, (2) a mirror, (3) a vajra chain, and (4) a head of Brahma with four faces, one face in each of the four cardinal directions.

Regarding the first two hands, which hold vajra and bell and embrace the consort, the vajra symbolizes great, supreme, immutable bliss, and the bell symbolizes the reality of emptiness, its nature being free of conceptual elaboration. The union of primordial wisdom of emptiness and bliss is symbolized by the vajra and bell, as well as by the embrace of the deity and consort. The deity Kālacakra embracing the consort is the provisional meaning. They symbolize immutable bliss and empty form. The definitive meaning is the nondual nature of these. Therefore, one's divine pride is associated equally with the deity and the consort.

The Legs

With my right, red leg extended and my white, left leg bent,
I dance in a hundred ways
Upon Māra and Rudra.

The word "dance" in this context means that Kālacakra stands on top of these two deities with a haughty stance. Kālacakra's right leg is red and extended. Beneath the right foot is a red god of desire, Māra. This god of desire has one face and four hands, holding (1) in the first right hand five arrows of flowers, (2) in the first left hand a bow, (3) in the bottom left hand a lasso, and (4) in the bottom right hand a hook. The arrows are called flower arrows because they incite the five poisons, which are the five mental afflictions. This god of desire casts such arrows at practitioners of Dharma to arouse in them these five afflictions.

The left leg of Kālacakra is white and bent. Beneath the left foot lies Rudra, with one face, three eyes, and four hands holding (1) in the first right hand a trident, (2) in the first left hand a ḍāmaru, (3) in the bottom right hand a skullcup, and (4) in the bottom left hand a khaṭvāṅga.

The consort of Māra is Priyā. She is red and is holding onto a foot of Kālacakra. The consort of Rudra is called Madhyamā. Both of them are tugging at the feet of Kālacakra with their heads somewhat inclined downward.

The Appearance

My body, adorned with a multitude of ornaments,
Like the expanse of space beautified by the constellations,
Stands in the midst of a blaze of five stainless lights.

The appearance of the deity is like an extremely clear night, with the stars shining very brightly. The blaze of five stainless lights refers to the rays of light of the five colors being emanated in all directions. They are emitted from the body and represent the five primordial wisdoms.

The Consort

Facing the Lord is Viśvamātā,
Of the color of camphor, with four faces and eight hands
Holding various hand symbols such as a curved knife and skullcup.
With her left leg extended, she embraces the lord.

The consort is generated by means of the threefold process. Initially, in front of the deity Kālacakra there is the syllable *phreṃ*, which transforms into a curved knife. The knife transforms into light, and the light becomes Viśvamātā. She is facing Kālacakra and is yellow. As the male deity has his right leg extended, the consort has her left leg extended, and they are standing in union. The verse says she is "of the color of camphor," which means a yellow-red or orange color, while the *Vimalaprabhā* refers to her yellow color.

She has four faces. In clockwise direction, they are yellow, white, blue, and red. These colors are the opposite from Kālacakra. Each of the faces has three eyes. For any male deity with a third eye at the forehead, it looks like a left eye, pivoted up. For a female deity, the right eye is pivoted up. The eyelashes appear on opposite sides.

She has eight hands. In her right hands, which are on Kālacakra's left side, she holds (1) a curved knife in the hand that is embracing Kālacakra, (2) a hook held aloft, (3) a drumming ḍāmaru, and (4) a rosary.

In her four left hands she holds (1) a skullcup in the hand embracing Kālacakra, (2) a lasso, (3) a hundred-petaled lotus, and (4) a jewel. This jewel is actually composed of three jewels facing each other. It looks like one set of three jewels, with the middle one higher than the other two.

She is endowed with the five mudrās, or adornments, which include the one at the crown. Viśvamātā has the eight-spoked wheel on the crown of her head, as does Kālacakra. The five spokes coming forward end in the five plates of the panels of the crown. Her hair is also tied up in a fashion similar to that of Kālacakra.

Generating ourselves as the deity with consort does not mean that we are generating ourselves as a deity only, who is with consort. Rather, our pride is for both equally—we are both the male and the female aspect.

The Eight Śaktis

Surrounded by eight śaktīs upon the platforms of auspicious petals
In each of the cardinal and intermediate directions.

The term used here is "auspicious petals," but there is really nothing auspicious about the petals. The Tibetan word for "auspicious" is a symbolic term referring to the number eight, because there are eight auspicious signs. Such symbolic usage is often found in esoteric writings. For example, "rabbit" refers to the numeral one because it refers to the moon, and there is one moon. Likewise, "fire" refers to the numeral three because it refers to the triangle that transforms into the fire maṇḍala.

There are eight śaktīs, one on each petal, and they arise by means of the threefold process. The first four are in the cardinal directions:

- On the eastern petal is Kṛṣṇadīptā. On this petal arises the short syllable *a*. From *a* arises a container of incense, and from that arises Kṛṣṇadīptā. Black in color, she has four faces. Going clockwise from the front around the back, they are black, red, yellow, and white. She has eight hands. The four right hands, going from top to bottom, hold (1) a container filled with incense, (2) a container filled with sandalwood powder or paste and saffron, (3) a vessel of camphor, and (4) a container of musk. The four left hands, from top to bottom, hold (1) a bell, (2) a lotus, (3) a celestial tree, and (4) a garland of various flowers. Regarding the celestial tree, in the Buddhist description of deva realms, there is a tree around which the *asuras* at the base and the devas at the top fight. It is not to be confused with the wish-fulfilling tree.
- On the southern petal is Raktādīptā. On this petal arises the syllable *āḥ*. From *āḥ* arises a butter lamp, and from that, Raktādīptā. She has four faces, red, yellow, white, and blue, in a clockwise direction. She has eight hands. The four right hands, from top to bottom, hold (1) a lamp, (2) a jewel necklace, (3) a crown, and (4) a bracelet. The four left hands, from top to bottom, hold (1) a garment, (2) a belt, (3) an earring, and (4) anklets.
- On the northern petal is Śvetādīptā. On this petal arises the seed syllable *aṃ*. From *aṃ* comes food, and from that arises Śvetādīptā. Her four faces are white, black, red, and yellow. She has eight hands. The four right hands, top to bottom, hold (1) a container filled with milk,

(2) a container filled with water, (3) a container filled with the supreme medicine, and (4) a container filled with alcohol. The four left hands, top to bottom, hold (1) ambrosia, referring to the trunk of the *arura* tree, which has great medicinal properties, (2) a taste of siddhi, a type of elixir discussed in the *Kālacakra Tantra* that turns iron to gold and, if ingested, extends one's life span, (3) an arura fruit, and (4) a bowl of porridge.

- On the western petal is Pītādīptā. On this petal arises the letter *ā*, which transforms into a conch, which transforms into Pītādīptā. She has four faces, yellow, white, blue, and red. She has eight hands. Her four right hands, top to bottom, hold (1) a conch, (2) a flute, (3) a jewel, and (4) a ḍāmaru. The four left hands, top to bottom, hold (1) a lute, (2) a drum, (3) a gong, and (4) a trumpet.

These are the four cardinal directions. We also have the intermediate directions, which are referred to as the fire direction, the wind direction, and so forth.

- Āgneya is the Sanskrit name for the southeast and refers to the guardian for that direction. On the southeastern petal is Dhūmā. On this petal arises the syllable *ha*. From *ha* arises a black yak-tail fan, and from that arises Dhūmā. She has four faces, black, red, yellow, and white. She has eight hands, and each of them holds a black yak-tail fan.
- Nairṛtya indicates the southwest and is the guardian for that direction. On the southwestern petal is Marīci. On this petal arises the seed syllable *haḥ*. From *haḥ* arises a red yak-tail fan, and from that arises Marīci. She has four faces, red, yellow, white, and blue. She has eight hands and holds eight red yak-tail fans.
- Aiṣānī indicates the northeast and is the guardian for that direction. On the northeastern petal is Khagamanā. On this petal arises the seed syllable *haṃ*. This dissolves into a white fan, and from that arises Khagamanā. Her four faces are white, black, red, and yellow. In her eight hands she holds eight white yak-tail fans.
- Vāyavya indicates the northwest and is the guardian for that direction. On the northwestern petal is Pradīpā. On this petal arises the syllable *hā*. From that arises a yellow fan, and from that arises Pradīpā. Her four faces are yellow, white, blue, and red, and in her eight hands she holds eight yellow yak-tail fans.

The deities of the intermediate directions are guardians of the directions for the practice of Kālacakra. Altogether, there are ten guardians of the directions: one for each of the cardinal directions, one for each of the intermediate directions, one above, and one below. All of their faces have three eyes. They are all adorned with the five mudrās and they are all standing upright.

12

Deepening Your Understanding

Advice for Practice

The great Indian sage Āryadeva comments that although one may have an altruistic motivation to serve the needs of others, one lacks the capacity to do so. What he means here is that even though one has the motivation to be of service to others, one's altruism is still arising with effort.

When we view the training on the common path, the stages of generation, and the stages of completion, the practice can appear to our minds as a vast and distant undertaking. However, if we apply ourselves in a regular and persistent fashion, the path becomes nearer and nearer. This means that even though we may not feel that we are engaging in an authentic practice of the spirit of awakening or the stage of generation, by assiduously devoting ourselves, our facsimile of practice gradually turns into the real thing. For example, when meditating on impermanence, on emptiness, or on any other topic, the meditation may not seem very authentic at the beginning. As we become accustomed to the practice, though, it becomes more real, more actual.

This is true for any kind of activity. When we first set out, we are probably not doing it correctly; rather, we are doing merely an approximation. Gradually, with practice, our facsimile gets better and better until it becomes authentic. The door is closed if we fail to recognize this and instead think, "How could we ever gain an actual realization like the one that is being described? How can we even understand what is going on? Who can possibly do it!" Even though the practice may not go very well in the beginning, as we apply ourselves to it from month to month, from year to year, it will get better. This is the nature of reality. By reflecting upon this, one can be quite encouraged.

Another Look at the Outer and Inner Kālacakra

If we relate the etymology of Kālacakra to the external universe, kāla (time) refers to a year, and cakra (cycle) refers to the cycle of twelve months. Relating the etymology to internal reality, kāla is a single, complete breath. Within one breath, similar to the external monthly subdivisions of a year, there are twelve major shiftings, or internal alternating movements, of the breath, or vital energy. These twelve are further subdivided. For each of the twelve there are five minor shiftings of energy, making a total of sixty. These major and minor shiftings during each breath are also called cakra.

The purified external aspect of time in general, in other words, the external kāla aspect of Kālacakra, is the male deity Kālacakra. The purified internal aspect of the breath is also Kālacakra. The purified external aspect of cakra, the whole cycle of twelve months, is the female deity Viśvamātā. The purified inner aspect of the cycle of the twelve major or the sixty minor shiftings is also Viśvamātā.

In an astrological context, the sun moves in its cycle through the twelve signs of the zodiac. The twelve signs can be divided into two sets of six. The first pertains to the days getting longer or shorter, and the second to the sun going to the north or to the south. Internally, we have the twelve major shiftings of energy corresponding to the twelve astrological houses. Six shiftings go through the left nostril, and six through the right nostril. Internally, the duration of the breaths corresponds externally to the duration of the days. The internal two sets of six correspond in their purified aspect to the two legs of Kālacakra. The twelve shifts of energy are associated with the twelve links of dependent origination.

Dividing twelve into three sets of four gives us a triad, which in its purified aspect as outer and inner is represented by the three throats of Kālacakra. Twelve can also be divided into four groups of three, represented in their purified aspect by the four faces of Kālacakra. We can also divide twelve into six sets of two, and they correspond to the six shoulders on both sides. Then we have one set of twelve for the actual hands on both sides. They correspond to the twelve shiftings as well as the twelve signs of the zodiac.

One zodiacal sign corresponds to one month, and in one month the moon waxes and wanes. So we multiply the twelve months by two, which equals twenty-four. In its purified aspect, this is represented as the twenty-four hands of Kālacakra.

In the externally purified period of the twelve zodiacal signs, there are 360 days. The internal aspect, when purified, relates to the fifteen joints per hand on each of the twenty-four hands, equaling 360 joints. Internally, the joints symbolize the sixty shiftings. Multiplying the 360 joints by the sixty minor shiftings gives us 21,600.

Working with the Vital Energies

When grasping onto true existence motivates an action, the result is an accumulation of energy that leads one into future lives. In other words, karmic energy is generated. Through the purification of the 21,600 karmic energies, Kālacakra appears.

In order to bring about a cessation or purification of the 21,600 karmic energies during the stage of completion, one must directly generate 21,600 immutable blisses. To bring about these blisses, which are the direct antidote on the preceding stage of generation, one generates the entire body of Kālacakra.

Now we see a very clear dependent sequence of events. The generation of the entire body of Kālacakra is the cause that allows for the arising of the 21,600 great blisses, which consequently act as an antidote for the 21,600 karmic energies and lead to the actual attainment of Kālacakra. The causal sequence begins at the stage of generation and continues on through the stage of completion and the final fruition. During the stage of generation one must very consciously understand, practice, and apply to the meditation an awareness of the basis to be purified, the agents of purification, their function, and the results. One must do all of that very consciously, or the various types of immutable bliss in the stage of completion will not arise.

The explanation of purification is not yet complete in terms of the symbolism of the various aspects of the body. The red right leg, the white left leg, and the blue body pertain to the following.

For an ordinary being at the time of death, the indestructible drop separates into its red and white facets. The white drop goes down and is emitted from the lower orifice, and the red drop comes up and is emitted through the nostrils. During that process, the consciousness departs, and one wanders on to the next birth.

Even though a person may appear to be dead—that is, all the vital signs have stopped—there is no guarantee that the consciousness has actually departed. The person may appear to be stone dead for a week, or even two weeks, but the consciousness may not have departed, which means that the indestructible drop has not disintegrated. As long as the consciousness is present, the corpse cannot putrefy. As soon as the consciousness departs, the red and white drops separate up and down respectively, and then the body can start to putrefy. Tibetans often become awestruck when a great guru dies, and the drops are seen coming from the nostrils and the lower orifice. This is nothing unique to highly realized gurus. It is the case for everybody. If the body is disturbed at the time of death by being moved, burned, or having an autopsy performed on it, however, there is no certainty that the drops will be evident.

The yogi reverses that process through meditation. He or she stacks the white drops from the genital cakra all the way up to the crown of the head, like stacking pennies. Simultaneously, the yogi inversely stacks the red drops from the crown of the head down to the genital region. The yogi experiences the 21,600 immutable blisses and annihilates the 21,600 karmic energies.

The colors of the red right leg, the white left leg, and the blue body symbolize the process of the attainment of 21,600 immutable blisses, the exhaustion of the 21,600 karmic energies, and the attainment of the state of Kālacakra.

The stacking of the two types of drops occurs in the stage of completion. To accomplish that, one practices on the stage of generation by visualizing the different parts of the body, which ripens one's being for the practices and the arousal of the 21,600 immutable blisses in the stage of completion. Initiation facilitates meditation in the stage of generation, specifically the wisdom and secret initiations and the other initiations in which the channels and the energies are blessed.

The provisional Kālacakra—namely, the Kālacakra with consort in sexual union—symbolizes the definitive Kālacakra, which is the inseparability of the primordial wisdom of immutable bliss and the wisdom that realizes emptiness. That state is one in which there is no dualistic appearance, like one glass of water poured into another. By the very nature of reality, the inseparability of immutable bliss and the realization of emptiness is inevitable. It is impossible for it not to exist.

The definitive meaning of Kālacakra with consort is initially accomplished in the samādhi phase, the last of the six-phase yogas in the stage of completion, when one attains the union of the body and mind of Kālacakra. One first accomplishes the body aspect of that body-mind union at the recollection phase of the six-phase yoga. In order to ripen one's being so that one may engage in such a practice, one meditates on the stage of generation by visualizing the deity and consort embracing, and one imagines experiencing immutable bliss and wisdom.

The Symbolism of Kālacakra

The Kālacakra system has unique symbolism not found in the Cakrasaṃvara or Guhyasamāja systems, such as the several aspects of kāla and cakra regarding the outer environment, the year, and so forth. The following is another series of unique aspects of the Kālacakra system. First is the presentation of the four drops, together with the manner in which those four drops are purified during the initiation. Next is the manner in which one receives initiation in dependence upon the four maṇḍalas of body, speech, mind, and primordial wisdom, which are unique to Kālacakra. One receives initiation in dependence upon the four maṇḍalas for the practices of both the generation stage and the completion stage. In dependence upon the maturation process that takes place in the initiation, one goes on to visualize in the stage of generation the four faces and so forth of Kālacakra.

With respect to the dual classification of method and wisdom, the male deity Kālacakra is included in the element of consciousness, while the female deity Viśvamātā is included in the element of primordial wisdom. The fact that the deity and consort together have thirty-two hands, or four sets of eight, symbolizes the purification of the four drops.

The first two phases of the completion stage six-phase yoga, retraction and meditative stabilization, purify the drop at the forehead that produces the waking state. These two lead to the body vajra. The third and fourth phases of prāṇayāma and retention purify the drop at the throat that produces the dream state. These two lead to the speech vajra. The fifth phase, recollection, purifies the drop at the heart that produces the deep sleep state and leads to the mind vajra. Finally, the sixth phase, samādhi, purifies the drop at the navel that produces the fourth occasion and leads to the attainment of the primordial wisdom vajra. Ultimately, when one manifestly attains enlightenment, one does so in the forms of the four vajras of body, speech, mind, and primordial wisdom. The six elements are also purified in that same process. That concludes the explanation of the symbolic significance of the Kālacakra and the consort.

The visualization that has been discussed thus far in the six-session guru yoga is comprised of visualizing oneself as the deity with consort surrounded by the eight śaktīs. The eight petals of the lotus upon which Kālacakra with consort stands symbolize the eight branching channels of the heart cakra. The eight śaktīs who stand upon those eight lotus petals symbolize the eight energies that course through those eight subsidiary channels. These goddesses are visualized in colors that conform to the colors of the respective energies.

The lower portion of the center of the lotus seat symbolizes the lower portion of the central channel, that is, the portion below the heart. Through that flows the descending energy, which is included in the element of primordial wisdom, symbolized by Viśvamātā. The element of primordial wisdom is associated with the color yellow, and in that sense this is what Viśvamātā symbolizes. Primordial wisdom in this case means the immutable bliss that arises from the descending of the bodhicitta.

The upper portion of the center of the lotus symbolizes the upper portion of the central channel, the portion above the heart. Through that flows the life-sustaining energy, which is included in the element of space, symbolized by Kālacakra. The element of space is associated with the color blue, and in that sense this is what Kālacakra symbolizes. On occasion it is said that Kālacakra symbolizes the purified aspect of the consciousness element. In fact, the color associated with both the consciousness element and the space element is blue.

Preparing for the Completion Stage

At the time of the initiation, one generates the ten energies in the form of the ten śaktīs and thereby ripens them. The two principal deities, Kālacakra and consort, directly purify the left and right channels by blocking the flow of energy through them. This implicitly purifies the central channel. The principal deities directly purify the left and right channels, and indirectly purify the central channel.

During the initiation there are twelve deities, namely, the ten śaktīs and Kālacakra with consort. Of the two additional śaktīs, one is Vajradhātvīśvarī and the other is Viśvamātā, the consort of Kālacakra. At that time, both Vajradhātvīśvarī and Kālacakra symbolize the purification of the element of space. During the generation stage there are ten deities, namely, the eight śaktīs and Kālacakra with consort. In the generation stage, because the principal deity Kālacakra represents the purification of the space element, he also contains Vajradhātvīśvarī. In this way all of the twelve deities that are visualized during the initiation are included in these ten deities during the stage of generation. Among the ten types of energy, the life-sustaining energy is usually symbolized by Vajradhātvīśvarī. However, the respective element of consciousness, which includes the life-sustaining energy, is symbolized by Kālacakra, so there is no contradiction here.

Moreover, this practice acts to bless the ten energies that enter, remain, and dissolve into the central channel. In this fashion, the practice ripens one's being for the completion stage practice, when the chief deity with consort and all ten of the śaktīs appear. Thus, there is no real contradiction in the fact that there is a discrepancy between the initiation and the stage of generation, which leads to the stage of completion.

Drawing the karmic energies into the central channel is the principal agent for the attainment of the body and mind of Kālacakra. By causing the karmic energies to enter into the central channel, one accomplishes the empty form of the principal deity with consort. Initially there is only a facsimile of that accomplishment. The first two phases of the six-phase yoga, retraction and meditative stabilization, bring forth the facsimile of the empty form of Kālacakra with consort at the forehead. Then one practices in the third and fourth phases of prāṇayāma and retention, and by the force of those two, the empty form of the deity with consort is brought forth at the navel cakra, and one immutably holds the energies at the navel cakra. In the midst of the flaming of the tummo fire, the authentic empty form of the principal deity with consort appears.

During the fifth phase, recollection, the empty form of the deity and consort are in sexual union, and from this bliss arises. Rays of light emanate from the deity with consort, illuminating the galaxy. This is when one attains the body of Kālacakra. During the sixth phase, samādhi, one experiences immutable bliss in dependence upon the union of the empty form of the deity with consort. We have the body at the time of recollection, and in the very next phase we have the mind. Finally, the 21,600 immutable blisses exhaust the 21,600 karmic energies, and one attains the realization of Kālacakra. By means of the purification of the four types of drops, one manifestly attains the four bodies, which entails the state of Kālacakra.

This short six-session guru yoga sādhana includes all the essential points of the path. This is His Holiness the Dalai Lama's regular Kālacakra practice. When giving the Kālacakra initiation, however, His Holiness engages in a much more elaborate practice of the body, speech, and mind, visualization and preparation of the maṇḍala, self-initiation, and so forth.

This is a rough explanation of the symbolism involved. There are more elaborate explanations of the symbolic significance of all the deities of the maṇḍala, but we do not need to give them here.

There is a slight distinction between the texts of the six-session guru yoga and the initiation. Between the two elements of space and primordial wisdom, it is said that the element of space is included in the element of primordial wisdom. The buddha associated with the element of space is Akṣobhya, and Vajrasattva is the buddha associated with primordial wisdom. The text of the sādhana explicitly states that the deity visualized on the crown of the head of Kālacakra is Vajrasattva. I do not know whether there is some special meaning to this Vajrasattva crown or whether it is simply a mistake in the text. At the point in the initiation text that describes the bestowal of the initiation, the deity emerging from the crown of the head of Kālacakra is identified as Akṣobhya. Similarly, when the same process occurs for Vajravega, the wrathful form of Kālacakra, again the deity to emerge from the crown of the head is Akṣobhya. I cannot make a definitive statement about Vajrasattva, but in terms of meaning, it seems that Akṣobhya is more appropriate. In both the sādhana and the initiation text, Vajrasattva is the deity at the crown of the heads of Viśvamātā and the eight śaktīs.

The Five Tathāgatas and Their Attributes

A few more comments might be worthwhile regarding the five tathāgatas, or the five buddha classes. There are some differences between the general presentation and the one found in the *Kālacakra Tantra*. The discussion here follows the general presentation, so it will not necessarily accord with the *Kālacakra Tantra*.

When both types of obscurations, cognitive and afflictive, are totally dispelled, the five aggregates are purified. At the time of fruition, we have the five types of primordial wisdom and the five tathāgatas, which are of the same nature.

1. Delusion produces the form aggregate. Through purification, the affliction of delusion transforms[17] into the mirror-like primordial wisdom, which suggests the simultaneous general appearance of objects. The form aggregate transforms into Vairocana. Vairocana's body is white, and he holds a wheel. The symbolic meaning is that in order to dispel ignorance and delusion, the wheel of Dharma must be turned.
2. When the feeling aggregate is purified, it transforms into Ratnasambhava. Pride produces the feelings of pleasure and pain. By purifying the mental affliction of pride, the feeling aggregate is transformed into the primordial wisdom of equality, which entails even-mindedness. Ratnasambhava is yellow. In his hands he holds a jewel symbolizing the increase of Dharma and wealth.
3. Purification of the aggregate of recognition transforms it into Amitābha. It is chiefly desire that produces the recognition aggregate. Through the purification of desire, this aggregate is transformed into the primordial wisdom of discernment, which distinguishes between diverse objects. Amitābha is red and he holds a lotus. A lotus arises from mud, symbolizing that although the five primordial wisdoms arise from the desire for sensual objects, they are not tainted by such desire.
4. Through purification, the aggregate of compositional factors transforms into Amoghasiddhi. It is said that it is chiefly jealousy that produces the aggregate of compositional factors. Jealousy is transformed into the primordial wisdom of accomplishment, the wisdom that realizes what needs to be done. Amoghasiddhi is green and holds

a sword. The sword symbolizes the performance of various deeds, and is related to the cutting of the knot of jealousy.

5. The aggregate of consciousness is transformed into Akṣobhya. It is difficult to understand how it can be said that hatred produces the aggregate of consciousness. Be that as it may, hatred is transformed into the primordial wisdom of the absolute nature of reality. This primordial wisdom includes all the five forms of primordial wisdom, among which it is the principal one. The other four types of primordial wisdom are aspects or functions that it performs. Akṣobhya is blue and holds a vajra, which symbolizes a primordial wisdom that cannot be disturbed by hatred. Akṣobhya means "unmovable," and the vajra itself is a symbol of immutability.

Among the five mental afflictions, the one that provides the basis for the other four is delusion. Among the five aggregates, form provides the basis for the others. In dependence upon the form aggregate, pride, jealousy, hatred, and desire arise.

Vajrasattva is not included among the five tathāgatas; he is separate. Nevertheless, he is in the crown of the consort. I expect that he is associated with especially strong desire for sexual orgasm.

The extremely subtle life-sustaining energy goes through the central channel. It is said that this central energy is endowed with light rays of five colors. Blue is associated with Akṣobhya and symbolizes the energy flowing through the central channel. The white light ray symbolizes Vairocana. The other buddha classes have a corresponding relation to the remaining colors. The five subsidiary rays of light coming from the extremely subtle life-sustaining energy correspond to the five tathāgatas.

The five elements are symbolized by the five consorts. The earth element is of the Vairocana class. Water goes to two classes, Ratnasambhava and Akṣobhya. Fire is associated with the class of Amitābha, and air with Amoghasiddhi. We can say that space and consciousness are associated with Akṣobhya. The elements relate to those classes of tathāgatas, and in the purified form they arise as the consorts.

When one's meditation advances to a high degree, it is possible to see the five colors of light rays associated with the very subtle life-sustaining energy.

13

Hooking the Hearts of All Kālacakras

How Do We Benefit Others?

To paraphrase a quotation from the sūtras, "I bow to Gautama, the Buddha. With great compassion he taught the Dharma in order to dispel the obscurations and ignorance of sentient beings."

The point of attaining perfect awakening is to be of benefit to sentient beings by alleviating their suffering and bringing them to a state of genuine happiness. Does this mean that we should try to satisfy every desire of every sentient being? Not necessarily. There is no guarantee that satisfying every desire of an individual will truly be of benefit to that person. If satisfying our desires brought us to the culmination of the path, all the buddhas and bodhisattvas would surround us as servants. But if all our desires were met, our difficulties would become worse, and we would have more and more problems. Satisfying every desire would not be of greatest benefit to us.

Rather, the buddhas and bodhisattvas serve and benefit us by identifying the causes of our suffering, the very distortions of our minds, such as desire, anger, and delusion. If we do not recognize these as distortions of the mind, the buddhas and bodhisattvas cannot help us. In a frequently quoted statement, the Buddha said that the awakened ones are not able to cleanse with water our unwholesome deeds or habitual propensities, nor can they remove our suffering as if pulling out a thorn. Rather, they serve us by teaching the Dharma. The buddhas and bodhisattvas explain how to overcome our present mental state by cultivating a wholesome state of mind, which brings about well-being. Though all phenomena are in fact devoid of inherent existence, we nevertheless falsely grasp onto them as being truly existent. So the buddhas reveal this and show us the ultimate nature of existence, which is the lack of inherent existence of all phenomena.

It is difficult to alleviate the suffering of others, that is, to alleviate the sources of suffering that are the mental afflictions, if one is still subject to those mental afflictions. Therefore, the first task is to diminish the distortions of one's own mind. That is the supreme method for serving others.

SENDING OUT VAJRAVEGAS

The principal deities emit from their hearts terrifying Vajravegas
Holding various weapons,
Who draw in well a host of protectors dwelling in countless realms;
And they become of one taste with the samayasattvas.

The "principal deities" are Kālacakra, his consort, and the eight śaktīs. The fact that the deities "emit from their hearts terrifying Vajravegas" symbolizes that as soon as we are born from the womb, the energy of primordial wisdom starts to flow. On all the emanated Vajravegas we visualize the four syllables: the white *oṃ* at the forehead, the red *āḥ* at the throat, the blue *hūṃ* at the heart, and the yellow *ho* at the navel.

Vajravega's Form

The complete form of Vajravega is identical to that of Kālacakra except that he has two extra hands. The right one is red, and the left one is yellow, and they hold up an elephant skin behind him. The right hand of Vajravega holds the left foreleg of the elephant, and the left hand holds the left hind leg of the elephant. The symbolism of those extra two hands is as follows: Recall that Kālacakra has twenty-four hands, which represent the waning and waxing phases of the moon during the twelve months. According to the lunar-based astronomical system, occasionally there is an extra month per year. The extra month will have a waning and waxing phase of the moon as well, symbolized by Vajravega's two extra hands.

The Ten *Nāgas*

Vajravega has six types of bone ornaments, and coiled around those ornaments are snakes. When referring to the six types of ornaments, bear in mind that the anklets and the bracelets are included in one category. If we categorize those as two pairs, we would have four extra snakes, totaling ten snakes for the six types of ornaments. The ten snakes are in the aspect of nāgas, as described in chart 11.

Chart 11. The Ten Nāgas

Nāga	Location	Color
Jaya (Tib. *rgyal ba*)	crown	green
Vijaya (Tib. *rnam rgyal*)	ribbon	blue
Kulika (Tib. *rigs ldan*)	necklace	white
Ananta (Tib. *mtha' yas*)	belt	white
Karkoṭa (Tib. *stobs rgyu*)	ear	black
Padma (Tib. *pad ma*)	ear	black
Vāsuki (Tib. *nor rgyal*)	bracelet	red
Śaṅkhapāla (Tib. *dung skyong*)	bracelet	red
Takṣaka (Tib. *'jog po*)	ankle	yellow
Mahāpadma (Tib. *pad ma chen po*)	ankle	yellow

The Six Types of Bone Ornaments

At the crown of Vajravega is a wheel with eight spokes. In the center of the wheel is a blue half-vajra with five spokes. Three of the spokes of the wheel point to the front, three point to the back, and one points over the ears.

On the tips of the wheel spokes are five human skulls. The holes of the eyes are very big, and there are fangs in the mouth. On each of the skulls are five bone prongs from which the five buddha classes emerge. Two strings of bone beads are strung from mouth to mouth between the human skulls. In addition three bone pendants hang down from above the eyebrows of the skulls. The left pendant is a yak-tail, the handle of which is wrapped with a gold thread; the middle pendant is a bell; and the right pendant is a lotus.

On the top of the head, the hair falls loosely through the spokes of the wheel. Both the wheel and the hair are transparent. At each ear there is a bone wheel with six spokes from which hang three bone pendants. At the neck there is a bone wheel with sixteen spokes. On the back side of the neck and on each shoulder is a bone wheel with six spokes. The strands of bone beads that hold the wheels together form a diagonally woven band. Three pendants hang from each of the four bone wheels. The bracelet on the inside of the arm has a bone wheel with six spokes, and the one on the outside of the arm has a bone wheel with three spokes. The two wheels are again connected with bone rosaries that form a diagonally woven band. Again, three pendants hang from the inside of the bracelets.

There are also armlets at each upper arm with two bone wheels. The outside one has six spokes, and the inside one has three spokes. These are connected with diagonally woven bands of beads. Three pendants come from the front and back wheels.

There are two anklets with wheels. The one on the outside has six spokes, and the inside wheel has three spokes. The connection between the two wheels is the diagonally woven band of two strands of beads. On the top of the anklets are three pendants facing upward.

The breastplate is in the form of a wheel with eight spokes. Another wheel at the back also has eight spokes. Two bands of diagonally woven beads crisscross from front to back to hold the wheels together. One set goes under the arms, and the other over the shoulder. From the bottom of the wheel three pendants hang, and three face upward. The same pendants are at the back wheel.

There is a bone belt that has a front wheel with four spokes and a back wheel with six spokes. Over each hip is a wheel with six spokes each, making a total of four wheels connected with the diagonally woven bands of three strings of beads. From the belt hang bone beads long enough to form a short skirt. At the ends of these strands are again pendants of yak-tails, bells, and lotuses.

These ornaments are described in the Yamāntaka generation stage. On the basis of the description of the wheel of protection, which is not included in the Kālacakra text, it seems that Vajravega does not have a consort.

Vajravega's Activity

Like Kālacakra, Vajravega suppresses Māra and Rudra beneath his two feet. This is a kind of wrathful activity, and its significance implicitly relates to both Kālacakra and Vajravega. Suppressing Māra beneath the right foot symbolizes the overcoming of the four *māras.* The way of understanding the four māras in the Kālacakra system is different from that in other systems:

- ❖ The obscurations of the body are called the māra of the aggregates.
- ❖ The obscurations of speech are called the māra of the mental afflictions.

- The māra of the Lord of Death refers to the obscurations of the mind.
- The māra known as Devaputra refers to the ignorance that gives rise to karma.

Suppressing the god Rudra beneath the left foot symbolizes the overcoming of the four mental afflictions: desire, hatred, ignorance, and pride.

The suppression of Māra and Rudra beneath the feet also symbolizes the blocking of the left and right channels. The energies in the left and right channels are brought into the central channel, and the left and right channels become empty because the energy is flowing entirely through the central channel.

At this point in the practice, we visualize ourselves as Kālacakra with consort. At the *hūṃ* syllable at the heart, visualize a Vajravega and send him out with an exhalation. I surmise that since it is going out with the exhalation, we might send it out through the nostrils. We can send out either one Vajravega or many. In the latter visualization, innumerable Vajravegas are emitted in all directions, like bees out of a bee hive. Alternatively, simply visualize one Vajravega going out with innumerable rays of light emanating from his heart. Either way, Vajravega invites all of the Kālacakras with consorts from all directions. Vajravega holds in his dominant right hand a hook and in his left hand a lasso. He symbolically hooks the hearts of Kālacakras in all directions and binds them with his lasso. All of those Kālacakras with consorts and the eight śaktīs are invited to the space before you. Offerings are made, and then they dissolve into you, the chief deity with consort.

The deities we have already generated are called the samayasattvas. The ones we have invited are called the jñānasattvas. Then the two become of the same taste, which means of the same nature.

The jñānasattvas may be dissolved into the samayasattvas in one of two ways. We can invite countless beings and imagine them converging into ten groups of ten, corresponding to Kālacakra with consort and the eight śaktīs. Then we can have each of the ten dissolve into each of the ten samayasattvas. This is one possibility. Alternatively, we can have them all converge into one set of ten, in which case it is as if each jñānasattva is a replica of a samayasattva. One comes right above the other and then dissolves into it. The ferocious way in which Vajravega invites beings, with hook and lasso, is probably meant to suggest a very swift merging of the two. When Vajravega is doing all these impressive things, he seems quite awe-inspiring. When he comes back home, the only place he can go is back into our own heart, and that is where he dissolves.

Inviting the Initiation Deities

The empowering deities grant the initiation, and the lord of the class
Marks the tops of the heads of the principal deities and the entourage.

Once again, rays of light are emitted from the *hūṃ* at one's heart, inviting all the buddhas of the ten directions in the form of the initiating deities. These deities have different ornaments with which they bestow initiation. We may imagine this initiation in an elaborate way, including all seven of the initiations, or in a simple way, entailing just the water initiation.

Through the process of initiation, all internal impurities are dispelled, and all stains are purified. The ambrosia with which one is initiated comes to the crown of the head of oneself as Kālacakra and then overflows on the crown of the principal deity into the form of Akṣobhya, who is the lord of this class of Kālacakra. A similar process occurs for the consort; here the lord of the class is Vajrasattva. These are the complete forms of Akṣobhya and Vajrasattva, not just the head. They are, however, in their nirmāṇakāya aspects, so they are not replete with all of the adornments and ornaments of the sambhogakāya.

Recall that the phase of the practice with the eight śaktīs on the lotuses symbolizes birth, the emergence from the womb. The phase of practice starting with the Vajravega going out from the heart of Kālacakra up to the present point corresponds to the ordinary activity of an infant learning how to use the faculties of action.

The formation of the maṇḍala up to this point of the actual sādhana is called the supreme sovereign maṇḍala (Tib. *dkyil 'khor rgyal mchog*). The process is more elaborate in the actual extensive maṇḍala, entailing an elaborate presentation of supreme sovereign actions (Tib. *las kyi rgyal mchog*) of emitting light and so forth. What is being presented here is just the quintessence of the supreme sovereign actions.

14

Bindu Yoga and Subtle Yoga

Next there are two types of yoga to be practiced, the yoga of the drops, or bindu yoga (Tib. *thig le'i rnal 'byor*), and subtle yoga (Skt. *sūkṣma yoga*, Tib. *phra mo'i rnal 'byor*). Both the bindu yoga and the subtle yoga prepare one for the completion stage practices. Both yogas involve a practice exclusive to a tantra in which the experience of sensual objects is transformed into the path. For us, the practice is one of engaging in each of these phases by the power of imagination.

The Bindu Yoga

In the practice of bindu yoga, one visualizes for oneself as the principal deity and for the consort a white *oṃ* on the forehead, a red *āḥ* at the throat, a dark blue *hūṃ* at the heart, a yellow *ho* at the navel, a blue *haṃ* at the genital cakras, and a green *hā* at the crown of the head.

Then, as in the wisdom-gnosis initiation, one dissolves the genital region into emptiness. From emptiness one visualizes the syllable *hūṃ,* and that transforms into a blue, five-pronged vajra. The tip of the vajra is blocked with a yellow syllable *phaṭ*, and the top of the *phaṭ* is inserted into the tip of the vajra to block the descending energy. All downward expulsion, as in the processes of urination and defecation, is brought about by the descending energy. The idea is to block that downward motion.

Then one dissolves the genital region of the consort, and from emptiness there arises the syllable *āḥ*. That transforms into light, and the light transforms into a red, eight-petaled lotus. The center of the red, eight-petaled lotus is similarly blocked with a yellow syllable *phaṭ*. One chants the syllable *hūṃ* as if singing a song. Then, with the pride of being Vajradhara—Vajradhara refers here to Vajrasattva—one enters into union with the consort.

One should engage in the union with the three attitudes previously mentioned. When one experiences bliss, it is indispensable to meditate on emptiness.

According to the oral transmissions of the junior tutor of His Holiness the Dalai Lama, Kyabje Trijang Rinpoche, the central channels of the deity and consort are touching, and the descending energy emerges from the central channel of the consort. By the force of their union, the descending energy is actually emitted from the central channel of the consort into the central channel of the male deity. The energy strikes the *ho* syllable at the male deity's naval cakra, and this causes the tummo flame to blaze up from the navel like pure lightning.

That current of descending energy is now moving upward, pushing the tummo fire up through the central channel. The five maṇḍalas of the energies of the nature of the five aggregates course through the left channel. In the right channel flow the maṇḍalas of the energies of the five elements, which in their divine form are the five consorts. The heat of the tummo fire burns up the energies in the side channels, blocking the normal flow of these energies. As a result, one's sense faculties of vision and so forth are not able to function. The tummo fire then reaches up to the *hā* syllable at the crown of the head.

The *hā* syllable symbolizes the white bodhicitta. As if the moon were melting and dripping down moon droplets, the white bodhicitta at the crown is heated by the tummo fire and melts. When the drops of white bodhicitta descend from the crown of the head to the throat, one experiences bliss; when it descends from the throat to the level of the heart, one experiences supreme bliss; and when it descends to the level of the navel, one experiences extraordinary bliss. In each of these stages the bliss becomes greater, so a different name is given to each. When the drop of the white bodhicitta arrives at the tip of the jewel, it is blocked by the syllable *phaṭ*, and, as a result of its not being emitted, one experiences innate bliss. This practice is called bindu yoga. On the stage of generation, the four types of bliss that are experienced thereby are called the four descending blisses.

The Subtle Yoga

Much of the practice of subtle yoga is the same as bindu yoga in terms of the visualization, the union, and so forth. However, in the subtle yoga, the white bodhicitta, having arrived at the tip of the jewel of the vajra, now ascends. As it ascends to the level of the navel cakra, one experiences bliss; when it arrives at the heart, one experiences supreme bliss; when it arrives at the throat, one experiences extraordinary bliss; and when it arrives at the crown of the head, one experiences innate bliss. Bear in mind that this is not a stacking process, but simply the movement of the drop, up and down. If one has good habitual propensities for the practice of visualization with the divine pride, it will actually lead to such blisses.

In this practice, there is a special, quintessential instruction to prevent emission of the white bodhicitta. The two hands are clenched as vajra fists. The left hand is on the inside, the right hand is on the outside, and both are clasped over the two breasts. One draws one's abdomen in to flatten it against the spine, and gazes up to the sky. Then one forcefully clenches the toes, and very forcefully utters either *hūṃ* or *phaṭ*. With a bit of practice, this will certainly cause the white bodhicitta to turn around, if not the first time, then the second time. It will come with practice.

The situation is like this. In phase one there is a definite danger of white bodhicitta being emitted; in phase two you do all of the preceding practice, and you manage to reverse the white bodhicitta. Keeping everything contracted like that, however, will make one ill. Therefore, in phase three, a kind of diffusion yoga must follow. The diffusion yoga is done in this way: Clench the two hands in vajra fists at the base of the thighs. Then shake the body somewhat and simultaneously perform a little vase meditation at the abdomen. With that, you will have a sense of diffusion of the white bodhicitta.

Although it is not very clear in the text, I infer that the supreme sovereign maṇḍala practice purifies the drop of the waking state at the forehead; the supreme sovereign action purifies the drop of the dream state at the throat; the bindu yoga purifies the drop of the sleep state at the heart; and the subtle yoga purifies the drop of the fourth occasion at the navel. This is a logical inference, which is not explicitly stated in the text.

Bliss arises and one meditates on emptiness. From that emptiness again one visualizes one's own lotus seat, one's own body as the deity with consort and the various śaktīs. One thinks of all these as being of the nature of bliss-emptiness.

It is said that one's own primordial wisdom of bliss and emptiness should appear in the very form of the deities of the maṇḍala. Other people say that one focuses upon the divine form while ascertaining its non-inherent existence. The phrasing is different, but the essential point is really the same.

The deity yoga in the generation stage can be followed in two ways, one emphasizing the profound, the other emphasizing the vast aspects of the path. Profundity is emphasized by meditating on emptiness and having that very awareness of emptiness manifest in the divine form. In the practice of the profound, by the realization of emptiness, the accumulation of knowledge is completed. To emphasize vastness in the practice, meditate on emptiness, and as your awareness of emptiness arises in the various forms of the deities, have them arise without limitation of location or time. In other words, they have no borders. By the very appearance of that realization of emptiness as the divine forms, you accumulate merit.

Knowledge is accumulated in one way, and merit in the other. A uniquely profound aspect of tantric practice is that at the time of fruition, the body and mind of the buddha are of the same nature, and, similarly, during the path of practice, the accumulations of knowledge and merit are inseparable.

15

Mantra Recitation

Pure Vision and Divine Pride

At this point in the practice it is good to cultivate what is called pure vision. Pure vision and divine pride at the stage of generation entail suppressing ordinary vision and ordinary pride. Right now, we have an ordinary vision of our environment, body, and resources. These are supplanted by the visualizations of the maṇḍala and its inhabitants, and that suppresses the previous ordinary vision. The visualizations overwhelm ordinary appearances, and divine pride—the thought, "I am Kālacakra, and this whole maṇḍala is of the nature of my primordial wisdom of bliss and emptiness"—overwhelms ordinary pride.

By the cultivation of pure vision and divine pride, the immediate conditions for ordinary pride and ordinary vision are suspended. Those ordinary states are overwhelmed and replaced by pure vision and divine pride. Between the pure vision and the divine pride, the latter is more important, and the pure vision of the divine form brings forth a stable divine pride.

Ordinarily, we accumulate karma by distinguishing between one thing and another. On the stage of generation there are said to be practitioners of four types: those who lack both the divine pride and the pure vision; those who excel in divine pride, but lack pure vision; those who have pure vision but lack divine pride; and those who have both the pure vision and the divine pride. Whatever one's predisposition, whatever one's talent may be, one needs both in the process of the stage of generation. Practice will lead to the cultivation of both.

In order to cultivate pure vision, do a rough overall visualization and see what comes most clearly to mind. Focus upon that, and then as you develop stability, gradually extend the clarity that has been gained. If you put too much effort into getting a vivid visualization, though, it will be an obstacle rather than an aid to actual pure vision.

It is said that if you fail to get clarity, you must investigate and scrutinize the problem. If the visualization is lost, remind yourself of the form of the head, the arms, the legs, and so forth. After refreshing the memory and gaining some stability, abide there. When things start fading again, repeat the exercise, part by part, and re-establish the visualization. When you accomplish some stability in the visualization, awareness is brought in. You recognize that this is of the nature of the wisdom of emptiness and bliss, and you identify with it and develop divine pride. You should alternate between the pure vision aspect and the divine pride aspect.

The Maṇḍala Deities and Their Mantras

The seed syllables at the hearts of the principal deities and entourage
Are each surrounded by garlands of their own mantras,
Emitting a host of maṇḍala deities who serve the needs of animate beings,
Then return and dissolve into the seed syllable at their hearts.

The principal deities, of course, are Kālacakra and consort, and the entourage is comprised of the eight śaktīs. The maṇḍala deities are emitted from the seed syllables. They go into union and give the initiation of the bodhicitta to sentient beings, and make offerings to the buddhas and bodhisattvas of the ten directions. They bring all sentient beings to their own state of enlightenment.

Kālacakra's Mantra

Oṃ āḥ hūṃ ho haṃkṣamalavaraya hūṃ phaṭ

When we are not very well trained in the common path, it is a good idea to reflect upon its elements while reciting the mantras. Then there is a better chance of this practice being virtuous. In addition, just before the recitation of the mantras it is important to make a special point of visualizing oneself as, and identifying with, the deity.

Prior to reciting *oṃ āḥ hūṃ ho haṃkṣamalavaraya hūṃ phaṭ*, you can perform the so-called mental recitation. In this practice, you inhale and imagine the energy of the breath coming in and making the sound *oṃ*; you imagine the energy residing at your heart making the sound *hūṃ*; and as you exhale you imagine the breath making the sound *āḥ*. It is good to do this twenty-one times.

One visualizes at the heart of the principal deity the seed syllable *hūṃ* surrounded by *oṃ āḥ hūṃ ho haṃkṣamalavaraya hūṃ phaṭ*. Alternatively, one could visualize the *haṃkṣamalavaraya* in the center and *oṃ āḥ hūṃ ho phaṭ* around the periphery. Though it would be reasonable, it is not really clear whether or not the second procedure is correct.

Looking at the multicolored picture of the mantra in the Lanca script, we find the seed syllables of four elements within the *haṃkṣamalavaraya.* The internal reference is the seed syllables, and the external reference is the various maṇḍalas of the four elements. We have the following parts in *haṃkṣamalavaraya*:

- Black *ya.* Air maṇḍala and air element associated with the heart.
- Red *ra.* Fire maṇḍala and fire element associated with the throat.
- White *va.* Water maṇḍala and water element associated with the forehead.
- Yellow *la.* Earth maṇḍala and earth element associated with the navel.
- Four colored *ma.* Mount Meru associated with the spine or the space between genitals and navel.
- Green *kṣa.* Consciousness and the variegated lotus visualized but not actually present at the top of Mount Meru. This corresponds to the desire and form realms associated with the genitals.
- Blue *ha.* Space and moon, corresponding to the formless realm associated with the left channel.
- Moon crescent. Sun associated with the right channel.
- Bindu. Rahu associated with the upper part of the central channel.
- *Nāda.* Kālāgni associated with the lower part of the central channel.
- *Evam.* Method and wisdom.

The form maṇḍalas symbolize the four drops, and the ten signs symbolize the ten energies. Upon the basis of these, one generates the experience of bliss and emptiness in the stage of completion. At the time of fruition, these can be applied to the form bodies and the ten goddesses.

I am not entirely satisfied with the presentation given here, specifically the assertion that the color blue symbolizes the moon and the formless realm. Also, I feel that the head of the syllable *hūṃ* should be white, the crescent moon on top should be red, the bindu should be blue, and the nāda yellow.

Viśvamātā's Mantra

Oṃ phreṃ viśvamātā huṃ hūṃ phaṭ

At the heart of Viśvamātā you visualize the seed syllable *phreṃ*, surrounded on the periphery by the whole mantra. The *oṃ* symbolizes the body, the first *hūṃ* the speech, and the second *hūṃ,* the mind.

Mantras of the Goddesses

Oṃ dāna pāramitā huṃ hūṃ phaṭ

This mantra is associated with Dhūmā, who is in the southeast. At the heart of that goddess is the seed syllable *ha* surrounded by the mantra.

Oṃ śīla pāramitā huṃ hūṃ phaṭ

This mantra is associated with Marīci, who is in the southwest. At her heart is the seed syllable *haḥ*, around which is the complete mantra.

Oṃ kṣānti pāramitā huṃ hūṃ phaṭ

To the northeast is Khagamanā. At her heart is the seed syllable *haṃ* surrounded by the mantra.

Oṃ vīrya pāramitā huṃ hūṃ phaṭ

In the northwest is Pradīpā. At her heart, surrounded by the mantra, is the seed syllable *hā.*

Oṃ dhyāna pāramitā huṃ hūṃ phaṭ

To the east we have Kṛṣṇadīptā. At the heart of the goddess is the seed syllable *a*, and around that is the mantra.

Oṃ prajñā pāramitā huṃ hūṃ phaṭ

At the heart of the goddess Viśvamātā, we already visualized the syllable *phreṃ.* That syllable remains but we transform the surrounding mantra into *oṃ prajñā pāramitā huṃ hūṃ phaṭ.*

Oṃ upāya pāramitā huṃ hūṃ phaṭ

In the south is Raktādīptā, at whose heart is the seed syllable *āḥ* surrounded by the mantra.

Oṃ praṇidhāna pāramitā huṃ hūṃ phaṭ

To the north is Śvetādīptā, at whose heart we visualize the seed syllable *aṃ* surrounded by the mantra.

Oṃ bala pāramitā huṃ hūṃ phaṭ

To the west is Pītadīptā, at whose heart is the seed syllable *ā*, surrounded by the mantra.

Oṃ jñāna pāramitā huṃ hūṃ phaṭ

Then, once again, at the heart of Viśvamātā, leave the *phreṃ* as before and transform the previous mantra into *oṃ jñāna pāramitā huṃ hūṃ phaṭ.*

The One-Hundred-Syllable Mantra

Oṃ vajrasattva samayam anupālaya vajrasattva tvenopatiṣṭha dṛḍho me bhava sutoṣyo me bhava supoṣyo me bhava anurakto me bhava sarva siddhiṃ me prayaccha sarva karmeṣu ca me cittaṃ śrīyaṃ kuru hūṃ ha ha ha ha hoḥ bhagavan sarvatathāgata vajra mā me muñca vajri bhava mahāsamaya sattva āḥ hūṃ phaṭ

During the recitation of the one-hundred-syllable mantra, we visualize Vajrasattva above the crown of the head of each of the nine deities (counting Kālacakra and consort as one, plus eight śaktīs). At the heart of the Vajrasattvas we visualize the syllable *hūṃ* surrounded by the one-hundred-syllable mantra. As we recite the mantra, we imagine ambrosia coming down, purifying each of the deities, and thereby purifying any unwholesome habitual propensities to mistaken pronunciations, whether additions or subtractions, during the recitation of the preceding mantras.

Reciting the Mantras

You can recite the Kālacakra mantra somewhat more than the consort's mantra. If you want to do the recitations in accordance with the sādhana, then as you recite the mantra, you visualize rays of light coming from the mantras at the hearts of the deities, serving the needs of sentient beings, and making offerings to the buddhas and bodhisattvas of all directions. As you make these offerings, it is good to recite *oṃ āḥ hūṃ ho* three times. Because it is not appropriate to make ordinary offerings, visualize the offerings dissolving into emptiness and then from the nature of primordial wisdom arising in the nature of ambrosia. Then imagine the rays coming back and merging into the mantra.

Alternatively, as you recite the mantras you can reflect on other topics such as the cultivation of loving kindness, compassion, or the view of emptiness.

In the *hūṃ hūṃ phaṭ* at the end of each of these mantras, the second *hūṃ* always stands for the mind. The syllable *phaṭ* generally means "to set or place," but here it means "to eradicate," pertaining to the eradication of all conceptual elaborations and dualistic appearances. Some people interpret it as a supplication meaning "Please bestow siddhi." These two interpretations have almost the same meaning.

Mantra Recitation for a Propitiatory Retreat

In a propitiatory retreat (Tib. *snyen pa*), you recite the Kālacakra mantra *oṃ āḥ hūṃ ho haṃkṣamalavaraya hūṃ phaṭ* 100,000 times. It is probably sufficient to recite the Viśvamātā mantra *oṃ phreṃ viśvamātā huṃ hūṃ phaṭ* 10,000 times, and that should implicitly cover all the other mantras. On the other hand, there are some people who say that one does not need to give special emphasis to the Viśvamātā mantra, but that one should do all ten of them.

Once you have completed the propitiatory retreat, you are allowed to do other practices such as the self-initiation. A propitiatory retreat can be done with this six-session guru yoga text, but it is questionable whether it would count as a fully authentic propitiatory retreat, allowing you then to engage in the self-initiation practice. For this you would have to ask His Holiness the Dalai Lama.

To perform a propitiatory retreat I suggest that you do the entire guru yoga once in the morning, and for the later sessions throughout the day you can do a more abbreviated form. After reciting the principal mantra 100,000 times and the *oṃ phreṃ* mantra 10,000 times, you should slowly recite another 10,000 of what is called the mantra of descending wisdom, *oṃ āḥ hūṃ ho haṃkṣamalavaraya hūṃ ha a je hūṃ phaṭ.*

Recite the one-hundred-syllable mantra once or three times, as you wish.

16

Offerings

Next you make offerings, which have to be blessed first. The way to do this is to recite the syllables *oṃ āḥ hūṃ ho,* and then imagine the offerings transforming into the ambrosia of wisdom. In that process, you dissolve them into emptiness, and from emptiness you generate them into the wisdom of bliss and emptiness in the form of ambrosia.

The offerings have three qualities: they are of the nature of wisdom, they appear in the aspect of offering substances, and they have the function of bringing forth undefiled bliss (Tib. *zag med kyi bde ba*).

The Offering Substances

From my heart are emitted offering goddesses who make offerings:
Oṃ śrī kālacakra saparivāra arghaṃ pratīccha namaḥ
Oṃ śrī kālacakra saparivāra pādyaṃ pratīccha namaḥ
Oṃ śrī kālacakra saparivāra prokṣaṇaṃ pratīccha namaḥ
Oṃ śrī kālacakra saparivāra aṃcamanaṃ pratīccha namaḥ
Oṃ śrī kālacakra saparivāra puṣpe pratīccha namaḥ
Oṃ śrī kālacakra saparivāra dhūpe pratīccha namaḥ
Oṃ śrī kālacakra saparivāra āloke pratīccha namaḥ
Oṃ śrī kālacakra saparivāra gandhe pratīccha namaḥ
Oṃ śrī kālacakra saparivāra naividya pratīccha namaḥ
Oṃ śrī kālacakra saparivāra śabda pratīccha namaḥ
Oṃ śrī kālacakra maṇḍala saparivāribhyaḥ namaḥ

From our heart we emanate these ten offering goddesses who hold the offering substances. *Arghaṃ* is water for drinking; *pādyaṃ* is water for bathing the feet; *prokṣaṇaṃ* is water for washing the genital area; *aṃcamanaṃ* is water for cleansing the mouth; *puṣpe* are flowers for the hair; *dhūpe* is incense; *āloke* are butter lamps; *gandhe* is fragrant water for anointing the chest; *naividya* is food; *śabda* is music.

The word *namaḥ* suggests different things in different contexts, sometimes name, sometimes obeisance, and sometimes offering. Here it means offering.

The Offering Mudrās

For each of the offerings, while reciting *oṃ śrī kālacakra saparivāra,* we snap our fingers in front of our heart and simultaneously emanate these goddesses who make offerings to us while we are in the form of Kālacakra.

In the Kālacakra system, unlike other tantras, we use the index finger when snapping the fingers. When emanating a goddess, the right hand is facing forward and the left hand is facing backward. The left hand is out in front. Imagine pushing off the offering goddesses with the right hand. The hands turn over, so they are both facing forward. You say *oṃ* and snap your fingers. Then you rotate the two hands and continue the phrase, saying *arghaṃ,* with the palms up together and the thumbs tucked in. As soon as you have said *arghaṃ pratīccha namaḥ,* both of your palms are facing toward you, with the right hand out front and the left hand closer to your body. Snap your fingers again with the index finger and draw the offering goddess back into your heart. This movement is called the lotus cycle. As soon as you have snapped the first one in, snap the second goddess out, then do the lotus cycle. Do this for each offering goddess.

The mudrās, or hand gestures, for each substance are done like this:

- With arghaṃ, the palms are up together with the thumbs tucked in.
- With pādyaṃ, the left hand is down, the fingers dangle, and the fingers of the right hand open like a fan.
- For prokṣaṇaṃ, the small fingers and the ring fingers are held in with the thumb, and you throw out the index finger and the middle finger together. This flicking is for the cleansing water.
- Aṃcamanaṃ is for cleansing the mouth. Here the ring finger and the thumb are touching, and you fan the other fingers with the sense of sending out water.
- For puṣpe, the flowers, the fingers explode out, as if tossing the blossoms out into the air.

- With dhūpe, fan the fingers down, as if sprinkling powdered incense down onto the coal so that the fragrant smoke comes rising up.
- For āloke, the middle finger is up, touched by the thumb, and the other fingers are curled around.
- For gandhe, the two index fingers point straight forward, the thumbs are tucked into the hands, with the fingers and palms up.
- Naividya is very simple: the thumbs are tucked in, and the palms face upward. The difference between this and arghaṃ is that for the latter, the fingers are straight, and for naividya they are a little bit bent.
- With śabda, the index and the middle fingers are upright, the thumb touches the ring finger, and the ring finger and the little finger are bent. This symbolizes hand drums.

This is a time when a picture would be worth a thousand words!

Inner Offering

The final line, *Oṃ śrī kālacakra maṇḍala saparivāribhyaḥ namaḥ*, is for the inner offering. The inner offering is comprised of two groups of ingredients that are blessed by the syllables *oṃ āḥ hūṃ ho.* The syllables dissolve the offerings into emptiness and then generate them out of primordial wisdom. One of the groups is called the five fleshes: flesh from a bovine animal, an elephant, a horse, a dog, and a human. The bovine creature is a powerful animal, like a king of beasts, with a square head, possibly a buffalo. The elephant is quite extraordinary, for it is the mount of a *cakravartin*, a world emperor. The horse is called a supreme steed. What is called a dog is, in fact, a lion. The human flesh is from what is literally called a seven-lived brahmin, which refers not to an actual brahmin, but to a person who has taken rebirth as a human being in seven consecutive lifetimes.

The other group is the five ambrosias: semen, marrow, blood, urine, and excrement. They symbolize the five tathāgatas, and they symbolize the five elements in the following way. In the body we have energies associated with the five aggregates and energies of the five elements. Through meditation we seek to stop these energies flowing through the side channels and to bring them instead into the central channel, which leads to the experience of great bliss. This is the actual process symbolized by the various fleshes and ambrosias and their transformations. In the Kālacakra system, the five fleshes symbolize the five consorts, and the five ambrosias symbolize the five tathāgatas.

We bless the ingredients of the inner offering by saying the four syllables *oṃ āḥ hūṃ ho,* dissolving the ingredients into emptiness, and generating them, as before, out of primordial wisdom. They are thereby transformed into the five fleshes and the five ambrosias.

Then we make the offerings to the lineage gurus, to Kālacakra, and to the various deities. We can also offer them to all sentient beings, whom we imagine as Kālacakra. Imagine the principal deity and all of the surrounding deities experiencing undefiled bliss.

Secret Offering

You may also make the secret offering in the following way. Visualize yourself with consort, as done previously in the bindu yoga, and bless the two genital regions. Then, in union, experience the four descending blisses and the four ascending blisses, and offer that experience.

Rasavajrā, the offering goddesses associated with taste, is emanated for this final offering. Upon completion of the secret offering, she is drawn back into the heart.

17

Praise and Dedication

HOMAGE TO KĀLACAKRA

Homage to the glorious Kālacakra,
Having the nature of emptiness and compassion,
Who is without birth or destruction in the three realms of cyclic existence,
The embodiment of unified consciousness and the object of consciousness.

In this context, compassion refers to the immutable bliss that realizes emptiness. The phrase "without birth or destruction" refers to the blocking of the extremes of both existence and of quietism. Saying that Kālacakra is without birth in cyclic existence suggests the absence of saṃsāra, which is one of the extremes of existence. Being free of destruction refers to the absence of the extreme of quietism. Freedom from these two extremes is the essence of emptiness and compassion.

The fourth line refers to the special qualities of both the body and mind of Kālacakra. Consciousness refers here to immutable bliss, and the object of consciousness is empty form. This does not imply that immutable bliss knows the object of empty form, but rather, that immutable bliss and empty form are of the same nature. Immutable bliss might be likened to a television screen, and empty form to the images that appear on the screen.

Describing Kālacakra as glorious means that he is endowed with the glory of the body and mind of the buddha, and also with the glory of immutable bliss. I have already explained the outer, inner, and other aspects of Kālacakra. Here, Kālacakra refers to Kālacakra at the time of fruition, namely, the Buddha Kālacakra, not the outer or the other Kālacakra.

I bow to Kālacakra,
Whose embodiment is born from the immutable,

Even though the absorption of the āli *and* kāli
As well as such syllables as hūṃ *and* phaṭ *have been eliminated.*

Āli symbolizes the masculine gender, the vowels, and skillful means. *Kāli* symbolizes the feminine gender, the consonants, and wisdom. To the practitioner on the stage of generation, the visualized Kālacakra arises from *āli* and Viśvamātā arises from *kāli*. From the union of those two arises *hūṃ*. From the *hūṃ* arises the vajra of the male deity, which is blocked at the tip by the syllable *phaṭ*. The implication is that the lotus of the consort arises from *āḥ* and is also blocked by *phaṭ*.

In the process of the generation stage, the deity and consort, as well as the vajra and lotus, are generated from the *āli* and *kāli* syllables. In the stage of completion, even in the absence of this process, the body of Kālacakra arises from immutable bliss. It arises in dependence upon the completion stage practice by the experience of the 21,600 immutable blisses.

Homage to the Consort

I bow to Mahāmudrā,
Who transcends the reality of atoms,
Having the nature of an apparition,
And bearing all supreme qualities.

The term apparition (Tib. *pra phab*) refers to a kind of illusion produced by the use of a mantra, a kind of material substance, the practice of samādhi, and a mirror to see the past, present, and future. One sees images that are not composed of atoms. This is the description of the body of Mahāmudrā, who is, of course, Viśvamātā, who "transcends the reality of atoms." Her body is not composed of material particles. "Having the nature of an apparition" refers to having the nature of the images in the magical mirror. That she bears "all supreme qualities" means that her body cannot be measured; one cannot determine where it begins and where it ends.

Among the three types of mudrās, the karma mudrā, that is, the actual consort, and the wisdom mudrā, the visualized consort, bring about merely mutable bliss. It is only Mahāmudrā who is able to bring about immutable bliss. Therefore, the consort, Viśvamātā, is called Mahāmudrā.

Homage to Viśvamātā,
Mother of all the buddhas,

Who has eliminated birth and destruction,

And who performs the deeds of Samantabhadra.

In the Kālacakra system, there are two forms of mother deities, those with and those without aspects. Emptiness that is free of dualistic appearance and apprehended by immutable bliss is the definitive meaning of the mother, the aspectless mother deity. The preceding verse, in which we bowed to Mahāmudrā, refers to the mother deity with aspects.

The text says, "Homage to Viśvamātā, mother of all the buddhas," because before their enlightenment all buddhas meditate on emptiness and cultivate the perfection of wisdom. Therefore, in that sense, emptiness can be said to be the mother of all the buddhas. Moreover, all of the deities of the maṇḍala arise from the wisdom of emptiness and bliss. In this sense, too, such wisdom is the mother of these buddhas.

Viśvamātā is free of "birth and destruction" because she is free of all the elaborations of dualistic appearance. Therefore, she is called the "all good."

The provisional meaning of the consort symbolizes the definitive meaning, which is emptiness itself. So the first verse, "I bow to Mahāmudrā," complements the second, "Homage to Viśvamātā."

The etymology of Viśvamātā is as follows. *Viśva* often means various, and it also means all. *Mātā* means mother. On the one hand, she arises from the wisdom of emptiness and bliss and appears in different fashions, in her principal fashion and as the eight śaktīs. On the other hand, she is regarded as the mother of the entire universe.

Because the union of immutable bliss and the realization of emptiness is free from all elaborations of dualistic appearances, and since it arises and abides forever, at the time of fruition it is symbolized by Kālacakra in union with consort.

One can imagine these verses of praise either as being uttered by the offering goddesses or as coming from space itself. Upon hearing them, imagine experiencing immutable bliss.

Dissolving the Maṇḍala

The śaktīs with their platforms melt into light and dissolve into myself.

I also melt into light, and from the nature of non-objectified emptiness

I again transform into the aspect of the great Kālacakra

With one face and two hands.

This is the retraction of the maṇḍala. The dissolution process is as follows. The stem of the lotus dissolves into the lotus seat, the lotus dissolves into the throne, and the throne dissolves into the śaktīs. Or, both the śaktīs and the lotus may dissolve into the throne simultaneously. Then the seat dissolves into light, which dissolves into the principal deity with consort. The principal deity and consort are in union, the primordial wisdom of great bliss arises, and one imagines the consort dissolving into the principal deity. The principal deity also dissolves into the nature of the primordial wisdom of great bliss. One meditates for a while on the experience of emptiness and bliss.

Then, like a bubble emerging from the water, one arises from that as Kālacakra. You can generate oneself as Kālacakra either with or without consort. If you find it a little difficult to regenerate oneself with consort, you can be single. However, because the bliss and emptiness are forever of the same nature, which is symbolized by the union of the deity and consort, it is better to visualize the two in union.

This is where the six-phase yoga completion stage practices are implemented, if you wish to do them.

Dedication

By the power of the pure virtue derived from this,
May I, through the influence of Vajradhara,
Come to the culmination of the stages of the two-stage path,
Without ever transgressing the ethical discipline in all my lifetimes.

In summary, due to the accumulation of the mass of pure virtue such as this,
May I soon be born in Śambhala,
The treasury of jewels, and come to the culmination
Of the stages of the path of highest yoga tantra.

In all lifetimes may I enjoy the glory of Dharma
Without ever being separated from genuine gurus,
And upon perfecting the virtues of the grounds and the paths,
May I swiftly attain the state of Vajradhara.

The results of the common path and uncommon path arise in dependence upon the spiritual mentor, so this is the final prayer of dedication.

Part 3

Completion Stage Practices

18

The Nature of Phenomena

The Channel System

Inside the body, from the level of the genitals up to the crown of the head, are three channels. The central channel has its upper aperture in the middle of the forehead. The two side channels, the right and the left, have their upper apertures at the nostrils. Ordinarily, one speaks of three channels from the level of the navel up and three channels from the level of the navel down. In that sense, there are six channels.

It is said that the channels come down through the center of the torso, but not right in the middle of the body as measured from the front and back. The channels are located about sixty percent in from the front and forty percent in from the back. The channels are described as follows:

- The central channel (Skt. *avadhūtī,* Tib. *rtsa dbu ma*) from the level of the navel up is green and is sometimes called the rāhu channel. It is principally energy that moves through the central channel above the navel.
- The right channel (Skt. *rasanā,* Tib. *ro ma*) from the navel up is also called the wisdom or sunshine channel. It is red. It is principally blood that moves through the right channel.
- The left channel (Skt. *lalanā,* Tib. *rkyang ma*) is white, and through it flows principally the white bodhicitta. The left channel is also called the skillful means or moonshine channel.
- The central channel from the level of the navel down to the tip of the sexual organ is sometimes called *śaṅkhapāla* (Tib. *dung skyong*) and kālāgni (Tib. *dus me*). This channel is blue, and white bodhicitta descends through it.

- Below the navel, the right channel veers over to the left side and ends at the anus. Below the navel it is called *piṅgalā* (Tib. *dmar ser can ma*), and it turns from red to yellow.
- The left channel moves to the right side of the central channel below the navel and is called *meṣa* (Tib. *lug*). It culminates at the orifice for urination. Below the navel it is black, and urine flows through it.

According to other tantric systems, at the time of the ground, while one is starting out in the practice, there is no energy passing through the central channel at all. In contrast, the Kālacakra system uniquely states that even in our present state, 675 energies pass through the central channel.

Cakras and Branch Channels

In the Kālacakra system there are six cakras. At the level of each of the cakras there is a knot; that is, the two side channels coil around the central channel and thereby constrict it. There is one such constriction for each of the cakras. There is a difference here with the Guhyasamāja system, which states that there are three such knots at the heart.

At each of the cakras where the constrictions exist, there are horizontal channels from which the energy branches out from the central channel. This accounts for the fact that as one mentally focuses upon the cakras, it is possible to bring energy into the central channel through the small openings on the side. At each of these cakras, there are many more small subsidiary channels branching out from the main horizontal channels, as follows:

- The cakra at the very crown of the head has four channels branching out from the central channel. They are green in color.
- The forehead cakra has sixteen subsidiary branching channels, which are white in color. These sixteen branch out into smaller channels, and from them branches out a whole network of channels. The forehead cakra does not refer to the forehead, but to the cakra in the central channel at the level of the forehead. The forehead cakra is circular.
- At the throat there are thirty-two branch channels, which are red. The cakra is triangular in shape with the apex facing forward.
- At the heart are four black branch channels and each of them splits to make a total of eight. The heart cakra is in the shape of a bow, that is, more or less semicircular.

- The cakra at the navel has sixty-four branch channels, and they are yellow. The shape of the cakra is square.
- At the genital cakra there are thirty-two branch channels, blue in color.

In other systems, such as Cakrasaṃvara and Guhyasamāja, the number of the side branch channels in the forehead and throat cakras is reversed, so there are thirty-two at the forehead and sixteen at the throat.

The commentary does not mention anything about the shapes of the cakras at the crown of the head or at the genital region. It is unclear what to infer from this omission. In the Cakrasaṃvara and Guhyasamāja systems, it is said that from the top, the cakras look somewhat like an umbrella, and that there is something corresponding to that shape at the bottom. The cakras are roughly horizontal.

Another way that the shape of the cakra could be understood is in terms of the manner in which the branch channels merge into the central channel. Think of the central channel as being like a tube with the branches entering into it. The way the branch channels enter into the central channel determines the shape of the cakra.

The Channel Network

At the genital cakra the six root branch channels come directly out of the central channel. Two branch out to either side, one goes out in the front, and one out to the back. The front and back channels do not subdivide, but the two to either side do. These make the first round. Each of the two side branch channels splits into four, making the second round. Now we have two times eight on both sides. In terms of the primary branch channels, we have six, and then in terms of the next phase we have ten. Added together, we get sixteen. The sixteen split again. Sixteen plus sixteen equals thirty-two. You count the front and back channels for the inner circle and for the intermediate circle, but you do not count them for the tertiary circle.

The channels protruding to the front and back are quite short. There are a lot of very small branch channels, but because they are so short, one does not speak of them splitting like the others. The sixteen branch channels on each side in the third circle arborize out into a whole network. The arborization process occurs at all the cakras, so these very tiny channels pervade the entire body.

Channels of the Twelve Shiftings

Kālacakra has a unique presentation of the so-called channels of the twelve shiftings. In closest proximity to the central channel at the navel are four horizontal branch channels. Each of these splits to make eight, and each of those splits to make sixteen. Out of these sixteen channels, four are said to be empty channels. This leaves us with only twelve, six on each side. These are the channels in which the twelve shiftings occur. Each of the twelve shifting channels branches into five smaller channels. Twelve multiplied by five equals sixty, making thirty on either side. By adding the four empty channels, we have a total of sixty-four channels at the navel.

There are twelve shiftings of energy, and for each of the shiftings there are 1,800 energies. The twelve shiftings occur during a twenty-four-hour period, corresponding to the number of complete cycles of respiration per day. Twelve multiplied by 1,800 equals 21,600. This is the number of energies that flow through the twelve shifting channels per day. Out of the 1,800 shiftings for every two-hour period, 56.25 energies go into the central channel. In a twenty-four-hour period, 675 energies (12 x 56.25) course through the central channel.

If we subtract 56.25 from each set of 1,800, we get 1,743.75. When that is divided by five, the resultant 348.75 represents the five elements of earth, water, fire, air, and space flowing in the respective small branch channels. In other words, for each shifting we have 348.75 energies of each of the five elements going through the shifting channels into the left and right side channels, and 56.25 energies going through the empty channels into the central channel within every two-hour period ((5 x 348.75) + 56.25 = 1,800).

There is a specific sequence for the shiftings of energy. There are six shifting channels on the right side and six shifting channels on the left side. In the first shifting, all 1,743.75 energies flow through the right shifting channel at the back (348.75 each for earth, water, fire, air, and space) in their respective small branch channels. When these have flowed through, 56.25 go through the empty channels into the central channel.

The second shifting goes to the left shifting channel at the back, repeating the process described above. The third shifting goes to the right shifting channel in front of the back channel. The fourth shifting goes to the left shifting channel next to the back channel. It continues in this way until the energies have flowed through all the twelve shifting channels from the back to the front, right, left, right, left, and so forth.

As this is happening, the breath is going through the right nostril for the shifting channels on the right, and through the left nostril for the shifting channels on the left. This is the basis for calculating the sum total of the 21,600 energies.

Though I said previously that energy does not flow in the empty channel, this is not completely correct. Primordial wisdom energy (Tib. *ye shes kyi rlung*) flows through it. It is so called because it is the energy that flows through the empty channel into the central channel. When the strength of the breath flowing through both nostrils is equal, this is an indication of the primordial wisdom energy flowing into the central channel.

The Energies that Move in the Channels

There are ten types of energies, including the life-sustaining energy. They arise from the heart cakra. Most of the following discussion explains where these energies go. In short, the energies course through all of the minute branch channels throughout the body, as follows:

- The life-sustaining energy moves in all three channels—central, right, and left—from the level of the heart up. It performs all of the functions that occur with upward movement, such as articulation, and all the functions in the upper part of the body, like wiggling one's ears and so forth. It is green.
- The descending energy flows from the level of the heart downward. It is blue, and it performs all of the functions of the lower processes.
- The fire-accompanying energy comes out from the branch channels at the heart in an eastern direction, and it is black.
- The tortoise (Skt. *kūrma*) energy goes through the branch channels in a southeastern direction, and it is black.
- The ascending energy flows to the south, and it is red.
- The lizard (Skt. *kṛkara*) energy flows to the southwest, and it is also red.
- The pervasive energy goes to the north and is white.
- The devadatta energy flows to the northeast, and it is also white.
- The nāga energy is to the west, and it is yellow.
- The dhanaṃjaya energy flows in the northwest, and it is also yellow.

The text does not state the specific functions of the last eight energies.

Other systems, such as Guhyasamāja and Cakrasaṃvara, speak of the primary and secondary energies, usually five of each. In contrast, in the Kālacakra system, there is no dual classification of primary and secondary energies. Tagtsang Lotsawa, a great Tibetan master who wrote a general commentary to Kālacakra, explicitly states that there is no such dual distinction.

Although it can be said that all ten of the energies circulate throughout the entire body, it can also be said that the life-sustaining energy moves from the heart upward, and the descending energy moves from the level of the heart downward.

The etymologies of the names for the five energies—life-sustaining energy, descending energy, fire-accompanying energy, ascending energy, and pervasive energy—are not found in the Kālacakra system, so the following explanations are taken from the Guhyasamāja and Cakrasaṃvara systems:

- The life-sustaining energy is so called because it performs the function of providing a locale for the life force. This energy is located at the heart.
- The descending energy is so called because it evacuates the feces and the urine downward. It moves from the level of the heart downward.
- The fire-accompanying energy is instrumental in the digestion of food, and it is located at the level of the navel.
- The ascending energy is located from the level of the throat up and it is involved in the ascending actions, such as coughing, spitting, and speaking. All of these upward-moving activities are done with the ascending energy.
- The pervasive energy, as the name implies, is pervasive throughout the body and is instrumentally involved in such functions as the extension and contraction of the limbs.

The Red and White Bodhicittas

The red and white bodhicittas are located in the channels. To review the functions of the four bindus, or drops, that have been discussed thus far:

- The function of the drop at the forehead (sometimes said to be at the crown) is to avoid confusion. It produces the waking state.
- The drop at the throat produces the dream state.

- ❖ The drop at the heart produces the deep sleep state.
- ❖ The drop at the navel has two functions: sexual intercourse, or the fourth occasion, and also the waking state.

In addition, according to Kālacakra:

- ❖ There is a drop at the genital region that produces the dream state.
- ❖ Along the shaft of the male organ, there is a drop that produces the deep sleep state.
- ❖ In a man, the drop at the tip of the jewel produces the fourth occasion, and in a woman, that drop moves along the central channel in the sexual region. The drops occur in the same sequence for men and women. The drop at the very tip of the woman's sexual organ corresponds to the drop at the tip of the jewel for a man.

All those drops are a mixture of the red and white fluids. The white bodhicitta is predominant at the forehead, at the shaft of the jewel, and at the tip of the jewel, whereas the red bodhicitta is less dominant. At the navel, at the base of the genital region, and at the throat, the red bodhicitta is stronger.

The white bodhicitta is principally located at the level of the forehead, and the red bodhicitta is principally located at the navel. All those drops are located in the cakras. The drop at the heart is said to have equal aspects of the red and white bodhicittas.

Each of these four drops has an impure aspect. The drop at the forehead produces impure appearances of objects. Through purification, impure appearances turn into nonconceptual primordial wisdom. The drop at the throat is for the speech, and the impure aspect produces improper speech. The impure aspect of the drop at the heart is dreamless sleep. By purifying this sleep, it turns into nonconceptual wisdom. The impure aspect of the drop at the navel produces the pleasure from orgasm. By purifying the impurities of the four drops, they are transformed into the four bodies of the buddha. The drop at the forehead transforms into the vajra body; that at the throat transforms into the vajra speech; that at the heart transforms into the vajra mind; and that at the navel transforms into the vajra primordial wisdom.

This is a concise account of the bodhicittas that are located in the channels.

19

The Six-Phase Yoga

Overview

I will begin this discussion with a general presentation that pertains equally to all six phases of the six-phase yoga of the completion stage—retraction (Skt. *pratyāhāra*), meditative stabilization (Skt. *dhyāna*), prāṇayāma, retention (Skt. *dhāraṇā*), recollection (Skt. *anusmṛti*), and samādhi. Of initial importance is the samādhi of the vajra body, followed by the samādhi of the vajra speech, and finally the samādhi of the vajra mind.

The first two of the six phases, retraction and meditative stabilization, are included in the first of those three categories, the vajra body. These two phases are called "the first virtue." The chief function of these two phases is to actualize empty form. It is the function of retraction to freshly actualize the empty form, and meditative stabilization stabilizes the empty form that has already been realized.

The next two phases are prāṇayāma and retention, called "the second virtue." They actualize the vajra speech. The chief function of these two phases is to gain mastery over the energies. Prāṇayāma freshly causes the energies to flow through the central channel, and the practice of retention has the function of stabilizing that flow.

Finally there are recollection and samādhi. These two phases are called "the third virtue," and they actualize the vajra mind. It is the function of the recollection phase to bring forth the pure vision of the empty form bodies of the father and mother deities in union. This is not something that is visualized or created. Rather, it spontaneously appears. It appears to the mind's eye in a fashion somewhat similar to the sign (Skt. *nimitta*, Tib. *mtshan ma*) in the practice of mindfulness of breathing.

The union of the empty form of the father and mother deities brings forth immutable bliss, and as that immutable bliss is brought to its culmination, it transforms into the nature of the vajra mind. From that moment the samādhi phase of the practice begins. The recollection phase brings forth the actual appearance of the union of the empty form father and mother deities. The samādhi phase produces the supreme immutable bliss.

For the actual, spontaneous appearance of the union of empty form father and mother deities to occur, one must have mastered the energies, and that is brought about by the phases of prāṇayāma and retention. Mastery over the energies occurs when one brings them into the central channel. In order to master the energies by bringing them into the central channel, it is necessary to purify the central channel. This is done by means of the first two phases of retraction and meditative stabilization. This mastery over the energies entails the purification of the central channel so that the energies can easily flow through it.

We purify the central channel by focusing our awareness on its upper aperture, which arouses the ten signs, all arising as empty form.

The cultivation of empty form has two functions: to purify the central channel, and to provide a foundation for the later appearance of the actual empty form of the father and mother deities in union.

This is called the six-phase yoga on the stage of completion. Yoga means to join, or put together. These phases are called yoga because they entail a necessary, sequential process. If the earlier phases are not accomplished, the latter ones will not be realized.

I will now offer specific presentations of each of the six phases of the yoga, in which I shall explain (1) the etymology, (2) the time for practice, (3) the way to meditate, (4) an analysis of whether the verifying cognition produced in each of these phases is perceptual or inferential, (5) the manner of purification of the basis to be purified, and (6) the temporal and ultimate results of each phase.[18]

Retraction

In order to cultivate the initial phase of retraction, six conditions are necessary. The first of these conditions is place. At first, for the night yoga phase of practice, one meditates in a completely dark dwelling; later, for the daytime yoga, one meditates in the light, under a cloudless sky. Ideally, one should engage in the nighttime yoga in a three-storied house, and meditate on the second floor so that one is meditating off the ground. One's meditation room could also be on stilts or blocks, as long as there is empty space underneath. The reason is that one's practice may be detrimentally influenced by vapors from the ground, so this creates a buffer zone.

Outside one's meditation dwelling there should be a wall that covers it like a shell. The windows in this outside shell are not parallel to the wall but are at a steep angle, allowing for ventilation. A little bit of light can come through, but not much. That is the crucial point. They are baffled windows. If one meditated in a room without proper ventilation, one would get sick, but no light should filter into the room. This phase of practice could last for six months. Even though one would not have to stay in that dark room all the time during that period, one would spend a great deal of time in it.

The second necessary condition is the posture of the body. The legs are placed in the lotus posture, while sitting in the seven-point posture of Vairocana. This well-known posture entails keeping the spine erect, inclining the head, letting the lips be in the natural position, and so forth. The hands are clenched in vajra fists, with the back of the hands resting beneath one's navel or at the base of the thighs. The palms of the hands are facing up. This mudrā is said to be the mudrā of Vajrasattva.

The third necessary condition concerns one's gaze. One gazes with the eyes upward and focuses one's attention on a point in the middle of the forehead. One should focus specifically on the empty space inside the central channel.

The fourth necessary condition concerns the three immobilities: the body should not move, the mind should not be moved by conceptualization, and the eyes should not move. With these three immobilities, one focuses on the central channel. The eyelashes should not be flickering, as this would impair one's ability to actually see what is happening there. In the beginning, until one gets accustomed to this practice, it is a bit difficult, for the eyes tend to move up and down.

The fifth necessary condition is keeping the mind in a state free of all thoughts. One's attention should be entirely focused on the aperture of the central channel on the forehead.

The sixth necessary condition is the experiential realization (Tib. *nyams rtogs*) in this practice, which is described below.

The Etymology of Retraction

In the Tibetan word translated here as retraction (Tib. *sor sdud*), the first syllable means individual, and the second normally means retraction. But in this context, the second syllable refers to cutting, so the whole word suggests the individual severance of the connection between the sensory faculties and the objects of the senses.

In order for the sensory faculties to operate, the energies have to course through the left and right channels. In this phase of meditation, we retract the energies from the left and right channels and cause them to go into the central channel. When they cease flowing into the two side channels, then the connection between the sense faculties and the objects of the senses is severed.

The Time for Practicing Retraction

It is said that each session of this practice should begin when the breath starts to go through the right nostril. It is not to be done whenever one feels like it. Rather, one needs to see how the breath is flowing through the nostrils. When one sees that it is going predominantly through the right nostril, one should begin the session.

The reason is that the breath in the right channel is associated with the earth energy. If one starts the session in that way, it makes it easier for the energies to retract. Recall that the energies of all the five elements flow in the shifting channels, and the first of them to flow is the earth energy. It is best to start the meditation when the earth energy is moving.

The Way to Meditate on Retraction

If we want to engage in the practice of retraction separately from the six-session guru yoga, then, after cultivating the motivation, we visualize our guru in the form of Kālacakra with consort in the space before us. Since we are about to practice the stage of completion, we renew our previous motivation, "Might I attain perfect awakening by means of the following practice of the stage of completion." We then make the offerings and prayers of supplication. The supplications are: "Please bless me, bless the channels, and bless the energies so that they may be made serviceable. By so doing, may immutable bliss arise, and may the state of perfect awakening be swiftly attained."

Then the guru with consort comes to the crown of the head and dissolves into us. Imagine experiencing immutable bliss, focus upon emptiness, and then arise in the form of Kālacakra with consort, with one face and two hands.

It is said that if one visualizes one's form as being transparent, brilliant, and purely of the nature of light, and also visualizes one's channels, energies, and the five elements as being of the nature of transparent light, one will experience fewer obstacles regarding one's channels and energies.

Having done that, one visualizes the three channels from their upper apertures down to the lower apertures, as described previously. It is said that when one is actually meditating, it is not necessary to visualize the various points of constrictions at the cakras, but it would be good to visualize the six cakras. However, if one can visualize only the central channel, that alone is probably sufficient for the phase of retraction. Nevertheless, if one can do the more elaborate visualization of all the cakras, it will be easier to retract the various energies. It is said that highly realized yogis are actually able to see the cakras and the different energies together with the colors and the channels.

The Nature of Experiential Realization

The following describes the nature of the sixth condition, experiential realization. Recall that the central channel at the forehead is green, but do not visualize it as such. Just focus on the inside of the channel, which is hollow and dark. It is said that after focusing on that point for a while, one will start to see certain visions. As one perseveres in this practice, the energies gradually start coming into the central channel, and various visions appear to the mind. Once one achieves a little stability in this practice, certain signs and visions will appear, such as smoke and a mirage. They will appear as if they were out in space. When that or a variety of other visions appear, it is said that one is not to regard these as the authentic appearances of empty form.

Other events may occur. One's body may start trembling, it may start jerking around, or it may feel numb. Also, words may be expressed spontaneously. One may find certain mental events, thoughts, and so forth, occurring chaotically, such that one cannot really tell if they make sense or not, or whether they are good or bad. It is not as if one were following a train of thought. It is just a kind of mental jumble.

These various events are an indication that the energies are beginning to go into the central channel. However, one should not place credence in these, thinking that they indicate some kind of realization. If one does, they turn into obstacles. One should not think of any of those occurrences as being something special. The yogi who is beginning in this practice, who does not know the practice properly and does not have proper guidance, may do exactly that when these things arise. That can lead to insanity. Even if there is a qualified teacher there, and the student receives proper instructions, the student may still ignore what the teacher says, in which case again there is no benefit. That is why it is best to come to one's mentor to receive advice if problems are encountered in the practice. One should heed the advice, and then the problems can be surmounted. Otherwise, one may run into real difficulties.

For this practice it is indispensable for the student to follow the instructions. In other words, if you have a qualified teacher, do what the guru says to do and do not do what the guru says not to do. If you do not have a qualified teacher, it is not so important to follow what he or she says.

One really needs to take responsibility for this oneself. As one engages in the meditation and sees certain types of behavior starting to arise that do not conform to one's ordinary behavior, do not succumb to such conduct. For those who are meditating seriously, this is very, very important. The crucial point is to recognize when such anomalous behavior arises and not to go along with it. Do not identify with it, do not indulge in it, do not give energy to it. Leave it, but continue meditating. If you can deal with the experiences I have just described, this is very helpful for the whole path, as well as for abandoning grasping onto the affairs of this lifetime.

You may also experience itching or shooting pains, like being pricked with needles in the upper torso, in the head, or all over the body, but that is likely to occur for only a couple of days.

Ascertaining the Signs

Eventually the signs of smoke and so forth will become more and more vivid. At that point, the energies have begun to enter into the central channel. Then the signs of smoke and so forth will start to appear in the central channel, whereas previously they might have been up in the space above you. The more the energies are drawn into the central channel, the more these visions also appear at the aperture of the central channel. This is not to say that one needs to try to make them do so. One should not visualize them. They will occur in that place spontaneously. When such visions appear at the aperture of the central channel, appearances of the external environment will cease.

One may not be able to ascertain those visions as soon as they arise, but only right after they have vanished. This is a kind of delayed reaction. However, as one becomes more and more familiar with the practice, there is a greater continuity of realization of what is appearing to the mind. In the early phase of this practice, the visions will be of very short duration, like flashes, but later on they last longer, and one may be able to ascertain them while they occur.

Other sensations may also arise. One may have a sensation of something like a snake moving through one's central channel, either coming in from the top and going down or coming up from the bottom. Such a sensation can go in any direction. One may have the sense of a stick being prodded through the central channel. One may feel as if oneself or some other creature is being squeezed through a small hole. Of course, these are merely subjective feelings or sensations.

In addition, one may have the sense of one's body being covered with insects, some of them biting. Also, while sleeping at night, one may have the sense of being hugged by another person. One may also have the sense when asleep, not quite in the dream state, of being hemmed in, either by sentient beings or other things, which can be oppressive.

At that time, much fear arises. It is very important to anticipate such states, to anticipate these experiences and think that if they occur, one will not succumb to the fear, which can be quite strong. Otherwise, when that happens in the middle of the night, one may find oneself running out of the house, screaming. It can be dangerous. If instead one can anticipate these experiences and embolden oneself, thinking, "I will not be afraid, I will not succumb to terror, I will hold fast," there is tremendous benefit.

There are many accounts of people becoming terrified when they practice tantra. One antidote to this is the practice of severance (Tib. *gcod*). There was once a practitioner who was having terrifying experiences of this type. He did not yet have any deep realization, and he felt he was being visited by demons and spirits. Once he was practicing under a window with the moonlight shining in. Right in front of him was the pillar that held up the roof, and there were stones at the base of the pillar, polished smooth by people sitting on them, making a nice smooth shiny surface. When the light of the moon struck that shiny surface, he saw it while he was practicing and thought this was another demon. He began screaming, *"phaṭ, phaṭ, phaṭ,"* trying to expel it with the realization of emptiness, but it would not go away.

One may also confuse such subjective impressions with objective reality. For instance, a yogi was once sitting in meditation, and in front of him there was a tiny pool of water with a bug in it with its legs up, squirming around, unable to get away. In his mind's eye, the yogi saw this as a lake with a large animal like a yak thrashing about in the water.

The great Indian Buddhist teacher Atīśa was once meditating, and a huge nine-headed scorpion appeared to drop right in front of him. He responded by embracing it as his chosen deity, and the scorpion immediately transformed into Tārā.

If one can accept such experiences and transform them into the path, they can be of great benefit. But if one cannot do so, there is danger. That needs to be borne in mind. One should bolster oneself repeatedly, anticipating how one will respond.

Having said all this, it should also be mentioned that there is no guarantee that these unpleasant sensations will appear. If one is very well prepared for this phase of the practice, one may go through it much more easily.

A sign that the energy has entered into the central channel is that the force of breath that flows through both nostrils is of equal magnitude. When the energy associated with the five sense faculties ceases to function, the energy dissolves into the central channel.

We should understand that the word "dissolve" used here is the same word that is used when speaking of the energy of earth dissolving into the energy of water. This term should not be taken literally. It is not to say that the energy of one is actually merging into the other, like salt dissolving into water. Rather, the energy of the earth actually ceases, and in its absence the energy of the water element manifests more dominantly.

When the energy of the two side channels dissolves into the central channel, it is not that it flows from the side channels like water from a tube; rather, the energies cease flowing in the two side channels and they manifest in the central channel. When the energies dissolve into the central channel, the actual meaning is that the energies vanish in the right and left channels and freshly arise in the central channel.

Similarly, at other times of practice, one sends out rays of light in all directions from the heart and then draws them back in and brings them into the *hūṃ* syllable. This is not as if one were rolling them up like a carpet. Rather, it is like drawing them in as if they were on a string that vanishes at the end. The vanishing process continues until everything has vanished and there is only the *hūṃ* left. This is what is meant by dissolving them.

The Nighttime Signs

The first of the ten signs are the four signs for the night yoga, as follows:

- ❖ Smoke.
- ❖ A mirage.
- ❖ Fireflies.
- ❖ A butter lamp.

At a certain stage of the practice, just the sign of the smoke appears, and it appears with greater and greater continuity. Some people say that one experiences each of the four signs immediately, one after the other. But my sense is that they occur sequentially and gradually over a period of time. However, different people may have different experiences.

I expect that the process would normally take place over a period of several days. One would have the experience of smoke, and then after a few days that would be replaced by the appearance of a mirage. After a few more days fireflies would appear, and finally after several more days a butter lamp would appear.

For some people, these signs may appear before the energies have stopped flowing through the two side channels and emerged into the central channel. If that happens, the signs will appear out in the space before one. When the special empty form does actually begin to appear, it arises in the aperture of the central channel.

When these four night signs appear regularly—that is, whenever one sits down and engages in the retraction, the signs arise sequentially—that is the time to begin the daytime practice.

What is the reason for making the distinction between nighttime and daytime yoga? The reason is that in the daytime it is more difficult for the signs to arise. However, it is not impossible for the six daytime signs to appear at night. When one practices in the daylight, the light gives a greater stability and regularity to the daytime signs, which will eventually appear after the regular experience of the four night signs.

The Daytime Signs

The daytime yoga posture, the way to begin the practice, the motivation, and the visualizations are the same as described previously for the night yoga. The place is different, of course: instead of meditating in the dark, you now meditate in the light, under a cloudless sky. In the morning, meditate while facing west, so that the sun is behind you. In the afternoon or evening, face east. The sun should always be behind you.

The focus of the meditation is right at the central channel. By continuing in the meditation during the daytime, the signs will appear again. The four night signs are followed by the six daytime signs:

- Like flame.
- Like a disc of the moon.
- Like the light of the sun.
- Rāhu, which, according to the text, is a vision of darkness. Sometimes it is referred to as blue, and sometimes as dark or black. The terms are used interchangeably.
- Like forked lightning, the supreme aspect.
- A pale blue drop, the size of a sesame seed, which appears at the upper aperture of the central channel.

There also appears a fine black circle, not a disc, but a fine black line going around the aperture. This appears in the form of clear light. For some people, the sambhogakāya together with the five definite attributes appears inside that drop with the little black line framed around it. This does not necessarily happen to everyone. According to Khedrub Je's writings and some of those of Je Tsongkhapa, the sambhogakāya appears in that drop. In another set of notes of Je Tsongkhapa, he simply speaks of the appearance of the drop and the black circle as an indication of the completion of the retraction phase of the practice. It appears from Je Tsongkhapa's writings that the drop appears first as the tenth sign, and then the sambhogakāya may appear with the black line around it.

In proper practice, these signs will appear regularly, and apart from them, many other types of visions will be experienced. Among the ten signs that occur during the retraction phase, the four night signs indicate the dissolving of the energies into the four intermediate-direction branch channels at the heart. The appearance of the first four of the six daytime signs—the flame, moon, sun, and rāhu—indicates the dissolving of the energies into the four cardinal directions of the branch channels at the heart.

The final two daytime signs—the appearance of the supreme aspect, which is the forked lightning, and the drop—are the final two of the ten signs, and indicate the dissolution of the energies flowing up and down. The forked lightning indicates the dissolution of the life-sustaining energy, and the drop indicates the dissolution of the descending energy.

The ten signs of smoke and so forth appear during the first two phases, retraction and meditative stabilization. During the phase of retention, the ten śaktīs appear. Recall the perfections associated with them, namely, generosity, ethical discipline, patience, and so forth. During the phase of recollection, the authentic wisdom body appears. If that practice does not yield results, special backup techniques are taught that are more forceful, but there is no backup technique for the retraction phase. Corresponding to the ten signs, one can make a tenfold internal classification within the phase of retraction.

Analysis of Verifying Cognition in Retraction

The verifying cognition (Skt. *pramāṇa*) produced in the retraction phase is called sensory perception, referring to one's vision of the above signs. I suspect that it is so called because one's experience of these various signs is very much like actually seeing them with one's own eyes. However, it is not actually a sensory perception because it does not rely on the five sense faculties. It is analogous to sensory perception, but in reality it is a non-conceptual, mental perception.

The Manner of Purification of the Basis

What is the purified aspect or result of this practice of retraction? It is the purification of the aggregate and element of primordial wisdom, as well as two sets of six phenomena. It seems that the aggregate of primordial wisdom and the element of primordial wisdom are synonymous. What they are referring to is the pleasure of orgasm at the time of the ground. Through this practice the aggregate of primordial wisdom and the element of primordial wisdom, which are actually one, are purified and sublimated.

I have checked four commentaries on Kālacakra, but I have not found two sets of six phenomena. Here is one possibility. There is an internal five-fold classification of each of the buddha classes, including Vairocana and so forth, and one may relate these to each of the six aggregates. Begin, for example, with the aggregate of primordial wisdom. First, recall that the form aggregate is of the nature of the aggregate of primordial wisdom. Then go through the other aggregates—feeling, recognition, compositional factors, and consciousness—and analyze how they also are of the nature of primordial wisdom. This would make one set of six. Then recalling that the six elements—earth, water, fire, air, space, and consciousness—are also of the nature of primordial wisdom, one could establish another set of six. Perhaps those are the two sets of six phenomena referred to in the text.

The Temporal and Ultimate Results of Retraction

The temporal, or mundane, benefit of having accomplished the stage of retraction is that one accomplishes a state called "words of truth," meaning that all one's words come true. For example, if a house goes up in flames, one can simply say, "May the fire go out," and the fire will die down. Or if someone has taken some poison, one may simply say, "May it be pacified," and the poison will be neutralized. One's speech itself has the power of truth.

There are techniques that are specifically designed to accomplish the eight siddhis, or paranormal abilities. It is not necessary to practice them when one is following these phases of practice, for they will automatically be accomplished as side effects of the main practice. Such abilities may also be accomplished by using alchemical or magical substances. But those techniques are ineffective if one has not attained the culmination of the stage of generation.

If one has accomplished the words of truth, then one may, for example, dispel a famine simply by the power of speech, but there must be a karmic relationship with the sentient beings with whom one is performing such a feat.

Within the six-phase yoga, the ultimate result of retraction is that one actualizes the body of Vajrasattva. As I mentioned already, when the drop, the tenth sign, has appeared with its surrounding black circle and possibly the sambhogakāya form, one is ready to go on to phase two, meditative stabilization.

Meditative Stabilization

The Etymology of Meditative Stabilization

Meditative stabilization is so called because this second phase stabilizes the accomplishment of the first phase of retraction and because it is similar to the fifth of the six perfections, namely, the perfection of meditation. However, there is a great difference in that in this phase of practice, the attention of the meditator is more stable and has many other qualities superior to that of the sūtrayāna practice of meditative stabilization.

The Time for Practicing Meditative Stabilization

The time for meditating in the phase of meditative stabilization is the same as for the phase of retraction.

The Way to Practice Meditative Stabilization

The locale and posture for the second phase are the same as they were in the first phase. In the first phase, though, the nighttime and daytime yogas entailed two different locations. It seems odd that both would be involved in the second phase, because after one has accomplished those signs for the nighttime yoga, those signs will appear during the day and the night. Nevertheless, the commentary says the locations are the same. While still engaged in this practice, one probably uses both locales, in the dark and in the light.

The motivation, posture, and direction of the gaze are all as they were in the first phase.

During the training in meditative stabilization, the ten signs (including the tenth sign followed by the black circle and sambhogakāya with the five definite attributes appearing in the drop) all occur regularly. In addition, one may have various hallucinations of such things as pots, articles of clothing, and so on.

During the practice of the second phase, the mind is so concentrated at the aperture of the central channel that all sense of duality has vanished. No mental imagery of one's body, face, head, and so forth appear to the mind, which has become absorbed into that spot at the aperture of the central channel. Therefore, during such periods of intense concentration, when images occur, they do not appear to be arising in that little hole in one's forehead. For that to occur, one would have to have some sense of one's body. Rather, the images, including but not limited to the ten signs, seem to be everywhere. As an analogy, while sleeping in a very small room, one may dream of elephants and forests and other large things without any of them being able to fit in that small room.

The empty forms appear as pervasive as space. As these various apparitions appear, they gradually transform into the different goddesses, who all dissolve into one goddess, who dissolves into the sambhogakāya with the five definite attributes. One identifies with this appearance of the sambhogakāya and develops divine pride, thinking, "I am Kālacakra."

When the various apparitions regularly transform into goddesses and dissolve into the sambhogakāya, one consistently develops divine pride by identifying with that sambhogakāya, and when one is well acquainted with this phase of practice, one has completed the phase of meditative stabilization and is ready to go on to the third phase of prāṇayāma.

It is said that there are five parts to the second phase of meditative stabilization, but nowhere do the texts discuss the different functions of the five parts.

An Analysis of Verifying Cognition in Meditative Stabilization

There are five factors of meditative stabilization: (1) investigation, which occurs when one sees coarse empty forms; (2) analysis, which is more subtle than investigation and occurs when one experiences subtler empty forms; (3) happiness, that is, the mental happiness brought forth by mental pliancy; (4) joy, which is the physical joy brought forth by physical pliancy; and (5) samādhi, which occurs when one's own awareness merges indivisibly into the nature of the sambhogakāya bearing the five definite attributes. In the great commentaries the last factor is called wisdom.

Verifying cognition at this point is called a sensory perception, though it is not actually sensory, as in the previous phase of retraction.

In accordance with the commentary on Kālacakra by Mahasiddha Śavaripa (Tib. *śa ra ba*), the tenfold internal classification of the phase of meditative stabilization corresponds to the ten signs.

The Manner of Purification of the Basis

The two sets of six phenomena are again identified as the objects of purification. One is a sixfold classification relating to the purification of the consciousness aggregate, the other a sixfold internal classification relating to the element of space. The sixfold classification is like the one in the first phase, which relates to Vajrasattva, while this one relates to Akṣobhya. The purification of the element leads to the realization of Vajradhātvīśvarī.

The Temporal and Ultimate Results of Meditative Stabilization

The temporal result of the practice is that one achieves all five forms of extrasensory perception, including the ability to see treasures beneath the ground. Ultimately, one attains the body of Akṣobhya. With the completion of the final two phases one attains the body vajra, also called the initial virtue.

Backup Techniques

According to Je Tsongkhapa, one does not need any backup technique for either retraction or meditative stabilization, but there are backup techniques for the next four phases and particularly for the retention phase.

In the first backup technique, your left heel is pushed against and blocks the anus. If that is difficult, then push the heel against a channel that is right between the base of the genitals and the anus. Press the left heel against that spot. The right heel goes beneath the left knee.

In the second technique, the left heel is either pressed against the anus or against the channel between the genitals and the anus. Then the right heel is placed on top of the left ankle. Both hands are clenched in vajra fists, the left hand over the right breast, and the right hand over that and the left breast. One sits upright with the eyes gazing upward. Then at the tip of the genitals, one visualizes the syllable *hūṃ* pointing inward. While inhaling, imagine that *hūṃ* ascending the central channel, head first, up to the navel. As soon as the *hūṃ* arrives at the level of the navel, simply focus on it. One can use this backup technique whenever one feels that one is not progressing in the practice.

Prāṇayāma

The Etymology of Prāṇayāma

The etymological meaning of prāṇayāma is that one blocks the life force, or the vital energies, from flowing in the two side channels.

The Time for Practicing Prāṇayāma

The time for engaging in this practice is when one has experienced all the ten signs in the meditative stabilization phase.

The Way to Practice Prāṇayāma

The posture is the same as before, except that the hands are now in the mudrā of meditative equipoise, held at the level of the navel with the right hand on top of left, palms up with thumbs touching.

In the phase of the prāṇayāma, the chief task is to bring the energies into the central channel. The task of the next phase, retention, is to firmly stabilize the energies that have been brought into the cakras by means of the phase of prāṇayāma. One must now hold them there unwaveringly.

One visualizes the cakras and the channels as in the preceding two phases. In the first two phases, the attention is focused at the upper aperture of the central channel. During the prāṇayāma phase, one focuses on the navel cakra in what is called the vajra recitation. In the very center of the navel cakra, there is the drop of the fourth occasion. In this practice, one has to feel that one is actually dwelling in that drop.

This practice is conjoined with the respiration. At the beginning of the inhalation, one brings one's awareness to the nostrils where the breath is coming in. As one identifies with the sambhogakāya form there, one sees it coming down the central channel with the sound *oṃ*. During the whole course of the inhalation, the deity with his consort descends, and one identifies with the movement, feeling as if one is inside an elevator and going down. One hears the sound *oṃ* all the way down.

When the elevator arrives at the drop at the navel, the deity with consort merges with that drop. That is, one comes down in the form of the deity with consort, and as soon as the figures strike the drop, they become inseparable from it. In one's mind's eye, the form of the drop vanishes, and just the two figures remain. As long as there is the inseparability of the drop and the deity with consort at the navel, one hears the sound *hūṃ*.

At the time of exhalation, the two figures come up, and as soon as they get above the level of the drop, the form of the drop re-emerges and the two deities start going up the elevator. As the deity and consort come up the central channel, the breath produces the sound *āḥ*.

One does not visualize these syllables, nor does one mentally recite them. Rather, one listens to these sounds. When one hears the sound *oṃ*, one does not have the sense that one is mentally reciting it or that it is being produced by the mind. One simply hears it. In this practice, one is blending the energies with one's mind and with the mantra.

In the beginning stages of this phase of practice, one alternates between two types of vajra recitations. The first is the one just described, from the upper aperture of the central channel down to the navel. The other is the lower vajra recitation. Here one starts the beginning inhalation at the lower aperture of the central channel and comes up from there. During that ascent, one hears the sound *oṃ*. When it gets up to the navel, one hears the sound *hūṃ*, and when it goes down again, one hears *āḥ*.

As one gets a little more accustomed to these two practices, one does them simultaneously. While energies descend from the head, other energies rise from the lower aperture of the central channel during the inhalation.

At the end of the inhalation, there is a meeting of these energies at the navel, and then they part again during the exhalation. It is like a dance. There is no specified visualization for what goes on from the navel down to the lower aperture of the central channel. Just think of that as being the vajra recitation itself.

As one becomes more advanced in this practice, the actual amount of vital energy that is expelled decreases, and more energy remains in the abdomen, at the navel. Eventually, the energy remains entirely in the navel cakra, and at that point one's external breath stops. When one gets to the point where the breath has stopped, one is ready to do the vase meditation. Generally speaking, during the stage of completion, the vase meditation should be done when the quantity of breath going through the left and right nostrils is evenly distributed. Here the breath has stopped, so there is a distinction between the general reference to the stage of completion practice and the one described here.

In this vase meditation, the life-sustaining energy that moves above the navel, and the descending energy that moves below the navel are united in the drop at the navel. Bear in mind that there is also the appearance of Kālacakra with consort.

An Analysis of Verifying Cognition in Prāṇayāma

When the mind has stabilized, the tummo fire blazes forth. As a result of the blazing of the tummo fire, the white bodhicitta at the crown of one's head melts and descends to the level of the throat, and one experiences bliss; at the level of the heart, one experiences great bliss; at the level of the navel, there arises extraordinary bliss; and at the tip of the vajra, innate bliss arises.

In Khedrub Je's writings it is stated that these blisses arise as a result of firmly conjoining the descending energy and the life-sustaining energy while steadily maintaining the appearance of deity with consort. At that point, one has completed the vase meditation and is ready to move on to the retention phase.

The Manner of Purification of the Basis

The aggregate of compositional factors is purified, and the energies flow through the central channel. The state of Amoghasiddhi is achieved in this phase of prāṇayāma.

The Temporal and Ultimate Results of Prāṇayāma

The temporal result is that the energies flow in the central channel. The ultimate result is that the left and right channels are purified, and the bodhisattvas give praise and make offerings.

Retention

The Etymology of Retention

The etymology of retention is that the energies are retained without movement in the cakras.

The Time for Practicing Retention

The time for engaging in this practice is when one has completed first the vajra recitation and then the vase meditation of the prāṇayāma phase.

The Way to Practice Retention

The way to practice retention is very similar to the preceding vase meditation in the sense that one is joining the two energies, the descending and the life-sustaining energies, and these are mixed with the appearance of the deity with consort. In our minds, we give effort to holding the energies together, but we are not giving any effort to maintaining a visualization of the deity with consort. They are simply present.

Recollect that the image of the deity with consort arises regularly as a result of the preceding phases of practice. During the phase of prāṇayāma, one is engaged in two meditations, the first being the vajra recitation and the second being the vase meditation, with one's mind focused at the navel cakra. In retention, one meditates in accord with the dissolution of the four elements, with earth dissolving into water and so forth.

The first step of the retention phase is to focus at the previous point in the navel cakra, joining the two energies and maintaining the awareness of the deity with consort. Next, one shifts the focus up to the heart. This may mean that one draws the appearance of the deity and consort and the conjoined energies up to the level of the heart. I expect that if, in this phase of practice, one directs one's awareness to the heart, then the appearance of the deity with consort will be there.

The navel cakra is associated with the earth element, and the heart cakra is associated with the water element. As one shifts the focus of one's awareness, one does so with the sense of earth dissolving into water. With the sense of water dissolving into fire, one focuses on the throat cakra. With the sense of fire dissolving into air, one shifts the focus of awareness from the throat to the forehead. With the sense of the air element dissolving into space, one shifts the awareness from the forehead to the crown of the head. With the sense of space dissolving into consciousness, one shifts the focus of the awareness from the crown of the head to the genital region.

One meditates on the unification of the two types of energy (descending and life-sustaining), one's mind, and the empty form of deity and consort, as before. As a result, one gains the ability to bring forth not merely the descending four blisses, but also the ascending four blisses. This practice should be done in conjunction with emptiness and bliss. This probably means that one should conjoin the descending and ascending four blisses with emptiness.

During the descending blisses, from the throat on down, it is said that the innate bliss cannot arise until the white bodhicitta gets to the tip of the jewel of the vajra. However, all the ascending blisses are innate bliss. One still uses the same four terms, but they are in fact all innate bliss.

It is said that in this phase of retention, before one engages in the vase meditation, one should very strongly project the thought, "I shall arise in the form of Kālacakra with consort." If one does so, then following the experience of the four blisses (including the ascending blisses), the empty form of Kālacakra with consort will appear extremely vividly, in a fashion similar to that of the actual wisdom body of Kālacakra with consort.

An Analysis of Verifying Cognition in Retention

In this process, one meditates on the indivisibility of the two types of energies. Empty form and the meditative state arise by simply directing one's mind there. When it gets to that point, one has completed the phase of retention.

The Manner of Purification of the Basis

This practice stabilizes the flowing of the energies through the central channel. The feeling aggregate is purified.

The Temporal and Ultimate Benefits of Retention

The temporal benefit of the retention phase is that one cannot be obstructed by māras and other interferences. All energies become one. The ultimate benefit is that one attains the state of Ratnasambhava. With the completion of prāṇayāma and retention one attains the speech vajra, called the intermediate virtue.

RECOLLECTION

We now begin the final virtue of recollection and samādhi.

The Etymology of Recollection

The fifth phase is called recollection because it bears a resemblance to the facsimile of empty form that occurred in the first two phases of retraction and meditative stabilization.

The Time for Practicing Recollection

As soon as the experience of the four blisses and the empty forms of Kālacakra and consort appear very vividly through meditating indivisibly on the two types of energy, one starts the phase of recollection.

The Way to Practice Recollection

In this phase, the actual forms of Kālacakra and consort appear at the navel cakra, and they radiate five-colored light in all directions.

A person of sharp faculties will experience the various blisses by means of the preceding practices of focusing on the facsimile of empty form of the consort. The experience of the blisses allows the actual empty form of the father and mother deity to arise. A person of medium faculties has to practice with a jñāna mudrā, who is visualized. The practice of a person of dull faculties requires a karma mudrā, an actual consort. The practitioner and the consort enter into union, and their energies are joined in the vase meditation. By familiarizing oneself with the bliss that arises from the melting of the bodhicitta, it is possible for the actual empty form of the father-mother deity to appear, and at this point the authentic empty form arises.

From the beginning of the completion stage practice up to and including the phase of retention, a facsimile of the empty form of deity with consort appears, and one is able to maintain the divine pride effortlessly. However, although one has those abilities, the appearance of the deity with consort in the earlier stages does not emanate rays of light from the pores of their bodies, illuminating the galaxy. Up to and including the phase of retention, focusing upon the empty form of the consort does not bring forth supreme immutable bliss. For that reason, the forms in those previous stages are called facsimiles of empty form. From this point on, when the authentic empty form of the deity with consort arises, innumerable rays of light are emanated from the pores of their bodies.

Many yoginīs are discussed in the context of Kālacakra. There are 360 life goddesses and sixty-four speech yoginīs. There are some thirty-six *icchās* (Tib. *'dod ma*) of body and speech, which are female embodiments of desire. In addition, there are mind yoginīs, which are the ten śaktīs and the five consorts in the mind maṇḍala. These yoginīs are actualized in their empty form in the recollection phase. By going into union with any one of them, one experiences immutable bliss. However, if a person of dull faculties is not able to bring forth the various types of bliss by means of these appearances to the mind, the person must practice with a karma mudrā.

As soon as one's practice is able to bring forth immutable bliss, one has completed the phase of recollection and is ready to move on to the sixth and final phase of samādhi.

An Analysis of Verifying Cognition in Recollection

By directly going into union with the consort of empty form, the first drop of fluid melts and comes down to the tip of the vajra, where it is held unwaveringly. Therefore, it is called Mahāmudrā, who gives immutable bliss. After that first drop resulting from the direct union with Mahāmudrā, the 21,600 drops are stacked from the tip of the jewel to the crown of the head. These 21,600 energies are purified, which means that they vanish. The 21,600 blisses are completed, the entire material constituent aspect is exhausted, and one manifestly attains the rainbow state of Kālacakra. As soon as that happens, one is in the samādhi phase of the practice.

The Manner of Purification of the Basis

The phase of recollection purifies the aggregate of recognition and the element of water.

The Temporal and Ultimate Results of Recollection

The temporal benefit of the phase of recollection is that one experiences the actual appearance of the empty forms of the father and mother deities. Five-colored lights emanate from the pores of that empty form. The ultimate result is that one attains the state of Amitābha, and one is praised by the bodhisattvas.

Going into union with the consort "with aspect" makes it is possible to go into union with the consort "without aspect," that is, to go into meditative equipoise focused upon emptiness that is similar to being devoid of dualistic appearance.

At the stage of retention, one unwaveringly maintains the descending energy, the life-sustaining energy, the drop of the fourth occasion, and the empty form of the deity with consort. Then, the tummo flame blazes upward, melting the white bodhicitta, which descends and leads to the four blisses. Once all that has occurred, one moves on to the phase of recollection. At that exact moment of the shift over to the recollection phase, there arises the actual empty form of the deity with consort.

In this recollection phase, one recalls the facsimile of empty form that occurred in the first two phases of retraction and meditative stabilization. But now it is the actual form and not a facsimile, and one attains the mind vajra.

Samādhi

Je Tsongkhapa says that there is no particular etymology in this context for the name of the sixth phase, samādhi. As soon as one experiences immutable bliss in dependence upon the union of the deity with consort at one's navel cakra, then one begins the transition from the recollection phase to the samādhi phase. The phase of samādhi lasts from the first moment of the experience of immutable bliss through the entire process of stacking the white bodhicitta and the experience of the 21,600 immutable blisses, until there arises the direct antidote for the most subtle of the cognitive obscurations.

The sixth phase of samādhi includes both the ordinary path and the ārya path. In the earlier part of this phase, you are still an ordinary being, not an ārya.

During the phase of samādhi, the meditative focal point is shifted from the navel cakra down to the genital region. In terms of the stacking of the drops, there are 3,600 between the tip of the jewel and the base of the genital region. At the midpoint of the jewel, the number of drops that has been stacked is 1,800. This corresponds to what is called the ground of imaginary action, and it corresponds to the bodhisattva paths of accumulation and preparation. It is called the ground of imaginary action because during that time a person is a bodhisattva but not yet an āryabodhisattva. Thus, the bodhisattva's actions are still only imagined to be chiefly directed to serving the needs of sentient beings. Because the emphasis lies in the training of the motivation at that time, it is called imaginary.

The final 1,800 of these drops act as a direct antidote for a corresponding specific karmic energy. The drops counteract the karmic energy, and in the very next moment one attains what is called the liberated path.

This resembles the attainment of the path of seeing in the Pāramitāyāna, which has two phases. The first one is called the uninterrupted path, which acts as a direct antidote to the acquired mental afflictions. Then, having eliminated these acquired mental afflictions, at the very next moment one attains the liberated path. It does not mean that one is an arhat, but it does mean that one has entered the path of seeing, whereby one becomes an ārya. According to the Cakrasaṃvara and Guhyasamāja systems, one simultaneously becomes an ārya, who directly realizes emptiness by means of one's innate mind, and an arhat, who has eliminated all acquired and inborn mental afflictions.

Simultaneous with the stacking of the white bodhicitta from the tip of the jewel to the base of the genital region, there is an inverted stacking of the red bodhicitta from the crown of the head to the forehead. The stacking process continues from the base of the genitals up to the navel cakra, and once again 3,600 white drops are stacked in the process. Simultaneous with that is an inverted stacking of the 3,600 red drops from the forehead down to the throat.

During the initial phase, due to the stacking from the tip of the jewel to the base of the genitals, one attains the first two āryabodhisattva grounds. By the stacking that occurs from the base of the genitals up to the navel cakra, one attains grounds three and four. Although one has attained four grounds, it is said that one achieves only the third ground.

This process then continues: from the level of the navel up to the heart there are another 3,600 drops; from the heart to the throat there are another 3,600 drops; from the throat to the forehead there are another 3,600 drops; and from the forehead to the crown of the head there are another 3,600 drops.

Simultaneously, there is an inverted stacking of the red bodhicitta from the forehead to the throat, from the throat to the heart, from the heart to the navel, from the navel to the base of the genitals, and finally, from the base of the genitals to the tip of the jewel.

In each of these phases one attains two grounds, for a total of twelve grounds.

Five events occur simultaneously:

- ❖ The stacking of the first white drop.
- ❖ The inverted stacking of the first red drop.
- ❖ The experience of the first immutable bliss.
- ❖ The cessation of the first of the 21,600 karmic energies.
- ❖ The cessation of the first of the 21,600 material elements.

As the material elements are exhausted, the extinguishing process goes deeper and deeper. This can be likened to a snowman that has a blue core: the superficial whiteness gets thinner and thinner, until only the blue remains. During this process, the outer and inner transparent element of one's body (Tib. *stong pa phyi gsal la nang gsal*) is the basis for one's wisdom body, and it is at the core of the body. As that starts to manifest, the material elements on the outside get thinner and thinner. Like dry ice, the material elements just vanish. Likewise, the material constituents of the body vanish totally. The material aspects of the drops that are being stacked are also extinguished. What is left over is one's full form. One has now arisen in an empty form body, which is a primordial wisdom body.

It is said that until that material element is totally exhausted, it is impossible to emanate one's empty form. When meditating, one's empty form arises, but the material constituent of the drops has not yet been extinguished, so when one rises from meditation, one's empty form vanishes.

When all of the karmic energies have been extinguished, all cognitive obscurations have been abandoned. With the purification of all the karmic energies and material elements, one attains the union of body and mind, the empty form of the deity with consort, and one attains immutable bliss. One purifies the form aggregate and the earth element. Both have a sixfold classification. One experiences immutable bliss and attains the state of Vairocana.

The temporal benefit is that the subjective mind and its objects become one. The ultimate benefit is that one attains the actual primordial wisdom vajra. It is in reference to this state that there is the praise:

Homage to the glorious Kālacakra,
Bearing the nature of emptiness and compassion,
Who is without birth or destruction in the three realms of cyclic existence,
The embodiment of unified consciousness and the objects of consciousness.

From that point on, there is no moment in which this being, the Buddha Kālacakra, is not dedicated to the welfare of sentient beings. One's body, speech, and mind pervade space. Even if we should encounter Kālacakra as the size of a sesame seed, it would still be the complete body, speech, and mind of the Kālacakra. In fact, they are always ready to be met.

The mind of Kālacakra with consort is of the same nature as emptiness, and there is nothing that is not pervaded by emptiness. The text states in the practice, "like bubbles arising from water," suggesting that the bubbles that arise are of the same nature as the water from which they arise. In a similar fashion, Kālacakra can be encountered anywhere and he takes on these forms.

This concludes a rough explanation of the stages of generation and completion of the Kālacakra practice.

As an auspicious gesture, I once again quote the initial verse of this practice:

With great adoration I take refuge in the Buddha,
The master from whom supreme empowerment is received,
The Dharma of indivisible method and wisdom that he reveals,
And the two types of Saṅgha who abide therein.

20

Questions and Answers

Q: Within the threefold classification of father, mother, and nondual tantras, where does Kālacakra fit?

A: According to Je Tsongkhapa, there is no threefold classification of tantras: there are just mother and father tantras, with no nondual tantras. I have already explained the distinction between mother tantras and father tantras. All highest yoga tantras lead to the attainment of the body of the buddha as well as the mind of the buddha. But among the different tantras there are different emphases. The tantras that emphasize the body of the buddha are called father tantras, whereas those tantras that emphasize the mind of the buddha are called mother tantras. There are no tantras that emphasize neither. All the tantras principally emphasize one or the other, but they all lead to both the body and mind of the buddha.

Q: What is the text upon which this explanation of the Kālacakra Six-Session Guru Yoga *is based? Is it Khedrub Je's commentary?*

A: There is no specific commentary to the *Kālacakra Six-Session Guru Yoga*, which was composed by His Holiness the Fourteenth Dalai Lama and versified by Kyabje Ling Rinpoche. I have been drawing from the writings of Khedrub Je and Gyeltsab Je, and the *Vimalaprabhā* as well as other texts, taking whatever I find relevant to different passages in the sādhana.

Q: Please comment on the issue of practicing even at the cost of one's life in the verse:

> *In order to liberate all sentient beings from the dangers of cyclic existence and quietism,*
> *From now until buddhahood is achieved*

I shall maintain the attitude of wishing to achieve perfect enlightenment,
And not forsake it even at the cost of my life.

Whenever I come across this verse, it always strikes me that it is very serious. It always makes me wonder what circumstances could arise that might make one hold to this commitment at the cost of one's life.

A: Let's clarify what is meant by this phrase "at the cost of my life." If someone were to ask, "What would you rather do: give up the spirit of awakening, or die?" then the appropriate response would be to opt for the latter. However, it is not very likely that someone is going to ask you this question. That being the case, why say it in the first place? The reason is that sometimes one may get discouraged and feel that it is probably impossible to carry through with this commitment. Reading that verse may pull one out of the discouragement and revitalize one's aspiration. If one actually were to relinquish this aspiration, then the commitment would be broken, and one would fall to the Hīnayāna path. It would be extremely unwholesome to turn away from that commitment.

It is said that it is nonvirtuous to turn away from concern for even one sentient being's well-being. Since the spirit of awakening is directed to the well-being of all sentient beings, to turn away from that motivation would be all that much more unwholesome. So when reciting this verse, one prays that one may maintain that commitment even in the most dire of circumstances.

Q: Having meditated on this, I had the thought that "even at the cost of my life" refers to my giving up the life that is incompatible with the spirit of awakening.

A: Good! His Holiness the Dalai Lama comments that it is inappropriate to divide one's life into a mundane portion devoted to worldly pursuits and into a Dharma portion. Rather, one should see how one can transform the mundane aspects of one's life and integrate them thoroughly into spiritual practice.

Q: When the Chinese invaded Tibet, many Tibetans were forced to give up their Buddhist vows of refuge. Some died, some committed suicide, some fled. In such a case, is it legitimate to verbally give up one's refuge in the Buddha, Dharma, and Saṅgha without actually doing so mentally?

A: There were two lamas in Tibet. One of them was the renowned tutor of Dromo Geshe Rinpoche (Tib. *gro mo dge bshes rin po che*), and the other was a monk who was the chanting leader in the Lower Tantric College in Lhasa. To the latter, the Chinese communists said, "Are you willing to renounce your respect and devotion to the Dalai Lama and his two tutors?" The lama said, "This is a very tough question. I have to really give it serious consideration. Please give me seven days to think it over."

After the seven days had passed, the lama came back to the Chinese and said, "This is a difficult question. If you ask me to speak of the excellent qualities of His Holiness the Dalai Lama and his two tutors, I could go on for months. But when you ask me to speak about their faults, I do not have anything to say at all. However, it would really be excellent if you did not kill me, because I am a little afraid of dying. But if you do kill me, then I am just going to die. Whether or not you kill me, it is just a matter of ten to fifteen years. Do what you like."

During those seven days he had requested to think over the question, he met the tutor of Dromo Geshe Rinpoche, who said, "Since in our hearts we can find no fault with His Holiness and his two tutors, it may not be so important whether or not we verbally renounce them." The chanting leader's response was to spit in disgust. He said, "You spent your whole life studying the Buddhadharma, but it does not seem that you have a drop of wisdom."

It is difficult to say what to do on such occasions, when one's life is actually being threatened. What is going to be stronger: your spirit of awakening or your fear of death? The issue is very simple. It is a matter of *when* we die, and not *whether* we die. This is what it boils down to.

By the way, the Chinese eventually released the chanting leader, whereas the tutor of Dromo Geshe Rinpoche was horribly beaten, forced to submit to a public inquisition, and then thrown into a concentration camp.

The blessing of the spirit of awakening is such that if one can maintain it like that chanting leader did, it is possible that even though people say they will kill you, they will not actually do it. In most cases of the Chinese threatening, "Either give up Dharma or we will kill you," when people responded, "I don't really want to die; you do what you have to do, but I am not giving up the Dharma," the Chinese let the people go.

Q: Please clarify the dangers of quietism in the phrase "The dangers of cyclic existence and quietism."

A: Quietism refers to nirvāṇa, which seems rather odd. On one occasion, Mañjuśrī was teaching five hundred disciples, and they were just about to attain arhatship. At that point, if they had been taught about emptiness in accordance with the Mādhyamika view, they would have succumbed to false views. Mañjuśrī saw that they could either continue on the path as they were and attain nirvāṇa, or they could be taught the Mādhyamika teachings on emptiness and be led to false views. In terms of attaining perfect enlightenment, Mañjuśrī saw that their path to awakening would be shorter if they were led to wrong views, so he gave them those teachings on emptiness. Consequently, they all did develop false views and abandoned Dharma.

The disciples of the Buddha who were aware of what had occurred were stunned by this! They reported to the Buddha that Mañjuśrī had made a great mistake by leading these people away from the very near-term attainment of arhatship to developing false views and abandoning Dharma. The Buddha responded that in fact Mañjuśrī had been very skillful, for he recognized that in the long run this would turn out to be a more direct path to perfect awakening.

By leading these five hundred to a swifter attainment of perfect awakening, each of them would be able to be of great benefit to sentient beings. This is what the Buddha had in mind when he praised Mañjuśrī. If they had attained arhatship, they would have dwelled for an extremely long time in nirvāṇa, and at the end of this long samādhi, they would have had to be aroused from it to follow the Mahāyāna path. However, after one has abided for such a long time in the state of nirvāṇa, it is very difficult to be aroused from that and to relate to sentient beings. One is so saturated with the peace of nirvāṇa that it is difficult to feel any heartfelt compassion for others. Therefore, the text speaks of the dangers of cyclic existence and the dangers of quietism, for the latter can obstruct one's attainment of perfect awakening.

If one has not already been saturated with the peace of nirvāṇa and freshly cultivates the spirit of awakening, then it takes about three countless eons until you attain buddhahood by following the Pāramitāyāna, whereas if you first attain arhatship and dwell for an immeasurably long time in nirvāṇa, and then are aroused from that and follow the Mahāyāna, it takes much longer to attain buddhahood. It takes many, many countless eons, not just three.

Q: Please explain all the kāyas of the buddha in the context of Vajrayāna and Pāramitāyāna.

A: The presentations of the four kāyas, or the four bodies of the buddha, in the two systems is about the same. It is not possible for sentient beings to encounter the jñānakāya (Tib. *ye shes chos sku*) and the svabhāvakāya (Tib. *ngo bo nyid sku*); only the buddhas can experience them. Both the jñānakāya and the svabhāvakāya are called the dharmakāya.

The dharmakāya is the awareness of all the buddhas. The ultimate, empty nature of that awareness is known as the svabhāvakāya, due to the purity of its nature, meaning its absence of inherent nature. The svabhāvakāya is also so called because of its freedom from the two types of adventitious obscurations. They are called adventitious because they are not in the essential nature of the mind; they are simply veils that can be dispelled.

The form of the buddha that is uniquely apparent to āryabodhisattvas is known as the sambhogakāya (Tib. *longs spyod rdzogs pa'i sku*). The form that appears to beings of pure karma is called the nirmāṇakāya (Tib. *sprul sku*). It is said that the four bodies of the buddha are of the same nature.

Q: Please explain the classifications of the kāyas as two, three, four, or five.

A: The classification of the five kāyas is made in terms of the five types of primordial wisdom of a buddha. The four kāyas are the nirmāṇakāya, sambhogakāya, dharmakāya, and svabhāvakāya. When the svabhāvakāya is included in the dharmakāya, then there are three bodies: the nirmāṇakāya, sambhogakāya, and dharmakāya.

Sometimes the body, speech, and mind of a buddha are referred to as the three kāyas of a buddha. There is also a twofold classification of the kāyas: the dharmakāya and rūpakāya. The latter refers to both the nirmāṇakāya and the sambhogakāya.

Q: Please clarify the classification of external, internal, and secret offerings, as well as the common and uncommon offerings.

A: The ten inner offerings and the next thirty-seven offerings are all inner offerings. They are called inner because they are part of one's being. They are not like flowers, which are outside your body. Among the inner offerings there are both common and uncommon offerings. The word *common* does not mean the offerings are vulgar or ordinary; rather, that these are offerings that are common with other tantric systems. Then there are offerings that are unique to the Kālacakra system, which are called *uncommon.* Among the outer offerings, the offerings of fruit and the great fruit are uncommon, for these are unique to Kālacakra. There are different inner offerings: some of them are common with other tantric systems and some are unique to Kālacakra.

Q: Who is Vajravega?

A: The wrathful form of Kālacakra is known as Vajravega, whereas the peaceful form is Kālacakra.

Q: How might desire for the form and formless realms arise?

A: Some non-Buddhist meditators may long for rebirth in such realms. For example, a teacher might praise the qualities of various states in the formless realm, such as infinite space, infinite consciousness, and nothingness, pointing out that you may remain in such a state for hundreds of thousands of years. To some people this may appear very attractive, and they strive in samādhi to get there. We, too, have the habitual propensities for such desire for form and formless realms.

Q: What is the distinction between wisdom (Skt. prajñā, *Tib.* shes rab*) and primordial wisdom (Skt.* jñāna, *Tib.* ye shes*)?*

A: There are important differences between the two. Wisdom is included in primordial wisdom, but primordial wisdom is not included in wisdom. Primordial wisdom refers to the realization of emptiness, whereas wisdom includes all kinds of wisdom. In some contexts, it is better translated as *intelligence,* which may come under the domination of mental afflictions. In those contexts, wisdom, or intelligence, is the faculty of the mind that is able to clearly discriminate between phenomena.

Q: It was stated that intelligence is the capacity to discriminate. It seems paradoxical that we seek in our practice to attain a type of wisdom that realizes emptiness, and while in that meditative equipoise, we cannot discriminate between phenomena.

A: Even when one attains a nonconceptual realization of emptiness, one is still focused upon a specific object. The discriminating ability that is able to distinguish is the means of gaining the realization of that particular object. It distinguishes between that which is and that which is not emptiness, and then proceeds to ascertain it.

Q: What is the nature of the innate mind that is free from conceptualization? If it is free from conceptualization, how can it give rise to conceptualization and make possible the appearances of objective and subjective phenomena?

A: One needs to understand the distinction between the manner in which something exists and the things that may arise from it. For example, in the nature of the sky itself there are no clouds, but clouds do arise from the sky. Just as the appearance of clouds does not obliterate space, and the absence of clouds does not bring about an end to space, similarly the appearance of conceptualization does not obliterate the innate mind. And the absence of conceptualization does not annihilate the innate mind.

To give another analogy: during the daytime when the sun is shining, although the light of the moon and the stars may be present, they are not seen because they are overwhelmed by the light of the sun. Similarly, when conceptualization is present, although the innate mind is present as well, it is not evident because it is overwhelmed by conceptualization.

Just as with the waning of the light of the sun, the light of the stars and the moon becomes more evident, so the waning of the strength of conceptualization causes the presence of the innate mind to become more and more evident.

Q: Are the five buddhas, the five consorts, and so forth, in their purified aspects to be taken literally? Are we made out of these deities? What should we take this to mean? When they transform, are they aspects of the mind or are they literally beings in sambhogakāya form?

A: It is said that the purified aspects of these aggregates and so forth appear in the form of these various deities, the five buddhas and consorts, and so forth. For example, as the five mental afflictions are purified as one develops along the path, their purified aspects arise in the forms of the five types of primordial wisdom. Just as one speaks of the five aggregates in their purified form appearing as the five classes of buddhas, so does one speak of the five mental afflictions in their purified form appearing as the five types of primordial wisdom. For example, it is said that the form aggregate in its purified form appears as Vairocana. Along these same lines, it is said that delusion in its purified form arises as the mirror-like wisdom.

Tantric practice is designed for specific disciples. A disciple in whom delusion is especially dominant will emphasize Vairocana, and the buddha will appear in the form of Vairocana for this disciple. If the disciple suffers predominately from pride, the buddha will appear in the form of Ratnasambhava. Similarly, the buddha will appear in the form of Amitābha to a disciple in whom desire is especially strong. For one whose main negative emotion is jealousy, the buddha will appear in the form of Amoghasiddhi. A disciple in whom anger is especially predominant will see the buddha in the form of Akṣobhya.

The fact that the buddha appears in these different forms of Akṣobhya and so forth is the result of the different capacities and predispositions of the trainees. Just as gold can take different forms yet remains gold, so from the side of the buddha there is only the wisdom of emptiness and bliss, which takes on these different forms for the sake of sentient beings.

Q: Are the drops simply conceptual constructs, or are they real physical phenomena?

A: The four drops exist whether or not you are visualizing them. As I mentioned before, they are composites of the red and white bodhicittas, which are physical. The white bodhicitta is certainly related, if not exactly identical, to semen. Similarly, the red bodhicitta is closely associated with blood and is comparable to blood. In this sense they are physical, and they exist in those four places mentioned earlier.

Q: Could we just have a few words of clarification of the meaning of the vajra body?

A: The Sanskrit word for body is kāya, which means an aggregate, or something compounded. This vajra body is called a kāya because it is created in dependence upon the accumulation of the two collections of merit and knowledge.

Vajra usually refers to diamond, and the connotation of diamond is that it is able to crush other things but is itself uncrushable. Because the vajra body is free of the two types of obscurations, nothing can vanquish it, and so it is similar to a vajra.

The vajra body is the supreme body that arises as a result of the culmination of the two collections, of merit and knowledge. Actually, the vajra body is identical to the rūpakāya, which includes both the sambhogakāya and nirmāṇakāya.

Q: Is primordial wisdom defined as the union of immutable bliss and empty form?

A: In the context of Kālacakra, at the time of fruition, primordial wisdom is inseparable from empty form. In a broader context, primordial wisdom refers to the realization of emptiness, and it is not correct to say that it is generally of the same nature as empty form. But in the Kālacakra system at the time of fruition, that is the case. In this context, that which is designated as nondual bliss and emptiness is primordial wisdom. In our present practice we simply imagine nondual bliss and emptiness, but that is not yet the actual indivisible bliss and emptiness.

Q: What is the relationship between emptiness and empty form?

A: In the context of Kālacakra, emptiness is called the "mother without aspect," for when one gains a direct realization of emptiness, it appears without aspect. In the context of Kālacakra, the term *empty form* refers to events that have apparent shape and color but are in fact free of materiality. That is the crucial point: they have no material substance. Having merely the appearances of shapes and colors, they are like rainbows. Bearing that in mind, in terms of the dual classification of ultimate truth and conventional truth, emptiness is ultimate truth, and empty form is conventional truth.

Q: Is there a relationship between the four high and very high initiations and the four kinds of bliss?

A: The terms bliss, supreme bliss, extraordinary bliss, and innate bliss are not commonly used in the Kālacakra literature, though they do appear in the sādhana. Within the Kālacakra system, the discussions of initiation and the stage of generation are different.

In the initiation, the bodhicitta descends from the crown of the head to the forehead. This is associated with bliss. When it descends from the forehead to the heart, it is associated with supreme bliss. From the heart to the genitals, it is associated with extraordinary bliss, and from the genitals to the tip of the jewel it is innate bliss.

The process in all the other tantras is different, and it is also different in the generation stage presentation even in Kālacakra. In the sādhana, when the white bodhicitta descends from the forehead to the throat, one experiences bliss; from the throat to the heart, supreme bliss; and from the heart to the navel there is extraordinary bliss. When it moves from the navel cakra to the genital cakra, which in this case is the same as the tip of the jewel, it is innate bliss.

Q: What are the eleventh and the twelfth grounds according to this system?

A: In the Pāramitāyāna, there are ten grounds, while in tantra there are eleven āryabodhisattva grounds. The name of the tenth tantric bodhisattva ground is the same as that in the Pāramitāyāna. The eleventh ground is called the "omnipresent light," and the twelfth ground is called the "incomparable." In the Pāramitāyāna, one dwelling on the tenth bodhisattva ground is called an āryabodhisattva, and on the eleventh ground one is said to be a buddha.

There are nine degrees of cognitive obscurations, ranging from gross to subtle. Of those, the ninth, the most subtle, has two facets, a grosser aspect and a more subtle facet. It is said that the Pāramitāyāna is incapable of dispelling the more subtle of those two facets of the ninth cognitive obscuration. Therefore, it is said that the buddhahood attained by means of the Pāramitāyāna is called the ground of the omnipresent light. The more subtle of those two facets of the ninth cognitive obscuration—in other words, the most subtle of cognitive obscurations—can be eliminated only by means of tantra. Through the elimination of that degree of obscuration, one attains the twelfth ground, the incomparable ground, which in fact is the ground of a buddha. The twelfth ground is explained in the context of the stage of completion.

With every set of 1,800 immutable blisses that one experiences, one attains a ground, since each set of 1,800 blisses is a direct remedy for obscurations associated with a specific ground. With each 1,800, one attains a ground. If you divide 21,600 blisses by twelve, you should come up with 1,800. In other tantric systems there are references to fifteen or sixteen grounds. These are simply different classifications of the same process of spiritual awakening.

Q: When visualizing the central channel, it is sometimes said that we are to imagine its upper half, from the navel up, as green, but elsewhere it is said we should visualize it only at the heart. Why is this?

A: Generally speaking, it is green from the navel up, but in the initial formation of these energies, the heart is the focal point. Like two tendrils, the section coming up from the heart is green, and the section going down is blue.

Q: Of the four interpretations of haṃ, *the second one corresponds to the generation stage, in which you made reference to the bardo being. It was my understanding that bardo beings are not discussed in the Kālacakra system. Please explain.*

A: This does refer to the process of the bardo being taking birth, but it is not actually a purifying agent for that bardo state. In other sādhanas, that of Yamāntaka for instance, one actually transforms the sambhogakāya into the path, and there is a separate visualization of a deity that relates to the bardo being. There is a phase in those sādhanas in which you generate yourself either as a syllable or as a deity. Then you cultivate the pride of being the sambhogakāya in order to transform that into the bardo state. This separate phase of the practice does not occur in Kālacakra.

Q: Is this a lesser purification?

A: It is not less potent. They both accomplish the task. It is just that one system can be more appropriate than another, depending on the disciples. For example, for those disciples for whom Guhyasamāja is the most appropriate, the Kālacakra system would appear inadequate. Whereas those who find the Kālacakra system most appropriate might consider the forms of meditation in the Cakrasaṃvara and Guhyasamāja systems to be superfluous in this particular phase.

Q: What is the difference between the sādhana and the six-session guru yoga?
A: This is called a six-session guru yoga because it includes all the pledges that must be kept six times a day. If you do this properly six times a day, you are keeping all these pledges.

This practice can also be called a sādhana, in the sense that you are generating yourself as a deity with consort along with the eight goddesses. First of all, you do the practice of transforming the dharmakāya into the path in reference to death. Then, as you transform the nirmāṇakāya into the path in reference to birth, you generate yourself as the deity with consort. The other practices of making offerings and reciting the mantras also entail parts of a sādhana. For a sādhana to be complete, it must have the initial stages of refuge and the spirit of awakening, at least a brief visualization of the field of merit, and guru yoga; it also has to conclude with the dedication of merit. This six-session guru yoga has all of that.

Q: Is the visualization to be done in stages? For instance, does one visualize Kālacakra first, then visualize Viśvamātā embracing him, or does one see them both at once?
A: When you read the sādhana, everything proceeds sequentially, of course. You cannot describe everything in that visualization at once. The sequence is that you generate the various parts of Kālacakra first, and then Viśvamātā.

There are different interpretations, though, of the actual meditation process. The sequential approach is one way to do it, but Khedrub Je states that it is very potent to visualize the deity with consort instantaneously, and as powerfully and as vividly as you can. His approach for beginning practitioners is to try with a great burst of the mind to create the whole thing and maintain this with intense clarity. Then, as one stabilizes in that, one can gradually fill out the details.

If one is intent on cultivating the stage of generation, then the process is to first of all generate a general visualization of the whole thing. Then, maintaining that in a rather vague fashion, give special emphasis to the two faces and the main two hands of each of the deities. Establish clarity there, while maintaining a somewhat nebulous surrounding visualization.

At that point, if the visualization of the hands is not clear, try to establish clarity of the faces and be satisfied with that. Moreover, if the whole face does not appear clearly to the mind, try to maintain a somewhat nebulous visualization of the whole face. But if some part of the face appears vividly, focus on that. Whatever appears vividly, give that special emphasis and maintain clarity in that.

When one can maintain this with clarity and continuity, one gradually extends clarity in all directions, including all the faces and all the arms, and eventually one establishes that clarity for the whole maṇḍala with its deities. According to the text, upon having fully and authentically received tantric initiation, it is possible within six months to attain a clear vision of the maṇḍala. That means that your generation of the maṇḍala, with the deities and so forth, appears to the mind's eye about as vividly as if you were looking at it. Moreover, you will be able to hold the visualization for four hours.

Q: Is there anyone nowadays who has accomplished that?
A: Maybe so. Fully and authentically receiving the initiation does much to eliminate the obscurations and unwholesome habitual propensities in the mind. Upon that basis, if one then very assiduously guards the precepts and the pledges, the clarity of one's mind is tremendously enhanced. If one does this, it seems quite possible to attain a clear vision of the maṇḍala in six months.

Remember the different eras, the era of fulfillment, the era of conflict, and so forth. It is in the era of fulfillment that people very easily attain realization. It is said that in the era of fulfillment, reciting the mantra *oṃ āḥ hūṃ ho haṃkṣamalavaraya hūṃ phaṭ* 100,000 times suffices to make the mind serviceable for the full practice of Kālacakra.

In the age of conflict, which is the present age, one needs to recite the mantra 400,000 times to make oneself serviceable for the practice, or to complete the propitiatory retreat. Bearing in mind the fourfold degeneration, it appears that if at the time of fulfillment it was possible to attain such clarity in six months, that might now take two years. To rephrase this, if people like us were to fully and authentically receive initiation and very diligently guard the precepts and pledges, there is much hope that we could attain a clear vision of the maṇḍala in two years. If one has some mental habitual propensities for this, then it could happen faster. Some people who have never meditated sit down in meditation and very swiftly gain realization. There is no way to predict the influence of hidden habitual propensities.

Q: Do we view this visualization from in front?
A: This is a self-generation. It is not something in front of you. On the other hand, think of the reflection of the moon appearing in water; liken your own mind to the water and the visualization to the moon's reflection. Just as the reflection of the moon appears in the water, so does this reflection of the visualization appear in your mind.

Q: Is a proper visualization like a solid image, or a rainbow-like, transparent image?
A: It is purely an image of light, like a hologram. You are not visualizing something solid. Remember that the whole thing is of the nature of wisdom, and that wisdom is your own wisdom. All of this is an emanation of your own mind. For everything in the maṇḍala you develop divine pride. All of these are to be regarded as displays of the primordial wisdom of bliss and emptiness. They all come from the same origin, and you identify with everything.

Q: Is there any significance in the different number of spokes in the wheels at the cakras?
A: The spokes of the wheels are in multiples of four. Usually there are eight. Symbolically, the eight-spoked wheel refers to the eight branch channels at the heart cakra.

Q: When generating the divine pride and the pure vision, do you imagine looking out from the eyes of Viśvamātā or from the perspective of Kālacakra?

A: Where are you now? Are you inside or are you outside?

Student: I am inside myself now.

A: So there are two of you? It is important to determine where you are right now. Are you inside your body or outside your body? When you think, "I am Kālacakra," you don't need to think of inside or outside. You think, "I am here," without making any distinctions of inside or outside. Why do we tend to think that we are positioned behind the eyeballs? Why is it such a persistent tendency, even while meditating, to think that we are up there in our head? It is because in terms of our experience, the visual sense is very powerful, and it is located in the head. For meditation this perspective is irrelevant.

If you imagine yourself down at the navel during the recitations, that is where you are. In fact, this tantric practice is in accord with reality, because the very subtle mind pervades all of reality. Even for ordinary experiences, as we gaze around the world, wherever the mind is, whatever is ascertained, the mind goes there. If we are looking at a mountain, the mind goes there and locks onto the mountain.

Consider the actual relationship between the mirror and the reflections in the mirror. We tend to grasp mentally onto the appearances in the mirror as if they had their own nature. We tend to view the appearances as if they were separate from the mirror, but that is not the case at all. The reflections in the mirror are inseparable from the mirror itself.

Q: Is there a correlation between karmic energies and the karmic habitual propensities?

A: There is a causal relationship between the two: that is, the karmic habitual propensities act as the cause for the karmic energies. An energy itself cannot be a propensity, and a propensity is not necessarily some kind of energy.

Unlike the Kālacakra literature, some texts of the Kagyü and Nyingma orders state that the appearances of the environment are themselves habitual propensities of energy as well as propensities of the mind. The reason for that is that the nature of the mind itself is clear and transparent. The things that arise in it are displays of its own habitual propensities.

In terms of tantra, it is correct to say that the appearances to the mind are habitual propensities of energy (Tib. *rlung gi bag chags*). For example, fire, water, earth, and air are all specific expressions of energy. Science states that the temperature of any substance determines whether it is a liquid, gas, or solid. This is analogous to the theory of Buddhist tantra. In this system, if one draws in all the karmic energy, then one draws in the whole universe.

Q: The Kālacakra system says that by means of the 21,600 immutable blisses, the 21,600 karmic energies are obliterated. Does this mean that they vanish without a trace?

A: In the Prāsaṅgika system, it is said that the extinction of the afflictive and cognitive obscurations is omniscience. It is not that they vanish and there is nothing left. Rather, their very extinction is omniscience. To relate this to the Kālacakra system, the very extinction of the 21,600 karmic energies is Kālacakra. That is to say that these energies are transformed into buddhahood, and without such a sublimation of the 21,600 karmic energies, enlightenment is impossible.

Q: What does it mean to say that "The lord of the class marks the tops of the heads of the principal deity and the entourage"?

A: Marking the top of the head in that way is sometimes called "making a seal impression." To make a seal impression generally means to make a contract, a bond, which is immutable, or sealed. This seal of immutability is symbolized by Akṣobhya on the crown of the head of the chief deity, and Vajrasattva on the crown of the heads of the consort and the śaktīs.

Recall that in the initiation, the disciples cast a flower after having entered into the maṇḍala. Where the flower lands in the maṇḍala indicates the class of buddhas in which they are to attain enlightenment, and that corresponds to the mental afflictions that are chiefly dominant in the disciples. Akṣobhya represents the overcoming of the mental affliction of hatred. As Akṣobhya appears on the crown of the head, he is appearing as one's own guru.

Q: If one is able to visualize any of these mantras at all, does it make any difference whether one visualizes them in Sanskrit, Tibetan, or English?

A: I feel that since the practice itself has been translated into English, it would be good to visualize English letters. You are reciting the whole practice in English anyway. If you were reciting the whole practice in Sanskrit, then it would be reasonable to visualize Sanskrit letters. The stream of blessing of this practice was maintained when it was translated from the Sanskrit into Tibetan. But the stream of blessings for the Sanskrit recitation vanished a long time ago. In other words, it is not a living Sanskrit tradition.

Q: Correlations have been made between the syllables and the various locations in the body, such as the heart, the throat, the forehead, and the navel, pertaining to differing elements. While reciting the mantra, should we try to attend to those locations?
A: No, you do not need to try to remember the locations of the sections of the mantra as you recite it.

Q: How many times do we recite the mantras?
A: Recite the mantra for the principal deity one hundred, two hundred, three hundred, or five hundred times, and recite the other mantras twenty-one times. You may begin by reciting the first mantra one hundred times, and if you find you want to do more, you do so and keep reciting the others twenty-one times. Finally, recite the Vajrasattva mantra once.

Q: What is the relation between compassion and immutable bliss?
A: It is said that as one cultivates compassion to a high degree, it transforms into immutable bliss. The Sanskrit word for compassion is karuṇa, which literally means "happiness blocker." The word has this etymology because compassion blocks the happiness of quietism, and by counteracting that, one is brought to a state of immutable bliss.

Q: I question the use of the adjective "immutable," for I thought there was absolutely nothing that was permanent and not in a state of flux.
A: Immutable bliss arises in dependence upon the stacking up of the drops of the white bodhicitta. Because the white bodhicitta is not being emitted but is rather stacked up, the basis of such bliss is the unmoving bodhicitta. Therefore, it is called unmovable or immutable. This does not suggest that it is noncomposite, or totally without any kind of change whatever.

Q: Please explain the verse starting with "Without transgressing even in my dreams..."
A: There are two types of moral boundaries that should not be transgressed. There are the natural, unwholesome deeds that result in negative karma whether or not you have precepts. If you kill someone, it is nonvirtuous whether or not you have taken precepts. There are also misdeeds from violating Buddhist precepts. If a monk kills someone, it is both a natural nonvirtue and a transgression of his precepts. There are two types of moral transgressions, natural and created. Natural transgressions pertain to everybody, whereas the created ones pertain only to people who have taken *pratimokṣa,* bodhisattva, or tantric precepts. For example, if one drinks alcohol and one has not taken a precept not to do so, there is no downfall, for this is not a natural moral transgression.

Q: Is there a one-to-one correspondence between the 21,600 breaths and the number of energies flowing during the day, with an average of four seconds for each breath? This seems like a normal type breath, but what happens when we go jogging and we breathe more rapidly?
A: There is a one-to-one correspondence between those breaths and the movements of the vital energies. The figure of 21,600 breaths or movements of vital energy per day is for an average person in good health.

Certainly there is a difference between a person who exercises and breathes fast and a person who is ill in bed and breathes slowly. If you breathe more times per day, which certainly is possible, it means that more of these energies course each day, and this may shorten your life. If you breathe more slowly, this may lengthen your life. This is why, for example, one does the vase breathing, which tends to slow down the breathing. It is said that one of the effects of this is increased longevity. As the signs of death occur, the number of breaths per day slowly starts to diminish. Some of the channels start to dry up, and the energies don't flow through them.

Q: Is the movement of the vital energies a closed system? As I understand it, we inhale either through the right or left nostril, corresponding to the right or left channel. These energies then go down to the navel cakra, and from there branch out and go in various proportions into the branch channels. After that, do they

go out to a certain point in the body, or do they move back and forth along the same routes? For example, is this analogous to the circulation of the blood?
A: I have checked this out very carefully, and it is not clear in the texts whether or not, after the arborization, the vital energies come back into the major channels. During the process of respiration, vital energy also goes in and out of the pores of the body.

There is also something called life-sustaining energy (Tib. *srog gi rlung*), which determines one's longevity, and this is directly associated with the breath. The other types of energies also move with the breath, but they pervade the whole body. It is not clear whether or not this is a purely cyclical process.

There are also interrelationships of the energies coursing through this whole network at the heart and at the navel cakra. How these interrelate with the gross breathing process through the nostrils is not very clear in the Kālacakra literature.

Q: Why is it necessary to start on the right side, since the earth energy flows on the left side as well?
A: It is true that all energies of the five elements also go through the left channel, but the sequence with which the energies of these elements move is opposite. On the right side the order is earth, water, fire, air, and space, and on the left side the order is space, air, fire, water, and earth. Earth comes last, and it is better to pick it up on the ascension. The session should start right when that element begins to go through the right nostril. There are six such opportunities each day.

Q: What is the basis for this presentation of the stage of completion?
A: I am relying on notes on Je Tsongkhapa's teachings on the six-phase yoga, but it is not clear who wrote them down.

Q: If you are a woman, should you focus on Kālacakra or his consort?
A: Regardless of your gender, you still generate yourself as Kālacakra, who is male. Before doing so, you dissolve your ordinary form and gender into emptiness, so regardless of your gender, you visualize yourself as Kālacakra with his consort Viśvamātā. Moreover, you generate the unified divine

pride of being Kālacakra and his consort as one, and not the pride of being Kālacakra who has a consort.

Q: Is the Kālacakra at the crown the size of a sesame seed?
A: It is not clear in the Kālacakra literature itself, but generally speaking it is said that the width of the central channel is that of a wheat straw, about one-eighth of an inch. That is the size of the central channel, and inside of that you visualize Kālacakra with consort. Generally speaking, the smaller the visualization, the more powerful it is.

Q: After you have engaged in the practice of the stage of completion and recited the dedication, do you continue to visualize yourself as Kālacakra with one face and two hands, with consort, as you go about your daily activities?
A: Yes, it is excellent to maintain that sense of identity with Kālacakra with consort in his simple form, with one face and two hands. And, as mentioned before, imagine everything as the divine palace. Repeatedly identify yourself with Kālacakra, and when you encounter other sentient beings, think of them, too, as being Kālacakra with consort, and regard your inanimate environment as being the palace of Kālacakra.

Moreover, imagine your food as ambrosia, of the nature of primordial wisdom, and your clothes also as being of the nature of such wisdom. By doing this you are cultivating pure vision, which is very powerful for accumulating merit.

As your mindfulness and introspection become more stabilized, it is also good to regard all of your speech as being mantras, and all of your bodily movements as being mudrās and dances of the deity. This, too, is a very powerful means of accruing merit.

Q: What is the difference between the empty form body and the illusory body?
A: The ways of accomplishing them are different. To accomplish the illusory body, you work with the very subtle energy. The empty form is not generated out of the very subtle energy. Rather, it is a freshly created form.

One crucial point here is that while one is still a trainee, all of one's energy is material, even the very subtle energies, which means that they are composed of particles. When you generate the empty form, this is something nonmaterial. It is a form, but it is nonmaterial in the sense that it is not composed of atoms or material particles. In that sense it is a fresh form, and it is said to be a mere appearance of the mind.

Recall that the drop at the forehead has the capacity to produce two types of phenomena. One is the impure appearance of objects, and the other is the pure appearance of objects. By means of the practice, one stops the production of impure appearance, and one thereby brings forth pure appearances. The mere aspect of the appearance of the object is empty form. It needs to be emphasized that empty form is not form in the ordinary sense. It is not material. According to Buddhist psychology, there are three types of composites: cognitive, material, and abstract phenomena. Empty form would probably fit into the category of abstract composites that are neither cognition nor form.

It can be useful to relate these points to the inseparability of the vajra body, speech, and mind. There is a more explicit relationship here than is to be found in the Cakrasaṃvara and Guhyasamāja systems.

Q: It is said on the one hand that the very subtle mind is located in the drop at the heart, and on the other hand that it pervades all of existence. Are these two statements compatible?

A: At conception, when the consciousness enters into the union of the red and white constituents of the parents, the conjunction of the three occurs at the heart of what is going to be the embryo. In the dying process, at the very moment when the energy mind entirely dissolves into the indestructible drop, the innate mind manifests. The very subtle mind, or the innate mind, may be said to be located in the indestructible drop in the sense that when the energy-mind converges into the drop at the heart, the very subtle mind manifests.

The pervasion of all existence by the innate mind is said to be inconceivable and inexpressible. That very subtle innate mind is of the same nature as the emptiness of reality. The emptiness of reality pervades everything that exists; that is, everything has emptiness as its ultimate nature. The innate mind is of the same nature as the emptiness of reality, and the emptiness of reality pervades all of existence. Therefore, it also follows that there is nothing that is not pervaded by the innate mind.

This reality is inconceivable and inexpressible, but it can be experienced. When the innate mind manifests, one cannot speak of either existence or nonexistence, for it is inexpressible. As an analogy, it is impossible to speak of the center of space, yet space pervades everything that physically exists. On many occasions, the term *innate mind* is used synonymously with emptiness, reality itself (Skt. *dharmatā*, Tib. *chos nyid*), and the absolute nature of reality (Skt. *dharmadhātu,* Tib. *chos kyi dbyings*). A mere appearance to the mind is called emptiness. Therefore, Khedrup Norzang Gyatso commented that anything that exists is a composite. According to Buddhist philosophy, this is an outrageous statement. But what he had in mind was that everything, including space itself, consists simply of appearances to the mind.

Q: You have encouraged us to maintain divine pride throughout the day. So when we begin our practice of this six-session guru yoga, we should already be imagining ourselves as Kālacakra. However, at one point the text says I am to imagine that the guru dissolves into myself, and I become of the same nature as him. Does this mean that at that point both the guru and I are Kālacakra, and we become of the same nature? Or should I begin this practice with my ordinary sense of identity?

A: It is good to cultivate the divine pride between sessions, and at the point in the sādhana where the guru Kālacakra dissolves into yourself, you imagine that Kālacakra and you are of the same nature. But in reality, you two are not yet of one nature. That occurs only upon the stage of fruition, when you have experienced the 21,600 immutable blisses and have become perfectly awakened. It is for this reason that tantra is called "transforming the result into the path." One transforms the desired result into the path by means of imagination.

Q: The offerings are very complex. How shall we imagine them while we are beginners in this practice?

A: Do not try to visualize them very clearly with everything in its place. In a general way, simply imagine offering all these things. Gradually refine your practice as your understanding and experience improve. Eventually you will be able to make the offerings of Samantabhadra, in which the whole of space is utterly filled with all kinds of intricate offerings. As beginners, we cannot even imagine the offerings that are made by Samantabhadra.

Q: If sexual desire arises while stacking the white bodhicitta, should one cultivate it, suppress it, or ignore it?
A: There are two types of mental processes here. One is desire for sexual intercourse, and the other is simply sexual bliss. It is the latter that one should conjoin with the realization of emptiness. Desire for sexual intercourse disturbs one's peace, unlike sexual bliss itself, which can be both physical and mental. This is to be conjoined with meditation on emptiness. Sexual desire should not be blocked, nor should it be cultivated. Simply meditate on emptiness. If lust arises very strongly, it is unlikely that one will be able to maintain the visualization. However, if sexual bliss arises, this would be unlikely to obscure visualization, but rather would clarify it.

Q: How does one meditate on emptiness when bliss arises?
A: If you already have some familiarity with meditating on emptiness, then you recall your former experience, abiding in that nonconceptual state. When bliss arises, you do not engage in any type of investigation into the nature of emptiness. If you start investigating, it will stir up the conceptual mind, which will then disturb the energies, and the whole experience will dissipate.

Q: How is the sixth perfection of wisdom according to the Pāramitāyāna different from the tenth perfection of primordial wisdom in the Kālacakra Tantra?
A: Generally, it is possible to cultivate the perfections only if one's practice is motivated by the spirit of awakening.

The perfection of primordial wisdom refers to the perfection of such wisdom in buddhahood, specifically a buddha's realization of emptiness. The perfection of wisdom in the Pāramitāyāna refers principally to a bodhisattva's realization of emptiness, which is imbued with the spirit of awakening.

In the Kālacakra context, the perfection of primordial wisdom is something that cannot be overcome by conceptualization, and it bears all the aspects of the speech of a buddha, which implies that it cannot be overcome by the passage of time. It also transcends the three times: the past, present, and future. Finally, the tenth perfection of primordial wisdom is Kālacakra himself, whereas the sixth perfection of wisdom occurs on the stage of generation.

Q: Does the statement that tantra can lead to enlightenment in one lifetime apply equally to men and women?
A: There is no difference. If one is a suitable practitioner, there is no distinction based on one's gender.

Q: Is there a specific time of the year when the self-initiation should be done?
A: It is done in the third Tibetan month because the fifteenth day of the third Tibetan month, being a full moon day, commemorates the day that the Buddha gave the *Kālacakra Tantra.* It covers a span of seven to eight days, with the fifteenth being in the center. Kālacakra practitioners perform the self-initiation from the eleventh to the eighteenth of the third Tibetan month.

Dedication Prayer

By the power of the unified prayers of dedicating the virtue
Of the sentient beings here and throughout space
And of all the *jinas* and *jinaputras* of the three times,
May the teachings of the jinas, the source of benefit and joy, flourish and be preserved.

May those who are sustaining the teachings have long lives, and may their virtue spread forth in all directions.
In particular, may the life of the Protector of the snowy land of Tibet remain firm,
May his thoughts reach out over the beings in Tibet,
And spread to all the nations of the world.

May all the three realms of saṃsāra become empty,
And may we swiftly achieve spiritual awakening, in which our own and others' aims are ultimately fulfilled.

May my prayers extend throughout
The outmost reaches of space,
Over the full range of all sentient beings,
And across all karma and mental afflictions.

Like the great elements such as earth,
And as constantly as space itself,
May I be a source of sustenance
For immeasurable sentient beings.

Likewise, until the realms of sentient beings
Extending throughout space
Have all achieved nirvāṇa,
May I be the basis for their sustenance.

By the blessings of the jinas and jinaputras,
By the power of the infallible dependent origination of empty appearances,
And by the strength of my pure altruism,
May all these prayers be fulfilled!

May virture and goodness prevail!

A Lucid Presentation of the Kālacakra Six-Session Guru Yoga

by

His Holiness the Fourteenth Dalai Lama

Versified by Kyabje Ling Rinpoche

Translated by B. Alan Wallace

Namo Guru Śrī Kālacakrāya

Having bowed to the original Buddha, the union of the vajra of great bliss with the aspectless mahāmudrā, I will elaborate herein the mode of practicing the very profound guru yoga in connection with the six sessions.

With great adoration I take refuge in the Buddha,
The master from whom the supreme empowerment is received,
The Dharma of indivisible method and wisdom that he reveals,
And in the two types of Saṅgha who abide therein.

From this time until enlightenment
I shall develop the spirit of awakening
And the pure resolve,
And I shall cease grasping onto *I* and *mine.* [recite 3x]

I shall cultivate loving kindness wishing that sentient beings be endowed with happiness,
Compassion wishing that they be free of suffering,
Delight in their dwelling forever in joy,
And the equanimity of impartiality. [recite 3x]

In order to liberate all sentient beings from the dangers of mundane existence and peace,
From now until buddhahood is achieved
I shall maintain the attitude of wishing to achieve perfect enlightenment,
And not forsake it even at the cost of my life.

Gurus, jinas,[19] and jinaputras,[20]
Please attend to me.
Just as the sugatas[21] of the past
Have developed the spirit of awakening
And dwelt by stages in the trainings of the bodhisattvas,
I, too, shall develop the spirit of awakening for the sake of sentient beings
And shall gradually engage
In the trainings of the bodhisattvas. [recite 3x]

Now my life is fruitful.
Human existence is well achieved.
Today I have been born in the family of the buddhas
And have become a child of the buddhas.
Now, whatever happens,
I shall embark on deeds that accord with this family,
And I shall not contaminate
This flawless, noble lineage.

Within the clear light mahāmudrā free of conceptual elaboration,
In the broad pathway of the immortal gods in front of me,
Is displayed an ocean of offering clouds of Samantabhadra,
Luminous like rainbows.

In their center, upon a jeweled throne supported by eight lions
Is a lovely lotus blossoming with a thousand petals.
On this are the discs of the moon, sun, rāhu, and kālāgni,
Upon which is the compassionate guru,

Indivisible from the Lord Kālacakra,
In whom are unified all the innumerable forms of refuge.
Bearing the brilliance of sapphire and blazing with glory,
He has one face and two hands holding a vajra and bell.

To symbolize the uncommon path of the union of method and wisdom,
He is in union with Viśvamātā, who is of the color of camphor

And holds a curved knife and skullcup.
With his right, red leg extended

And his left, white leg bent,
He dances in a hundred ways upon Māra and Rudra.
Their bodies, adorned with wondrous ornaments,
Like the expanse of space beautified by the constellations,

Stand in the midst of a blaze of five stainless lights.
The three places of their bodies are graced
With the luminous forms of syllables
Of the divine nature of the three vajras.

From the seed syllables at their hearts are emitted terrifying Vajravegas
Bearing various weapons, who draw in well a host of protectors dwelling in countless realms;
And they become of one taste with the samayasattvas,[22]
Thereby transforming into the great beings who comprise all the refuges.

Reverent homage to the guru in whom the three embodiments are indivisible:
The dharmakāya of great bliss, primordially free of conceptual elaboration,
The sambhogakāya bearing the fivefold self-illumination of primordial wisdom,
And the dance of nirmāṇakāyas in the oceans of realms of animate beings.

With a perspective free of the three spheres,[23] without attachment or depression,
For the pleasure of the compassionate guru, the supreme field of merit,
I offer billowing clouds of outer, inner, and secret offerings
Actually presented and emerging from the play of samādhi,

Six pairs of beautifully adorned, bliss-bestowing goddesses
Whose lotus hands are graced with suitable offering substances,
As well as common and uncommon offerings,

Together with my body, possessions, and accumulations of virtue.

The body, speech, and mind of myself and others, together with our possessions and virtues accumulated during the three times,
As well as the excellent, precious maṇḍala with the mass of offerings of Samantabhadra,
I raise up with my mind and offer to the guru, the chosen deity, and the Three Jewels.
Please accept them out of compassion and grant me your blessings.
Guru idaṃ ratnaṃ maṇdalakaṃ niryātayāmi

From beginningless time, due to the untamed steed of my mind
Being intoxicated by the beer of the three poisons and negligence,
I have committed sins and downfalls and caused others to do so.
In particular I have disturbed the master's mind and disobeyed his instructions,

Broken the general and specific pledges of the five buddha classes,
And have failed to keep properly the twenty-five disciplines and so on.
Each of my mistaken deeds I disclose with intense remorse,
And I resolve to restrain myself in the future.

I rejoice in the ocean of good deeds of myself and others,
From which rise a thousand bubbles of fine consequences.
Please let fall the rain of Dharma of the three vehicles
In accordance with the interests and attitudes of inferior, middling, and superior disciples.

May the coarse embodiments of the buddhas steadily continue to appear
To ordinary beings for a hundred eons without being destroyed or changed.
I dedicate my accumulation of virtue, such as this,
To be causes for the swift attainment of the state of union of Kālacakra.

From this time until enlightenment
I shall develop the spirit of awakening

And the pure resolve,
And I shall cease grasping onto *I* and *mine.*

For the sake of the three accumulations[24]
I shall practice the perfections of generosity, ethical discipline, patience, zeal, meditative stabilization, wisdom, method, prayer,
Power, and primordial wisdom.

I shall cultivate loving kindness, wishing that sentient beings be endowed with happiness,
Compassion, wishing that they be free of suffering,
Delight in their dwelling forever in joy,
And the equanimity of impartiality.

I shall beckon others well with generosity,
Engage in pleasant conversation,
Nurture them with meaningful behavior,
And give them great counsel according to their needs.

I shall eliminate the ten nonvirtues:
The three kinds of bodily actions,
The four verbal ones,
And the three kinds of mental actions.

I shall eliminate the five hindrances
That obstruct the three trainings[25]:
Remorse, lethargy, drowsiness,
Excitation, and doubt.

I shall eliminate the four afflictions
That are at the root of cyclic existence:
Attachment, hatred,
Delusion, and pride.

I shall eliminate the four contaminants

That are the cause of saṃsāra:
The contaminants of desire, of becoming,
Of ignorance, and of false views.

I shall accomplish perfect enlightenment
By means of the four doors of liberation:
Emptiness, signlessness,
Desirelessness, and nonactivity.

I pray to the compassionate guru, the synthesis of the three refuges,
Who, if relied upon, is the greatest wish-fulfilling
Source of all virtue and excellence within cyclic existence and peace:
Please bless my mindstream.
Oṃ āḥ guru vajradhara mañjuśrī vagindra sumati jñāna śasanadhara samudra śrībhadra sarva siddhi hūṃ hūṃ

Guru Kālacakra,
Please grant me the complete empowerments.
Bless me so that the four types of hindrances may be cleared away
And that the four embodiments may be achieved. [recite 3x]

From the heart of Kālacakra are emitted sugatas with their consorts
As well as the circle of the maṇḍala, and the empowering deities
Bestow the empowerments of water, crown, crown ribbon, vajra and bell,
Conduct, name, and permission.

They likewise grant the four pairs of the high and very high empowerments
As well as the supreme empowerment of the vajra master.
As a result, the channels and vital energies of the body become functional,
And I am empowered to cultivate the two stages.

I come to have the fortune of actualizing in this lifetime
The sevenfold state of Kālacakra,
In which the 21,600 karmic vital energies
And all the material elements of the body are consumed.

When I earnestly, reverently pray to you,
Guru Vajradhara,
Embodiment of all the infinite refuges,
Please bless my mindstream.

Due to the power of such fervent prayer,
My primary Guru Kālacakra
Comes to the crown of my head
And joyfully dissolves, becoming of one taste with myself.
All phenomena—causes, effects, natures, and actions—
Are primordially empty of intrinsic nature,
Like illusions and dreams.

From the sphere of emptiness, like the emergence of a bubble,
The moon, sun, rāhu, and kālāgni
Appear in the center of a lotus in blossom.
Upon them are the moon and sun, of the nature of the white and red elements,

Adorned with a garland of vowels and consonants, of the nature of the signs and symbols of a buddha.
In the center are the syllables of vital energy and the mind, *hūṃ* and *hi*,
which become unified in the form of the syllable *haṃ.*
That transforms into myself as Kālacakra,

Bearing the brilliance of sapphire and blazing with glory.
I have four faces and twenty-four hands, the first two embracing my consort
And holding a vajra and bell symbolizing the vajra of supreme, immutable bliss
And the reality of emptiness of a nature free of conceptual elaboration.

The remaining right and left lotus hands
Are graced with such hand symbols as a sword and shield.
With my right, red leg extended and my white, left leg bent,
I dance in a hundred ways

Upon Māra and Rudra.
My body, adorned with a multitude of ornaments,
Like the expanse of space beautified by the constellations,
Stands in the midst of a blaze of five stainless lights.

Facing the lord is Viśvamātā,
Of the color of camphor, with four faces and eight hands
Holding various hand symbols such as a curved knife and skullcup.
With her left leg extended, she embraces the lord.

Surrounded by the eight śaktīs upon the platforms of auspicious petals
In each of the cardinal and intermediate directions,
The principle deities emit from their hearts terrifying Vajravegas
Holding various weapons,

Who draw in well a host of protectors dwelling in countless realms;
And they become of one taste with the samayasattvas.
The empowering deities grant the initiation, and the lord of the class
Marks the tops of the heads of the principle deities and the entourage.

The seed syllables at the hearts of the principle deities and entourage
Are each surrounded by garlands of their own mantras,
Emitting a host of maṇḍala deities who serve the needs of animate beings,
Then return and dissolve into the seed syllable at their hearts.

Oṃ āḥ hūṃ ho haṃkṣamalavaraya hūṃ phaṭ
Oṃ phreṃ viśvamātā huṃ hūṃ phaṭ
Oṃ dāna pāramitā huṃ hūṃ phaṭ
Oṃ śīla pāramitā huṃ hūṃ phaṭ
Oṃ kṣānti pāramitā huṃ hūṃ phaṭ
Oṃ vīrya pāramitā huṃ hūṃ phaṭ
Oṃ dhyāna pāramitā huṃ hūṃ phaṭ
Oṃ prajñā pāramitā huṃ hūṃ phaṭ
Oṃ upāya pāramitā huṃ hūṃ phaṭ
Oṃ praṇidhāna pāramitā huṃ hūṃ phaṭ

Oṃ bala pāramitā huṃ hūṃ phaṭ
Oṃ jala pāramitā huṃ hūṃ phaṭ

Oṃ vajrasattva samayam anupālaya vajrasattva tvenopatiṣṭha dṛḍho me bhava sutoṣyo me bhava supoṣyo me bhava anurakto me bhava sarva siddhiṃ me prayaccha sarva karmeṣu ca me cittaṃ śrīyaṃ kuru hūṃ ha ha ha ha hoḥ bhagavan sarvatathāgata vajra mā me muñca vajri bhava mahāsamaya sattva āḥ hūṃ phaṭ

From my heart are emitted offering goddesses who make offerings:

Oṃ śrī kālacakra saparivāra arghaṃ pratīccha namaḥ
Oṃ śrī kālacakra saparivāra pādyaṃ pratīccha namaḥ
Oṃ śrī kālacakra saparivāra prokṣaṇaṃ pratīccha namaḥ
Oṃ śrī kālacakra saparivāra aṃcamanaṃ pratīccha namaḥ
Oṃ śrī kālacakra saparivāra puṣpe pratīccha namaḥ
Oṃ śrī kālacakra saparivāra dhūpe pratīccha namaḥ
Oṃ śrī kālacakra saparivāra āloke pratīccha namaḥ
Oṃ śrī kālacakra saparivāra gandhe pratīccha namaḥ
Oṃ śrī kālacakra saparivāra naividya pratīccha namaḥ
Oṃ śrī kālacakra saparivāra śabda pratīccha namaḥ
Oṃ śrī kālacakra maṇḍala saparivāribhyaḥ namaḥ

Homage to the glorious Kālacakra,
Having the nature of emptiness and compassion,
Who is without birth or destruction in the three realms of cyclic existence,
The embodiment of unified consciousness and the object of consciousness.

I bow to Kālacakra,
Whose embodiment is born from the immutable,
Even though the absorption of the *āli* and *kāli*
As well as such syllables as *hūṃ* and *phaṭ* have been eliminated.

I bow to Mahāmudrā,
Who transcends the reality of atoms,

Having the nature of an apparition,
And bearing all supreme qualities.

Homage to Viśvamātā,
Mother of all the buddhas,
Who has eliminated birth and destruction,
And who performs the deeds of Samantabhadra.

The śaktīs with their platforms melt into light and dissolve into myself.
I also melt into light, and from the nature of nonobjectified emptiness
I again transform into the aspect of the great Kālacakra
With one face and two hands.

From now on, for the sake of all sentient beings, who have been my mother,
I give away without reservation
My body, possessions, and the mass of virtue
That I accumulate during the three times.

Without transgressing even in my dreams
The subtle training of the pure pratimokṣa precepts,
bodhisattva precepts, and Vajrayāna precepts,
I shall practice in accordance with the instructions of the Jina.

I shall well preserve all the sublime Dharmas of scripture and realization
Included in the three vehicles and the four classes of tantras
In accordance with the meaning intended by the Jina,
And I shall completely liberate animate beings by any appropriate means.

Just as Surya and the family of sages
Achieved primordial wisdom due to this tantra,
Due to the kindness of Kālacakra may the sentient beings
Dwelling in the three types of cyclic existence do likewise.

Just as my mind-vajra is present throughout the earth
For the sake of liberating sentient beings,

Due to the power of Kālacakra may pure sentient beings
Dwell in the pure three types of cyclic existence.

May those people who, due to evil companions,
Constantly walk in the darkness of deception
And whose ways are decadent reach this path
And swiftly come to the vajra-jewel mansion.

By the power of the pure virtue derived from this,
May I, through the influence of Vajradhara,
Come to the culmination of the stages of the two-stage path,
Without ever transgressing the ethical discipline in all my lifetimes.

In summary, due to the accumulation of the mass of pure virtue
such as this,
May I soon be born in Śambhala,
The treasury of jewels, and come to the culmination
Of the stages of the path of highest yoga tantra.

In all lifetimes may I enjoy the glory of Dharma
Without ever being separated from genuine gurus,
And upon perfecting the virtues of the grounds and the paths,
May I swiftly attain the state of Vajradhara.

Charts

1. Distinctions between Kālacakra and Other Tantric Systems (ch. 3)
2. Water Initiation (ch. 8)
3. Crown Initiation (ch. 8)
4. Crown Ribbon Initiation (ch. 8)
5. Vajra and Bell Initiation (ch. 8)
6. Conduct Initiation (ch. 8)
7. Name Initiation (ch. 8)
8. Permission Initiation (ch. 8)
9. Summary of the Seven Self-Entries of a Child (ch. 8)
10. Kālacakra Self-Generation (ch. 11)
11. The Ten Nāgas (ch. 13). *See page 180.*

The data in charts 2–10 are taken from the teachings given by Gen Lamrimpa, and complemented from data given in *Kalachakra Tantra: Rite of Initiation* by Tenzin Gyatso, the Fourteenth Dalai Lama (Boston: Wisdom, 1989).

Chart 1. Distinctions between Kālacakra and Other Tantric Systems

Term	*In Kālacakra*	*In Other Tantras*
Union of Body and Mind	Body: Empty form Mind: Immutable mind*	Body: Illusory body Mind: Great bliss/ primordial wisdom
Union of Two Truths	Conventional: Empty form Ultimate: Immutable bliss	Conventional: Body Ultimate: Mind
Union of Method and Wisdom	Method: Immutable bliss Wisdom: Empty form	Method: Illusory body Wisdom: Mind

* In the union of body and mind in both Kālacakra and Guhyasamāja the mind is based on the subtle primordial energy.

Chart 2. Water Initiation

Location	*Seed*	*Symbol*	*Consort*	*Faces*	*Tathāgata*
Southeast	*i*	Sword	Tārā, black	3 Black, red, white	Vairocana
Southwest	*r*	Jewel	Paṇḍārī, red	3 Red, white, black	Amitābha
Northeast	*u*	Lotus	Māmaki, white	3 White, black, red	Ratnasambhava
Northwest	*l*	Wheel	Locanā, yellow	3 Yellow, white, black	Amoghasiddhi
	a	Vajra	Vajradhātvīśvarī, green	3 Green, red, white	Vajrasattva

Four consorts with deities reside in the primordial consciousness maṇḍala in their respective intermediate directions. Vajradhātvīśvarī resides indifferentially with Viśvamātā, but separates out to bestow the initiation.

All tathāgatas and consorts have three eyes. They are in sitting posture, embracing their respective consorts. The consorts are facing the main deity Kālacakra, and the deities have their backs to the main deity.

The primordial consciousness maṇḍala is rectangular in shape and surrounded by a balustrade of green vajras. There are four black pillars, one on each corner.

Hands	*Element*	*At*	*Seal*
6 *R:* sword, curved knife, trident *L:* shield, skull, khaṭvāṅga	Air	Navel	Amoghasiddhi
6 *R:* triple arrow, vajra hood, resounding ḍāmaru *L:* bow, vajra noose, 9-faceted jewel	Fire	Forehead	Ratnasambhava
6 *R:* mallet, spear, trident *L:* white 8-petaled lotus, mirror, rosary	Water	Throat	Amitābha
6 *R:* wheel, staff, frightening vajra *L:* conch, vajra chain, ringing bell	Earth	Heart	Vairocana
6 *R:* vajra, curved knife, axe *L:* vajra and bell, skull, head of Brahma	Space	Crown	Akṣobhya

Chart 3. Crown Initiation

Location	*Seed*	*Crown*	*Symbol*	*Tathāgata*	*Consort*
East	*i*	Blue	Sword	Amoghasiddhi, black	Locanā, yellow
South	*ṛ*	Red	Jewel	Ratnasambhava, red	Māmaki, white
North	*u*	White	Lotus	Amitābha, white	Paṇḍārī, red
West	*ḷ*	Yellow	Wheel	Vairocana, yellow	Tārā, black
	a	Green	Vajra	Akṣobhya, green	Prajñāpāramitā, blue

The four tathāgatas with consorts reside in the primordial consciousness maṇḍala in their respective main directions. Akṣobhya resides indifferentially with Kālacakra, but separates out to bestow the initiation.

All tathāgatas and consorts have three eyes. They are in sitting posture, embracing their respective consorts. The tathāgatas are facing the main deity Kālacakra, and the consorts have their backs to the main deity.

The pristine consciousness maṇḍala is rectangular in shape and surrounded by a balustrade of green vajras. There are four black pillars, one on each corner.

Faces	*Hands*	*Aggregate*	*At*	*Seal*
3 Black, red, white	6 *R:* sword, curved knife, trident *L:* shield, skullcup, khaṭvāṅga	Compositional factors	Heart	Amoghasiddhi
3 Red, white, black	6 *R:* triple arrow, vajra hook, resounding ḍāmaru, *L:* bow, vajra noose, 9-faceted jewel	Feeling	Throat	Ratnasambhava
3 White, black, red	6 *R:* mallet, spear, trident *L:* 8-petaled lotus, wheel, rosary	Recognition	Forehead	Amitābha
3 Yellow, black, white	6 *R:* wheel, club, frightening vajra *L:* conch, vajra chain, ringing bell	Form	Navel	Vairocana
3 Green, red, white	6 *R:* vajra, curved knife, axe *L:* vajra and bell, skull, head of Brahma	Consciousness	Crown	Vajrasattva

Chart 4. Crown Ribbon Initiation

Location	*Seed*	*Symbol*	*Śaktī*	*Faces*
East	*a*	Vessel of incense	Kṛṣṇadīptā, Black Blazer (Tib. *nag mo 'bar ma*)	4 Black, red, yellow, white
South	*āḥ*	Butter lamp	Raktadīptā, Red Blazer (Tib. *dmar mo 'bar ma*)	4 Red, yellow, white, blue
North	*aṃ*	Food	Śvetādīptā, White Blazer (Tib. *dkar mo 'bar ma*)	4 White, black, red, yellow
West	*ā*	Conch	Pītadīptā, Yellow Blazer (Tib. *ser mo 'bar ma*)	4 Yellow, white, blue, red

This initiation is bestowed by the ten śaktīs, residing in the maṇḍala of great bliss on the eight petals of the lotus in their respective main and intermediate directions. The śaktīs have three eyes and five mudrās, and a crown with Vajrasattva. They reside in the posture of equality. The śaktīs are also called the ten pāramitās or the ten perfections.

Hands	*Ribbon*	*Energy*	*Pāramitā*
8 *R:* containers for incense, sandalwood and saffron, camphor, musk *L:* bell, lotus, celestial tree, flower garland	Black	Fire-accompanying	Dhyāna
8 *R:* butter lamp, jewel necklace, crown, bracelets *L:* garment, belt, earring, anklets	Red	Ascending	Upāya
8 *R:* vessels for milk, water, supreme medicine, beer *L:* vessels for ambrosia, taste of siddhi, arura fruit, food	White	Pervasive	Pranidhana
8 *R:* conch, flute, jewel, ḍāmaru *L:* guitar, drum, gong, trumpet	Yellow	Nāga	Bala

continued on next page

Chart 4. Crown Ribbon Initiation, cont'd.

Location	*Seed*	*Symbol*	*Śaktī*	*Faces*
Southeast	*ha*	Black yak-tail fan	Dhūmā, Black Fan Lady (Tib. *du ba ma*)	4 Black, red, yellow, white
Southwest	*haḥ*	Red yak-tail fan	Marīci, Red Fan Lady (Tib. *smig sgyu ma*)	4 Red, yellow, white, blue
Northeast	*haṃ*	White yak-tail fan	Khagamanā, White Fan Lady (Tib. *mkha' snang ma*)	4 White, black, red, yellow
Northwest	*hā*	Yellow yak-tail fan	Pradīpā, Yellow Fan Lady (Tib. *mar me ma*)	4 Yellow, white, blue, red
The remaining śaktīs are:				
	ho		Vajradhātvīśvarī, green	3 Green, red, white
	phreṃ		Viśvamātā, blue	3 Blue, white, red

Chart 5. Vajra and Bell Initiation

Location	*Seed*	*Implement*	*Deity*	*Color*
Top of maṇḍala	*hūṃ*	Vajra	Kālacakra	blue
	phreṃ	Bell	Viśvamātā	saffron color

Hands	*Ribbon*	*Energy*	*Pāramitā*
8 All holding black yak-tail fans	Black	Turtle	Dāna
8 All holding red yak-tail fans	Red	Lizard	Śīla
8 All holding white yak-tail fans	White	Devadatta	Kṣānti
8 All holding yellow yak-tail fans	Yellow	Dhanaṃjaya	Virya
6 *R:* vajra, curved knife, axe *L:* vajra bell, skull, head of Brahma	Blue	Life-sustaining	Jñāna
6 *R:* vajra, bell, axe *L:* bell, skull, head of Brahma	Green	Descending	Prajñā

Faces	*Hands*	*Purifies*	*Seal*
1	2 hands holding vajra and bell	Right channel	Akṣobhya
1	2 hands holding curved knife and skullcup	Left channel	Vajrasattva

Chart 6. Conduct Initiation

Location	*Seed*	*Symbol*	*Bodhisattva*	*Consort*
Right side of door				
East	*e*	Sword	Ākāśagarbha, black	Gandhavajrā, yellow
South	*ar*	Jewel	Kṣitigarbha, red	Rūpavajrā, white
North	*o*	Lotus	Avalokiteśvara, white	Rasavajrā, red
West	*al*	Wheel	Viṣkambhī, black	Sparśavajrā, yellow
Left side of door				
East	*am*	Vajra	Samantabhadra, blue	Dharmadhātuvajrā, green
South	*a*	Vajra	Vajrapāṇi, green	Śabdavajrā, blue

This initiation is bestowed by the six male bodhisattvas and the six female bodhisattvas, each in dual aspect, that is, twelve pairs. They are residing in the mind maṇḍala, left and right of the respective doors and in the four corners.

Faces	*Hands*	*Seal*	*Purifying*
3 Black, red, white	6 *R:* sword, curved knife, trident *L:* shield skull, khaṭvāṅga	Amoghasiddhi	Nose faculty
3 Red, white, black	6 *R:* triple arrow, vajra hook, resounding ḍāmaru *L:* bow, vajra noose, jewel	Ratnasambhava	Eye faculty
3 White, black, red	6 *R:* mallet, spear, trident *L:* 100-petaled lotus, mirror, rosary	Amitābha	Tongue faculty
3 Yellow, white, black	6 *R:* wheel, staff, frightful vajra *L:* conch, vajra chain, resounding bell	Vairocana	Body faculty
3 Blue, red, white	6 *R:* vajra, curved knife, axe *L:* bell, skull, head of Brahma	Akṣobhya	Mental faculty
3 Green, red, white	6 *R:* vajra, curved knife, axe *L:* bell, skull, head of Brahma	Vajrasattva	Ear faculty

continued on next page

Chart 6 Conduct Initiation, cont'd.

Location	*Seed*	*Symbol*	*Bodhisattva*	*Consort*
North	*ah*	Vajra	Śabdavajrā, blue	Vajrapāṇi, green
West	*a*	Vajra	Dharmadhātuvajrā, green	Samantabhadra, blue
Corners				
Southeast	*ai*	Sword	Sparśavajrā, yellow	Viṣkambhī, black
Southwest	*ar*	Jewel	Rasavajrā, red	Avalokiteśvara, white
Northeast	*au*	Lotus	Rūpavajrā, white	Kṣitigarbha, red
Northwest	*al*	Wheel	Gandhavajrā, yellow	Ākāśagarbha, black

Face	*Hands*	*Seal*	*Purifying*
3 Blue, red, white	6 *R:* vajra, curved knife, axe *L:* bell, skull, head of Brahma	Akṣobhya	Sound
3 Green, red, white	6 *R:* vajra, curved knife, axe *L:* bell, skull, head of Brahma	Vajrasattva	Mental objects
3 Black, red, white	6 *R:* sword, curved knife, trident *L:* shield, skull, khaṭvāṅga	Amoghasiddhi	Touch
3 Red, white, black	6 *R:* triple arrow, vajra hook, resounding ḍāmaru *L:* bow, vajra noose, 9-faceted jewel	Ratnasambhava	Taste
3 White, black, red	6 *R:* mallet, spear, trident *L:* 100-petaled lotus, mirror, rosary	Amitābha	Visual forms
3 Yellow, white, black	6 *R:* wheel, staff, frightful vajra *L:* conch, vajra chain, ringing bell	Vairocana	Smell

Chart 7. Name Initiation

Location	*Seed*	*Symbol*	*Wrathful Deity*	*Consort*	*Faces*
East	*ya*	Sword	Vighnāntaka, black	Stambhani *(see below)*	3 Black, red, white
	(*lā*	Wheel		Stambhani, yellow	3 Yellow, white, black
South	*ra*	Jewel	Prajñāntaka, red	Māninī *(see below)*	3 Red, white, black
	(*vā*	Lotus		Māninī, white	3 White, black, red
North	*va*	Lotus	Padmāntaka, white	Ḍombinī *(see below)*	3 White, black, red
	(*rā*	Jewel		Ḍombinī, red	3 Red, white, black

This initiation is bestowed by the six male and the six female wrathful deities (Skt. *krodhas*, Tib. *khro bo* [pronounced *trowos*] and *khro mo* [pronounced *tromos*]), that is, six pairs. Four deities with consorts reside in the doorways of the mind maṇḍala, one deity with consort resides above the eastern door of the mind maṇḍala, and one deity with consort resides in the body maṇḍala.

Hands	*Seal*	*Purifying*
6 *R:* word, curved knife, trident *L:* shield, skull, khaṭvāṅga	Amoghasiddhi	Mouth faculty
6 *R:* wheel, staff, frightful vajra *L:* conch, vajra chain, resounding bell)	Vairocana	Talking
6 *R:* 3 arrows, vajra hook, resounding ḍāmaru *L:* bow, vajra noose, 9-faceted jewel	Ratnasambhava	Arm faculty
6 *R:* mallet, spear, trident *L:* 100-petaled lotus, mirror, rosary)	Amitābha	Taking
6 *R:* mallet, spear, trident *L:* 100-petaled lotus, mirror, rosary	Amitābha	Leg faculty
6 *R:* 3 arrows, vajra hook, resounding ḍāmaru *L:* bow, noose, 9-faceted jewel)	Ratnasambhava	Going

continued on next page

Chart 7. Name Initiation, cont'd.

Location	*Seed*	*Symbol*	*Wrathful Deity*	*Consort*	*Faces*
West	*la*	Wheel	Yamāntaka, yellow	Ativīryā *(see below)*	3 Yellow, white, black
	(*yā*	Sword		Ativīryā, black	3 Black, red, white
Above East door	*ha*	Vajra	Uṣṇīṣacakravārtin, green	Atinīlā *(see below)*	3 Green, red, white
	(*haḥ*	Vajra		Atinīlā, blue	3 Blue, red, white
Body maṇḍala	*ham*	Vajra	Sumbharāja, blue	Raudrākṣī *(see below)*	3 Blue, red, white
	(*hā*	Vajra		Raudrākṣī, green	3 Green, red, white

Chart 8. Permission Initiation

Seed	*Symbol*	*Deity*	*Consort*
haṃ	Vajra	Vajrasattva, blue	Vajradhātvīśvarī
kṣa	Vajra	Prajñāpāramitā, blue	Akṣobhya

This initiation is bestowed by Vajrasattva and Prajñāpāramitā, residing in the great bliss maṇḍala. In the maṇḍala, Vajrasattva resides on Kālacakra's head, and Prajñāpāramitā is fused with Kālacakra's consort, Viśvamātā.

Hands	*Seal*	*Purifying*
6 *R:* wheel, staff, frightful vajra *L:* conch, vajra chain, bell	Vairocana	Defecation faculty
6 *R:* sword, curved knife, trident *L:* shield, skull, white khaṭvāṅga)	Amoghasiddhi	Defecating
6 *R:* vajra, curved knife, axe *L:* bell, skull, head of Brahma	Vajrasattva	Urination faculty
6 *R:* vajra, curved knife, axe *L:* bell, skull, head of Brahma)	Akṣobhya	Urinating
6 *R:* vajra, curved knife, axe *L:* bell, skull, head of Brahma	Akṣobhya	Supreme faculty
6 *R:* vajra, curved knife, axe *L:* vajra and bell, skull, head of Brahma)	Vajrasattva	Emitting semen

Seal	*Purifying*
Akṣobhya	Primordial wisdom aggregate
Akṣobhya	Consciousness element

Chart 9. Summary of the Seven Self-Entries of a Child

Initiation	*Location*	*Residing*	*Deities*	*Implement*
Water	White, Facing North	Primordial consciousness maṇḍala	5 consorts with deities	Vase
Crown			5 tathāgatas	Crowns
Crown Ribbon	Red, Facing South	Great bliss maṇḍala	10 śaktīs	Silk ribbon
Vajra & Bell			Kālacakra Viśvamātā	Vajra & bell

Purification	*Purifying*	*Brings Forth*
Five Elements	Drop at forehead,	Vajra body
1 earth	Waking state	
2 water		
3 fire		
4 wind		
5 space		
Five Aggregates		
6 form		
7 feeling		
8 recognition		
9 compositional factors		
10 consciousness		
Ten Energies	Drop at throat,	Vajra speech
11 fire accompanying	Dream state	
12 ascending		
13 pervasive		
14 life-sustaining		
15 descending		
16 nāga		
17 turtle		
18 lizard		
19 devadatta		
20 dhanaṃjaya		
Two Side Channels		
21 left channel		
22 right channel		

continued on next page

Chart 9. Summary of the Seven Self-entries of a Child, cont'd.

Initiation	*Location*	*Residing*	*Deities*	*Implement*
Conduct	Black, Facing East	Mind maṇḍala	6 male & 6 female bodhisattvas	Thumb ring
Name			6 male & 6 female krodhas	Bracelets/ anklets
Permission	Yellow, Facing West	Great bliss maṇḍala	Vajrasattva Prajñāpāramitā	Hand symbols

Purification	*Purifying*	*Brings Forth*
Six Sense Bases/Faculties 23 eye and form 24 ear and sound 25 nose and smell 26 tongue and taste 27 body and touch 28 mental sense and objects **Six Actions/Activities** 29 mouth/talking 30 arms/taking 31 legs/walking 32 defecation/defecating 33 urination/urinating 34 supreme faculty/emitting semen	Drop at heart Deep sleep state	Vajra mind
Two Factors of Wisdom 35 aggregate of primordial wisdom 36 element of consciousness	Drop at navel, Fourth occasion	Vajra primordial wisdom

Chart 10. Kālacakra Self-Generation

Kālacakra

Arising from the syllable *haṃ*

Blue in color

4 faces	Black, red, yellow, white. All faces have 3 eyes.

5-paneled crown of tresses

On top of the head is a crown of tresses, upon that an eight-spoked wheel, the hair coming through the spokes. In the center of the wheel is Akṣobhya. Five of the eight spokes point to the front and the sides. On the tip of these five are panels. On top of the crown of tresses is a four-pronged, variegated, crossed vajra, standing vertically.

6 mudrās	Vajra earrings, vajra bracelets, armlets, and anklets, vajra chest ornament, vajra belt, vajra scarf and vajra rosary, finger markings
3 throats	Center black, right red, left white
6 shoulders	Two front ones blue, two middle ones yellow, two back ones white
12 upper arms	First two black, second two red, back two white
24 lower arms	(From bottom) first eight black, second eight red, third eight white
24 hands	Outside of thumb yellow, index finger white, middle finger red, ring finger black, little finger green. Insides of first joints black, middle red, last white. Adorned with rings and emitting light.

Hand implements (from bottom)

8 blue hands	*R:* vajra, sword, trident, curved knife *L:* bell, shield, khaṭvāṅga, skullcup with blood
8 red hands	*R:* 3 fire arrows, vajra hook, resounding ḍāmaru, hammer *L:* bow, lasso, jewel, white lotus
8 white hands	*R:* wheel, spear, club, axe *L:* conch, mirror, vajra chain, 4-faced head of Brahma

Right red leg outstretched

White leg slightly bent

Right foot over Māra, red god of desire, one face
4 hands, holding 5 flower-like arrows, bow, lasso, iron hook

Left foot over Rudra, white, one face, 3 eyes
4 hands, holding trident, ḍāmaru, skullcup, khaṭvāṅga

Consorts of Māra and Rudra, Priyā and Madhyamā, hold on to Kālacakra's heels with lowered heads.

Viśvamātā

Arises from the syllable *phreṃ* in front of Kālacakra	
Saffron color	
4 faces	Yellow, white, blue, red. All have 3 eyes.
Crown with Vajrasattva	
5 types of mudrās (ornaments)	
8 hands	*R:* curved knife, hook, drumming ḍāmaru, rosary *L:* skullcup, lasso, white hundred-petaled lotus, jewel

Fused with Kālacakra

Akṣobhya	Green
Consort	Prajñāpāramitā
3 faces	Green, red, white
6 hands	*R:* vajra, curved knife, axe *L:* vajra bell, skull, head of Brahma
Vajrasattva	Blue
Consort	Dharmadhātuvajrā
3 faces	Blue, red, white
6 hands	*R:* vajra, curved knife, axe *L:* vajra bell, skull, head of Brahma

Fused with Viśvamātā

Vajradhātvīśvarī	Green
Consort	Vajrasattva
3 faces	Green, red, white
6 hands	*R:* vajra, curved knife, axe *L:* bell, skull, head of Brahma
Prajñāpāramitā	Blue
Consort	Akṣobhya
3 faces	Blue, red, white
6 hands	*R:* vajra, curved knife, axe *L:* bell, skull, head of Brahma

Glossary

(Skt. = Sanskrit; Tib. = Tibetan)

actions of power. Also called the four types of enlightened activity (Tib. *'phrin las bzhi*): (1) activity of peace; (2) activity of increase; (3) activity of power; (4) activity of wrath/force.

afflictive obscurations (Skt. *kleśāvaraṇa,* Tib. *nyon sgrib*). Obstacles to liberation.

ārya (Skt.). This is translated as *superior being* and refers to a person who has directly realized emptiness. There are four types of superior beings: the superior hearers and the superior solitary conquerors (Skt. *pratyekabuddha*) of the Hīnayāna lineage, and the superior bodhisattvas and superior buddhas of the Mahāyāna lineage. In all cases, one first becomes a superior being by developing a direct realization of emptiness. In this sense, all superior beings are born from emptiness and the wisdom that realizes emptiness. *Tibetan Buddhism from the Ground Up,* B. Alan Wallace (Boston: Wisdom, 1993), 5–6.

bhaga (Skt.). Refers to the womb.

bodhicitta (Skt.). In Tibetan, *byang chub kyi sems.* Translated here as the altruistic spirit of awakening. Ultimate or absolute bodhicitta is the union of emptiness and compassion, the essential nature of the spirit of awakening. Relative bodhicitta is the tenderness arising from a glimpse of ultimate bodhicitta that inspires one to train oneself to work for the benefit of others. In tantra, bodhicitta also refers to the subtle liquid energy, or drops (Skt. *bindu,* Tib. *thig le*), that exists in the channels of the body.

bodhisattva (Skt.). One in whom the spirit of awakening arises effortlessly.

cognitive obscurations (Skt. *jñeyāvaraṇa*, Tib. *shes sgrib*). Knowledge obstructions; obstacles to omniscience.

eight great siddhis. Also called the eight powers of the buddha: (1) body of the buddha; (2) speech of the buddha; (3) mind of the buddha; (4) magical power; (5) mastery over the three times and nirvāṇa and saṃsāra; (6) all fulfilling power, which means satisfying the needs of beings; (7) power of good qualities; (8) power of deeds.

eight worldly dharmas. The eight worldly concerns: (1) pleasure derived from gaining something; (2) displeasure at not gaining an object of desire.; (3) happiness caused by worldly pleasures; (4) sadness caused by displeasure; (5) pleasure at being praised; (6) displeasure at being abused or degraded; (7) pleasure at hearing pleasing words about relatives, friends, etc.; (8) displeasure at hearing unpleasant speech.

five aggregates (Skt. *skandha*, Tib. *phung po*). The components of the psychophysical personality on the basis of which beings commonly impute the false notion of self. They are: (1) form; (2) feeling; (3) discrimination or recognition; (4) consciousness; and (5) compositional factors or mental formations.

four defeats. (1) Killing human beings; (2) stealing; (3) sexual misconduct; (4) lying.

four means of assembly. (1) Give to disciples things they need; (2) say pleasant things; (3) work for their welfare; (4) be consistent in word and deed.

four remedial powers. Also called the four opponent powers: (1) disclosure or the power of object; (2) power of regret or remorse; (3) power of restraint; (4) power of the antidote, or purification. Purification entails (a) recitation of the one-hundred-syllable mantra; (b) prostration; (c) meditation on emptiness; and (d) meditation on compassion.

great compassion (Skt. *mahā karuṇa*, Tib. *snying rje chen po*). The root of the Mahāyāna and Vajrayāna paths. It engenders the intense desire to free others from suffering based on the realization of the essential identitylessness and interdependence of all beings, engendering spontaneous actions to eliminate beings' sufferings and bring them to the highest spiritual awakening.

Hīnayāna and *Mahāyāna* (Skt.). These terms are translated by Robert Thurman as Individual Vehicle and Universal Vehicle.

kleśa (Skt.). In Tibetan, *nyon mongs.* Mental distortion or affliction.

mudrā (Skt.). This term translates as *seal.* It refers to consorts or to specific ritual hand gestures. It can also refer to the ornaments of a deity.

maṇḍala (Skt.). In Tibetan, *dkyil 'khor.* The purified environment of a tantric deity; the diagram or painting representing this.

posture of Vairocana. The seven point posture of Vairocana: (1) lotus position, or half-lotus position; (2) right hand placed upon left hand with thumbs touching at level of navel; (3) arms bent bow-shaped; (4) back straight, to keep channels straight; (5) head slightly inclined forward; (6) tip of tongue touching roof of mouth to prevent saliva from forming and making you thirsty; (7) eyes gazing down about one foot in front of knees.

renunciation (Skt. *niḥsaraṇa,* Tib. *nges 'byung*). Other translations are emergent mind or spirit of emergence. It is the attitude of wishing to be rid of the sufferings of cyclic existence and their causes, and to attain liberation.

samādhi (Skt.). In Tibetan, *ting nge 'dzin.* Literally, mental stabilization. The state of deep meditative absorption of the yogi or yoginī who has achieved single-pointed concentration, which is the ability to focus effortlessly and for as long as one wishes on an object of meditation.

śamatha (Skt.). In Tibetan, *zhi gnas.* Meditative quiescence or calm abiding. A form of meditation that creates a stable mind capable of focusing single-pointedly on emptiness or any other phenomenon. *Calming the Mind,* Gen Lamrimpa (Ithaca, N.Y.: Snow Lion, 1995), 146.

seven-limb devotion (Tib. *yan lag bdun pa*). Also called the seven-limb pūjā: (1) prostration (Tib. *phyag 'tshal ba*); (2) offering (Tib. *mchod pa*); (3) disclosure (Tib. *bshags pa*); (4) rejoicing (Tib. *rjes su yi rang*); (5) entreaty (Tib. *bskul ba*); (6) supplication (Tib. *gsol ba 'debs*); (7) dedication (Tib. *bsngo ba*).

Śrāvakayana (Skt.). The Way of the Hearers.

six perfections. They are: (1) generosity; (2) ethical discipline; (3) patience; (4) zeal; (5) meditation; (6) wisdom. In tantra there are ten perfections. To the above six are added: (7) skillful means; (8) prayer or aspiration; (9) power; (10) primordial wisdom.

stream-enterer. One of the four levels of the Śrāvakayana, or the Way of the Hearers, which includes stream-enterer, once-returner, never-returner, and arhat.

tathāgata (Skt.). Term meaning "ones gone thus," or paraphrased as "one who has become one with the essence of what is."

ten energies. (1) Life-sustaining; (2) descending; (3) fire-accompanying; (4) ascending; (5) pervasive; (6) nāga; (7) turtle; (8) lizard; (9) devadatta, or gift of god; (10) dhanaṃjaya or victory over wealth.

ten nonvirtuous acts. (1) Killing; (2) stealing, taking what is not given; (3) sexual misconduct; (4) lying; (5) divisive talk; (6) verbal abuse, harsh words; (7) idle or senseless speech; (8) covetousness; (9) ill will; (10) wrong view. The ten virtuous acts are to refrain from the above.

torma (Tib. *gtor ma*). A type of religious offering.

tummo (Tib. *gtum mo*). Literally, ferocious female; also called inner fire. This term refers to a completion stage tantric meditation technique for bringing all the vital energies into the central channel. *The Bliss of Inner Fire*, Lama Thubten Yeshe (Boston: Wisdom, 1998), 206.

twelve links of dependent origination. (1) Ignorance; (2) karma; (3) consciousness; (4) name and form; (5) six sources; (6) contact; (7) feeling; (8) desire and craving; (9) grasping; (10) becoming; (11) rebirth; (12) death with aging and without aging.

Notes

(*trans.* = translator's note; all others are editor's notes)

1 In this book, the term *Kālacakra Tantra* refers to the Kālacakra literature, in particular, the *Kālacakra Mūlatantra,* or *Root Tantra* (also known as the *Paramādibuddha*), taught to King Sucandra of Śambhala by the Buddha Śākyamuni in his manifestation as the deity Kālacakra; the *Kālacakra Laghutantra,* or *Condensed Tantra,* composed by Yaśas Mañjuśri, the first of the twenty-one Kalkī Kings of Śambhala; and the *Vimalaprabhā,* or *Stainless Light,* a commentary on the *Condensed Tantra* composed by Yaśas Mañjuśri's son.

2 For a detailed explanation of the Vajrasattva practice, refer to *The Preliminary Practices of Tibetan Buddhism,* Geshe Rabten, Library of Tibetan Works and Archives, Reprint 1982, 79-85.

3 For an explanation of the distinction between empty form body and illusory body, please see chapter 20.

4 In the Tibetan calendar, the number of days in a year varies from year to year. The number 360 is merely an average.

5 *Mudrā* is a Sanskrit term meaning *seal.* It can also refer to ritual hand movements, or consorts.

6 Bodhicitta in this sense refers to energy drops (Skt. *bindu,* Tib. *thig le*).

7 The nineteen pledges of the five buddha classes are described in the confession part of the seven-limb devotion in chapter 5.

8 To facilitate understanding of the four nonvirtuous actions and the four virtuous actions, each nonvirtuous and virtuous action is discussed together. Traditionally in the teachings, the four nonvirtuous actions are explained first, and the four virtuous actions are explained after that.

9 For a further description of Vajravega, see chapter 13.

10 "In terms of the bases" refers to practitioners of Dharma.

11 The Tibetan word *byin rlabs* (pronounced *jin lap*) is translated as blessings. It has two syllables: byin refers to power, and rlabs refers to transformation. It means to transform into power. *Trans.*

12 The Tibetan term *zag pa* is translated as defilement, contaminant, or taint. In Tibetan it literally means to fall. The etymology is that a person falls into miserable states of existence and into the cycle of existence because a person is endowed with contaminants. *Trans.*

13 Lama Thubten Yeshe describes drops as red and white subtle liquid energy that exists throughout the channels of the body. The drops are always together in all the channels, but the red female drops predominate at the navel cakra, and the male white drops at the crown cakra. The Sanskrit word for drops is bindu; in Tibetan, drops are called thig le. In the tantras, drops are also referred to as *kun da lta bu byang sems,* literally, "moon-like bodhicitta," or simply "bodhicitta." (*The Bliss of Inner Fire,* Lama Thubten Yeshe [Boston: Wisdom, 1998], 84, 206–207.) In Tibetan, *byang sems* (pronounced *jang sem*) refers to the Sanskrit word bodhicitta, translated here as the spirit of awakening.

14 For a detailed description of khaṭvāṅga, see the section enumerating the hand implements of Kālacakra in chapter 11. In Tibetan, the Sanskrit word is used. To quote Chandra Das: "the Tantric staff with three skulls piled one above another at the top, the lowest resting on a pot. This was originally introduced into Tibet by Padma Sambhava." *A Tibetan-English Dictionary* (Delhi: Book Faith India, Reprint 1995).

15 When speaking of the subjective and objective, the usual translation is *yul* as objective and *yul can* (pronounced *yul chen*) as subjective. In this case, however, the words are *gzungs* (pronounced *zung*) and *'dzin* (pronounced *dzin*); gzungs means that which is apprehended, 'dzin, that which apprehends. So, gzungs, that which is apprehended, I am translating as objective energies, and 'dzin, that which apprehends, I am translating as subjective energies. *Trans.*

16 Generation through the five purifications is further explained in chapter 11 in the section on the process of birth, the generation of the consort, and the generation of the eight śaktīs.

17 The Tibetan word for transformation, *gnas 'gyur,* literally means a shifting, a movement of status or place, similar to the transformation of a seed into a sprout.

18 The six-fold presentation is not used in the phase of samādhi.

19 An epithet of the buddhas, literally meaning "the Victorious Ones."

20 An epithet of the bodhisattvas, literally meaning "the Sons of the Victorious Ones."

21 An epithet of the buddhas, literally meaning "the Well-Gone Ones."

22 Literally, "pledge beings," these are the beings who are originally visualized, into whom merge the jñānasattvas, or primordial wisdom beings.

23 These refer to the inherent existence of an agent, action, and object of the action.

24 Merit, ethics, and primordial wisdom.

25 These are the trainings in ethical discipline, samādhi, and wisdom.

Bibliography

"P.," standing for "Peking edition," refers to Suzuki, Daisetz T. (ed.), *The Tibetan Tripitaka: Peking Edition* (Tokyo-Kyoto: Tibetan Tripitaka Research Foundation, 1961).

"Tōh.," standing for "Tōhoku catalog" to the *sde dge* edition, refers to Hakuju Ui (ed.), *Complete Catalogue of the Tibetan Buddhist Canons* (Sendai, Japan: Tōhoku Imperial University, 1934).

Sūtras and Tantras

Kālacakra Root Tantra (Mūlatantra)
(not extant)

Kālacakra Condensed Tantra (Laghutantra)
paramādibuddhoddhṛta-śrīkālacakra-nāma-tantra-rāja
mchog gi dang po'i sangs rgyas las phyung ba rgyud kyi rgyal po dpal dus kyi 'khor lo
P. 4; Tōh. 362
Sanskrit edition: *Kālacakra-Tantra And Other Texts,* 2 vols. Edited by Raghu Vira and Lokesh Chandra (New Delhi: International Academy of Indian Culture, 1966).

Cakrasaṃvara Tantra
śrī-cakrasaṁvara-tantra-rājādbutaśmaśānālamkāra-nāma
dpal 'khor lo sdom pa'i rgyud kyi rgyal po dur khrod kyi rgyan rmad du 'byung ba
P. 57; Tōh. 413

Guhyasamāja Tantra
sarvatathāgata-kāyavākcittarahasya-guhyasamāja-nāma-mahākalparājā
de bzhin gshegs pa thams cad kyi sku gsung thugs kyi gsang chen gsang ba 'dus pa zhes bya ba brtag pa'i rgyal po chen po
P. 81; Tōh. 442

Sampuṭa Tantra
Sampuṭa-nāma-mahātantra
yang dag par sbyor ba zhes bya ba'i rgyud chen po
P. 26; Tōh. 381

Heart Sutra
prajñā-pāramitā-hṛdayā-nāma-sūtra
shes rab gyi pha rol tu phyin pa'i snying po'i mdo
P. 160; Tōh. 21/531

General Confession (spyi bshags)
byang chub ltung bshags dang spyi bshags sogs bzhugs so
excerpted from:
triskandhaka-sūtra
phung po gsum pa'i mdo
P. 950; Tōh. 284

Sanskrit and Tibetan Commentaries and Other Works

Aśvaghoṣa
Fifty Verses on the Guru
gurupañcaśīkā
bla ma lnga bcu pa
P. 4544; Tōh. 3721

Kulika Puṇḍarīka
Stainless Light (Vimalaprabhā) Commentary
vimālaprabhā-nāma-mūla-tantrānusāriṇī-dvādaśasāhasrikā-laghu-kālacakra-tantra-rāja-ṭīkā
bsdus pa'i rgyud kyi rgyal po dus kyi 'khor lo'i 'grel bshad rtsa ba'i rgyud kyi rjes su 'jug pa stong phrag bcu gnyis pa dri ma med pa'i 'od ces bya ba
P. 2064; Tōh. 1347

Nāgārjuna
Friendly Letter to the King
suhṛllekha
bshes pa'i spring yig
P. 5682; Tōh. 4182

Śāntideva
A Guide to the Bodhisattva Way of Life
bodhi[sattva]caryāvatāra

byang chub sems dpa'i spyod pa la 'jug pa
P. 5272; Tōh. 3871

Tenzin Gyatso, the Fourteenth Dalai Lama, and Thub-bstan-lung-rtogs-rnam-rgyal-'phrin-las (Glin Rinpoche)
Kalacakra Six-Session Guru Yoga, Dharamsala, 1977
thun drug dang 'brel ba'i dus 'khor bla ma'i rnal 'byor nag 'gros su mdzad pa

Tsongkhapa
Foundation of All Excellence
yon tan gzhir gyur ma
Tōh. 5275(1)/6995

English Titles

Andresen, Jensine, *Kalacakra: Textual and Ritual Perspectives* (Ph.D. dissertation, Harvard University, 1997).

Berzin, Alexander, *Kalachakra and Other Six-session Yoga Texts* (Ithaca, N.Y.: Snow Lion, 1998).

Berzin, Alexander, *Taking the Kalachakra Initiation* (Ithaca, N.Y.: Snow Lion, 1997).

Bryant, Barry, *The Wheel of Time Sand Maṇḍala* (San Francisco: Harper, 1992).

Grönbold, Günter, *The Yoga of Six Limbs: An Introduction to the History of Ṣaḍaṅgayoga.* Translated by Robert L. Hütwohl (Santa Fe, NM: Spirit of the Sun Publications, 1996).

Guenther, Herbert H. V., *The Life and Teachings of Nāropa* (Boston: Shambhala, 1986).

Mullin, Glenn H., *The Practice of Kālacakra* (Ithaca, N.Y.: Snow Lion, 1991).

Newman, John, *The Outer Wheel of Time: Vajrayāna Buddhist Cosmology in the Kālacakra Tantra* (Ph.D. dissertation, University of Wisconsin-Madison, 1987).

Ngawang Dhargyey, *Kālacakra Tantra.* Translated by B. Alan Wallace, edited by Ivanka Vana Jakic (Dharamsala: Library of Tibetan Works and Archives, 1985).

Sopa, Geshe Lhundup, Roger Jackson, and John Newman, *The Wheel of Time: The Kālacakra in Context* (Ithaca, N.Y.: Snow Lion, 1985).

Tenzin Gyatso, the Fourteenth Dalai Lama, *Kalachakra Tantra: Rite of Initiation.* Translated and edited by Jeffery Hopkins, 2nd ed. (Boston: Wisdom, 1989).

Tenzin Gyatso, *The World of Tibetan Buddhism.* Translated, edited, and annotated by Geshe Thubten Jinpa (Boston: Wisdom, 1995).

Wallace, B. Alan, *Tibetan Buddhism from the Ground Up* (Boston: Wisdom, 1993).

Wallace, Vesna, *The Inner Kālacakratantra: A Buddhist Tantric View of the Individual* (Ph.D. dissertation, University of California-Berkeley, 1995).

Yeshe, Lama Thubten, *Introduction to Tantra: A Vision of Totality.* Compiled and edited by Jonathan Landaw (Boston: Wisdom, 1987).

Index

afflictions, 6, 14, 19, 21, 39–41, 43, 45, 57, 70, 81–83, 142, 154, 176–77, 235, 244–46
  antidote to, 130
  four afflictions, 81–83
  māra of the mental afflictions, 181
aggregates, 2, 26, 29–30, 88, 93, 157–58, 176, 196, 226, 229–32, 245–46
  aggregate of primordial wisdom, 94, 126, 223
  as deities, 106–9, 176–77
  māra of the aggregates, 181
Akṣobhya, 4, 63, 65, 71, 97–99, 107–8, 122, 126, 175, 176–77, 183, 226, 246, 254
Amitābha, 4, 63, 71, 99, 104, 105, 107–8, 176–77, 234, 246
Amoghasiddhi, 4, 63, 69, 71, 99, 105, 107–8, 176–77, 230, 246
anger, 19, 48, 81, 178, 246
  See also afflictions; non-virtuous actions
appearance. *See* pure appearance
arhat, 82, 235, 242–43
āryabodhisattva, 25, 65, 125, 235–36, 243, 248
Āryadeva, 168
aspiration for awakening. *See* spirit of awakening, aspiration
astrology, 169
Aśvaghoṣa
  Fifty Verses on the Guru, 85
Atīśa, 219

bardo. *See* intermediate state
bhaga, 104–6, 110, 116, 122
bindu. *See* drop
bliss, 14, 28, 30–32, 37, 58, 78, 81, 93, 94, 97, 115, 162, 170–72, 196, 201, 213, 255, 260, 261
  of the dharmakāya, 64–65
  and emptiness, 53, 57, 60, 66, 69, 73, 95, 132, 134, 137, 146, 155, 185, 189, 190, 194, 198, 200, 231, 247–48, 252
  vajra of great bliss, 37
bodhicitta. *See* spirit of awakening; white bodhicitta
bodhisattva, 5, 13, 21–22, 48, 71, 76, 79, 118–19, 125, 140, 151, 178, 189, 192, 230, 262
  bodhisattva grounds, 106, 109, 114, 116, 119, 121, 124–25, 132, 134, 137, 236, 248–49
  bodhisattva precepts, 47–53, 65–66, 256
  with sharp faculties, 13, 232
  See also āryabodhisattva
brahmin, 196
Buddha, 18–19, 38, 41, 49–50, 178
  five families, 26, 71, 93, 176–77
  bodies of, 88, 92, 101, 243
    dharmakāya, 1, 64–65, 84, 91, 146–48, 150, 153, 243, 250
    jñānakāya, 243
    nirmāṇakāya, 64–65, 84, 147–48, 183, 243, 247, 250
    rūpakāya, 1, 243, 247
    sambhogakāya, 64–65, 84, 147–48, 183, 222, 225, 243, 247, 249
    svabhāvakāya, 65, 84, 243
    vajra body, 102, 104–6, 108–9, 125–26, 131, 138, 211, 247, 259
  Buddha Kālacakra, 8, 37, 198
  See also Akṣobhya; Amitābha; Amoghasiddhi; Ratnasambhava; Vairocana
Butön, 3

cakra, 169–72, 227–29, 252
crown cakra, 107, 206
forehead cakra, 91–92, 107, 184, 206
genital cakra, 91–92, 107, 134, 136–37, 171, 184, 207
heart cakra, 91–92, 107, 110, 136–37, 173, 184, 206, 209, 231, 248, 252, 257
navel cakra, 27, 31–32, 91–92, 100, 107–8, 129, 174, 184–5, 207, 227–35, 248, 256–57
throat cakra, 91–92, 107, 184, 206
Cakrasaṃvara, 28, 55, 83, 90, 102, 129–30, 148–49, 172, 207, 210, 235, 250, 259
channels, 7, 26, 91, 100, 110–12, 171, 205–16, 218–19, 257
branch channels, 206–9, 222, 252
central channel, 1, 27, 32, 61–62, 65, 77, 100, 110–11, 114, 124, 129, 133, 156, 173, 177, 182, 185, 190, 196, 205–8, 212–13, 215–21, 227–30, 249, 258
right and left (side) channels, 61–62, 114–15, 156, 182, 185, 190, 196, 205–6, 215–16, 221, 227, 256, 257
six channels, 205
See also drops; vital energies
Cilupa, 2
cognitive obscurations, 17, 22, 55, 176, 235, 237, 248–49
See also afflictions
compassion, 5–6, 13, 18–19, 41–46, 50, 54–57, 72, 76, 101, 140, 154, 178, 192, 198, 242, 255
completion stage, 1, 8, 16, 20, 27–31, 82, 86, 88, 91–92, 97, 100–2, 113, 121, 129, 138, 141–43, 149, 153, 157–59, 168, 173–75, 184, 190, 199–201, 205, 213, 215, 229, 233, 237, 249, 257, 258
compositional factors. *See* aggregates
confession, 70–72
consciousness. *See* aggregates; clear light
consort, 129–132, 199
craving. *See* afflictions

death, 5, 39, 89–91, 93, 129, 136, 140–54, 170, 241, 256
in the path, 146–48
deep sleep, 89, 92, 100, 125, 156, 172–73, 210
deities, 25–31, 55, 65, 69, 89, 92, 94–95, 97–99, 105–23, 130, 131, 137–39, 153, 163, 167, 175, 179, 182–83, 187, 189–92, 197, 200, 228, 234, 245–46, 250, 251, 254, 255, 257, 258
wrathful. *See* krodhas
See also Kālacakra, main deity
dependent origination, 169
desire. *See* afflictions
dhyāna. *See* meditative stabilization
Dignāga, 39
divine pride, 6, 138, 146, 150, 163, 186, 188–89, 225, 233, 252, 253, 258, 260
dream state, 92, 100, 109, 116, 125, 132, 156, 172, 186, 210–11, 218
drops, 7, 78, 82, 99–100, 105, 121, 125–26, 128–29, 132–37, 147, 150, 156, 171, 228–29, 233–35, 246, 255, 259
four drops, 91–93, 101, 190
indestructible drop, 129, 170, 259
See also channels; vital energies; white bodhicitta
Drukpa Kunla, 152
Dzogchen, 1, 90

empowerment, 101
emptiness, 45, 66, 77, 83, 89–90, 102–3, 104, 112, 114, 117, 155, 163, 192, 260, 261
and bliss, 53, 57, 60, 66, 69, 73, 95, 132, 134, 137, 146, 155, 185, 189, 190, 194, 198, 200, 231, 247, 252
as free of conceptual elaborations, 58, 89, 159, 162
and mahāmudrā, 37
realization of, 1, 55, 57–60, 83, 89, 128, 153, 187, 245
energies. *See* vital energies
ethical discipline, 22, 44–45, 71, 76–77, 80, 201, 222

faculties, 26, 68–69, 125, 185, 215, 219, 223
six faculties for action, 93–94, 119–20, 125, 183

faith, 39
five hindrances, 80
four immeasurables, 78

generation stage, 1, 16, 20, 26–30, 32, 61, 68, 86, 88, 91–92, 95–97, 100–2, 106, 110, 112, 114, 121, 129, 138, 141, 153–54, 155, 159, 168, 170–74, 181, 188, 199, 224, 237, 248, 249, 251, 262
giving. *See* perfections; pledges
Guhyasamāja, 28, 55, 83, 102, 114, 128–30, 148–49, 172, 206–7, 210, 235, 250, 259
  Guhyasamāja Tantra, 90, 107
guru devotion, 55–57, 84–85
Gyeltsab, 135–37, 239

Heart Sūtra, 49, 56
Hīnayāna. *See* vehicles
Hevajra, 54

inherent existence, 45, 59, 83, 101, 123, 143–45, 155, 178, 187
initiation, 66, 86–87, 97–103, 171–75, 183
  conduct initiation, 116–19, 125
  crown initiation, 106–9, 125
  crown ribbon initiation, 112–14, 125
  greatly higher initiations, 100, 127–28, 135–38, 248
  higher initiations, 100, 127, 130–34, 248
  initiation of permission, 122–23, 126
  inner initiation, 109–112
  meaning of, 101–3
  name initiation, 116, 119–21, 125–26
  self-initiation, 86, 175, 193, 262
  seven initiations, 124–26
  three types of, 29
  vajra and bell initiation, 114–16, 125
  vajra master initiation, 123–24
  water initiation, 101, 104–6, 125
intermediate state, 61, 93, 142, 147, 249

jñānasattvas, 64, 110, 118, 122, 182

Kālacakra
  Kālacakra Tantra, 1–3, 28–30, 33, 51, 71, 80, 81, 88, 94, 148, 166, 176, 261, 262
  Buddha Kālacakra, 8, 37, 198
  chapters of, 29–30
  cosmology, 27–28, 61, 151, 169–70
  etymology of, 27–28, 169
  generating oneself as, 134–37, 155–64, 200–1, 257, 258
  main deity, 97–99, 107, 109, 159–65, 173–74
  maṇḍala, 103, 155–56
  mantra, 189–93
  precepts, 52
  rainbow state of, 233–34
  sevenfold state of Kālacakra, 100–1, 141
  symbolism of, 172–73
  system compared with others, 28, 55, 83, 102, 108, 129–30, 148–49, 172–73, 206–7, 210, 235, 244, 247, 249–50, 254, 259
  and tantra classification, 239
  Vajravega, 63–64, 175, 179–83, 244
  See also completion stage; generation stage; *Vimalaprabhā*
Kalkī kings, 2
Khedrub, 136–37, 146, 222, 229, 239, 250
krodhas, 26, 94, 95, 98–99, 120–21, 125
Kṛṣṇa-pa, 131

Mādhyamika, 242
Mahāmudrā, 31, 58, 78, 90, 199, 233
  with and without aspect, 37
Mahāyāna. *See* vehicles
maṇḍala, 68–70, 97, 102–3, 124, 153, 155–60, 183, 189, 200–1, 233, 251, 254
  etymology of, 69–70
  offering, 65, 69–70
  primordial wisdom maṇḍala, 102, 107
mantra, 72, 123, 133, 199, 228, 251, 255
  of deities, 189–93
  name mantra, 85–86
  one-hundred-syllable mantra, 20, 192–93
meditative stabilization, 8, 32, 77–78, 97, 172, 174, 212–13, 224–27
  etymology of, 224
merit, 13, 44–45, 58–64, 77, 91, 124–25, 187, 247, 250, 258

mind
clear light, 1, 58, 83
innate mind, 28, 58, 89–90, 128, 131, 146–51, 235, 259–60
See also emptiness, realization of; primordial wisdom; wisdom
mindfulness, 79, 212, 258
motivation, 13–19, 20, 127, 168
mudrā, 31, 58, 71, 78, 123, 160–61, 167, 195–6, 199, 214, 227, 232, 258
action mudrā, 78
karma mudrā. *See* consort
primordial wisdom mudrā, 78
See also Mahāmudrā

Nāgārjuna, 40, 79
Friendly Letter to the King, 80
Naropa, 57
Ngulchu Dharma Bhadra, 153
nonvirtuous actions, 47–50, 79–80
Nyingma, 5, 253

offerings, 65–70, 196–97

pāramitā. *See* perfections
Pāramitāyāna. *See* vehicles
paranormal abilities. *See* siddhi
perfections, 6, 22, 77–78, 114, 200, 222, 224, 261–62
pledges, 70–71
prāṇayāma, 8, 32, 97, 172, 174, 212, 227–30
Prāsaṅgika, 254
pride, 81
See also afflictions; divine pride
primordial wisdom (jñāna), 28–31, 77, 85–86, 92–94, 96, 126, 128–29, 131–32, 148, 150–53, 155, 157–58, 163, 171–75, 177, 179, 187, 188, 192, 196–97, 201, 211, 223, 244, 247, 252, 258, 259, 261–62
element of primordial wisdom, 173, 223
five primordial wisdoms, 63–64, 163–64, 176, 243, 246
primordial wisdom body, 236, 243
primordial wisdom energy, 209
primordial wisdom maṇḍala, 102, 107
primordial wisdom mudrā, 78
vajra primordial wisdom, 121–24, 134, 138
pure appearance, 94–97

Ratnasambhava, 4, 46, 63, 71, 73, 99, 105, 107–10, 176–77, 232, 246
recollection, 8, 31–32, 97, 172–73, 212, 222, 232–34
refuge, 17–19, 37–41, 64–66, 71, 72, 84–85, 240–41, 250
retention, 8, 32, 97, 172, 174, 212, 230–32
retraction, 8, 32, 97, 174, 212–24

śaktīs, 26, 93, 98, 111–14 126, 135, 150, 165–67, 173–75, 179, 182–83, 186, 189, 192, 200–1, 222, 233, 254
samādhi, 8, 97, 172, 199, 212, 226, 234–237, 244
samayasattvas, 64, 179, 182
Śambhala, 2, 25, 102, 201
sambhogakāya. *See* Buddha
saṃsāra. *See* cyclic existence
Śāntideva, 41, 51, 54, 75, 127
A Guide to the Bodhisattva Way of Life 51
sense bases, 88, 93
sexual union, 23, 89, 92, 104–5, 129, 133, 261
definitive meaning, 100–1, 171
siddhi, 32, 60, 86, 106, 109, 114–16, 119, 121, 124, 136, 152, 193, 224
siddhi (elixir), 166
six phase yoga, 8, 31–32, 97, 138, 172–74, 201, 212–37
See also meditative stabilization; prāṇayāma; recollection; retention; retraction; samādhi
six-session guru yoga, 17, 27, 32, 37, 44–45, 53, 55, 57, 85, 98, 173, 175, 193, 215, 250, 260
spirit of awakening (bodhicitta), 5–6, 22, 42–44, 46–51, 72, 75–76, 88, 91, 133–34, 141, 143, 153, 168, 240–41, 242, 250, 261–62
subtle body. *See* channels; drops; vital energies

Sūtrayāna. *See* vehicles
Śavaripa, 226

Tagtsang Lotsawa, 210
tantra, 15, 16, 20–24, 28–29, 38, 56, 60, 71, 89, 116, 129–31, 151, 184, 187, 195, 206, 219, 239, 248–49, 253–54, 260, 262
  four classes of Buddhist tantra, 1, 23–24
  highest yoga, 1, 4, 13–14, 17, 23, 30–31, 88, 129, 141, 239
  See also Kālacakra; vehicles, Vajrayāna
Tilopa, 57
transgressions, 52, 131, 201, 256
  and alcohol, 256
two truths, 247
Tsongkhapa, 55, 135, 146, 222, 226, 234, 239, 257
  Foundation of All Excellence, 141
tummo, 129–30, 159, 174, 185, 229, 234

Vairocana, 4, 33, 39, 63, 71, 99, 105, 107–8, 122, 176–77, 214, 223, 237, 246
vajra, 37, 45, 91–92, 99–101, 116, 122–23, 133, 136, 159, 184–86, 229–34
  and bell, 33, 71, 162–63
  vajra body, 102, 104–6, 108–9, 125–26, 131, 138, 211, 247, 259
  pledge of the vajra, 71
  vajra sense base, 119
  vajra yoga, 97
  See also initiation
Vajradhara, 85, 141, 184
  etymology of, 85
Vajrasattva, 63, 94, 99, 105, 122–24, 126, 153, 160, 175, 183, 184, 192, 214, 224, 226, 254
  Vajrasattva Practice, 20–21, 37, 255
Vajravega. *See* Kālacakra, Vajravega
vehicles, 21–23, 71, 73
  Hīnayāna, 21–22, 49, 54, 89, 127, 141, 240
  Mahāyāna, 5, 13, 15, 18, 20–23, 48–49, 52, 54, 127, 140, 242
  Pāramitāyāna, 6, 18, 21–22, 56, 58, 65, 89, 125, 235, 242, 248, 261
  Sūtrayāna, 21–23
  Vajrayāna, 1, 5–7, 14, 16, 18, 21–23, 52, 56, 101, 128, 243
Vimalaprabhā, 2–3, 164, 239
vital energies, 1, 7, 30–31, 65, 77, 100–1, 112, 170–72, 196, 212–13, 230–31, 256–57, 258–59
  five energies, 210
  ten energies, 110–14, 125, 156–57, 173–74, 190, 209–10
  descending energy, 173, 184–85, 209–10, 222, 229–31, 234
  See also channels; drops

white bodhicitta, 61–62, 81, 93, 129–37, 185–86, 205–6, 209–10, 229, 235–36, 246, 248, 255, 261
  See also drops
wisdom (prajñā), 13, 21, 30, 76–77, 80, 85, 88, 119, 131, 133, 146, 172, 176, 189–90, 200, 226, 244–45, 261–62
  See also primordial wisdom
wrathful deities. *See* krodhas

Yamāntaka, 55, 96, 120, 181, 249
yoga
  bindu yoga, 184–85, 197
  deity yoga, 187
  subtle yoga, 185–87
  vajra yoga. *See* six phase yoga
  See also six-session guru yoga

zeal, 77

About Wisdom Publications

Wisdom Publications, a not-for-profit publisher, is dedicated to making available authentic Buddhist works for the benefit of all. We publish translations of the sutras and tantras, commentaries and teachings of past and contemporary Buddhist masters, and original works by the world's leading Buddhist scholars. We publish our titles with the appreciation of Buddhism as a living philosophy and with the special commitment to preserve and transmit important works from all the major Buddhist traditions.

If you would like more information or a copy of our mail-order catalog, please contact us at:

Wisdom Publications
199 Elm Street
Somerville, Massachusetts 02144 USA
Telephone: (617) 776-7416 • Fax: (617) 776-7841
Email: info@wisdompubs.org
www.wisdompubs.org

THE WISDOM TRUST

As a not-for-profit publisher, Wisdom Publications is dedicated to the publication of fine Dharma books for the benefit of all sentient beings and is dependent upon the kindness and generosity of sponsors in order to do so. If you would like to make a donation to Wisdom, please do so through our Somerville office. If you would like to sponsor the publication of a book, please write or e-mail us for more information.

Thank you.

Wisdom Publications is an non-profit, charitable 501(c)(3) organization and a part of the Foundation for the Preservation of the Mahayana Tradition (FPMT).